Born to SHOP

M E X I C O

Born to SHOP

MEXICO

▼

SUZY GERSHMAN
and
JUDITH THOMAS

Introduction by
VICTOR FOSADO

BANTAM BOOKS
NEW YORK • TORONTO • LONDON
SYDNEY • AUCKLAND

BORN TO SHOP: MEXICO
A Bantam Book / November 1989

Produced by Ink Projects

Library of Congress Cataloging-in-Publication Data

Gershman, Suzy.
  Born to shop. Mexico / Suzy Gershman & Judith Thomas :
introduction from Victor Fosado.
    p.   cm.
  Includes index.
  ISBN 0-553-34767-5
  1. Shopping—Mexico—Guide-books. 2. Mexico—
Description and travel—1981–   —Guide-books.
I. Thomas, Judith (Judith Evans)
II. title.
TX337.M6G47   1989
380.1'45'0002572—dc20   89-7028
                                                                   CIP

Published simultaneously in the United States and Canada

Bantam Books are published by Bantam Books, a division of
Bantam Doubleday Dell Publishing Group, Inc. Its trademark,
consisting of the words "Bantam Books" and the portrayal
of a rooster, is Registered in U.S. Patent and Trademark
Office and in other countries. Marca Registrada. Bantam Books,
666 Fifth Avenue, New York, New York 10103.

PRINTED IN THE UNITED STATES OF AMERICA

FG   0 9 8 7 6 5 4 3 2 1

The BORN TO SHOP Team:

reported by:
Suzy Gershman
Debra Chester Kalter, M.D.
Sy and Yvette Kalter
Aaron Gershman
editor: Jill Parsons
executive editor: Toni Burbank
assistant to executive editor: Ellen Powell
cover art: Dave Calver
book design: Lynne Arany
copy editor: Archie Hobson
proofreader: Lorie Young
maps by: David Lindroth

HOPE

Editorial Note

The Mexican *peso* fluctuates daily as it continues to seek stability. The prices quoted in this book are pegged to the exchange rate of $1 U.S. = 2,000 Mexican *pesos*. This means that all prices in this book may seem slightly higher than you were expecting, but the 2,000 = *peso* benchmark makes mathematics easier and allows one to budget accordingly. Sticklers will note that the *peso* generally trades from between 2,250 and 2,500 per dollar, but can go higher or lower.

This book was prepared under the same strict guidelines used for all *Born to Shop* books and following our own personal standards:

▼ At no time did any store or market know who we were or why we were visiting them.

▼ One of us, if not both, has been to every listing in this book at least once.

▼ The information presented here was verified prior to publication. While this book will be continually updated, it is impossible to guarantee that all stores are still in business. If you catch a change before we do, please drop us a note:

Born to Shop
Suzy Gershman & Debra Kalter
Bantam Books
666 Fifth Avenue, 25th Floor
New York NY 10103

Acknowledgments

This being a book by Texans, our list of thank-yous reaches across an area as big as the state of. This has been a family project; special thanks go to Sy (known as Grandpa Sy) and Yvette Kalter and Aaron Gershman, who helped us out with the reporting, legwork, driving, and research.

We're most appreciative of the time and effort given by Dr. Jill Vexler, a cultural anthropologist who curates museum exhibits and specializes in art, textiles, and crafts. She grew up with us in San Antonio; her mother makes the best pralines in Texas; she has curated several museum shows about Mexico; and she says she's willing to wait for the next edition of this book to add the 500 pages of notes about weaving that she thinks are important for you to read.

Thanks also to Joan Yurman, Eduardo Amezcoa, and Scott Sunshine, who helped organize part of the research in Mexico and to Donata Magipinto of Westin Hotels, who made sure we always had a luxurious place to sleep. Gunilla Rogers of Viking Travel made additional arrangements.

More thanks to Pat Olle, to David Goldfein of Sheraton Hotels in Mexico, to Linda Lake (from San Antonio, Texas!) at the Sheraton Hotel and Towers in Cancún, to Nancy Weiss of AARP, and to the incomparable Jill Joseloff, who cruised to Mexico and taught us everything there is to know about panniers.

Yet more thanks to Rita Glassman of Ramada Renaissance; to Karen Kandrin of Continental Airlines; to Anne Storch of Asti Tours;

to Max Hall and Jill Biggins from Princess P&O; and to all those on the "Love Boat" who made our research cruise so nice.

Abrazos to Victor Fosado.

Also, a nod of the head to American Express, whose Purchase Protection™ plan made it so much easier (and safer) for us to shop all over Mexico and have as much fun as we did. No doubt they'd like to thank us for spending as much as we did and going over our budgets.

CONTENTS

Preface

¡Ole!, ¡Hola!, and *¿Qué tal?* to all of you from all of us. Welcome to our Mexico book. In keeping with our usual practice of making the guide suitable to the location, you'll find this book somewhat different from other editions of *Born to Shop.* All of the reporting was done by Texans!

So Hook 'em, Horns! and Remember the Alamo! When Texans go to Mexico they don't consider themselves a tourists. They're just going home.

For those of you who are not quite up on your history, Texans were once Mexicans ... although back then they were called Texicans. So we bring you this book from a special point of view. We did not suddenly dash into Mexico, do a little Mexican hat dance, and say "*¡Olé!*—here's the book, *amigos.*" We have been working on this book for just about twenty-five years; it is part of our very fiber.

We grew up in San Antonio, Texas—an American city filled with pride of its Mexican roots and Mexican traditions. All our school holidays and long weekends were spent in Mexico. We grew up with little papier-mâché serving dishes shaped like watermelon (that's *sandía* to us); our birthday parties came complete with *piñatas* brought up from Nuevo Laredo. We ate off Mexican glass plates, drank from Mexican glasses, and stirred our iced tea with long silver straws brought back from shopping excursions down south in the big backyard of Texas. We wore the uniform of the proper Texas preppy: a hand-embroidered Mexican dress, a pair of Papagallo shoes (hot pink, with a silk flower on the toe), and a Collins of Texas handbag. (You had to see it to believe it.) No little flower prints or green whales for us—that's New England stuff. We were never Yankees, merely *yanquis*.

Our lives, our taste, our appreciation of art have been shaped by our love of the arts and crafts of Mexico, the talents of our southern brothers and sisters. Who we are is, in some small part, what Texas and Mexico are. So we bring you this book with *abrazos*—hugs. We speak Spanish, we know the territory, we are *hermanas* . . . sisters.

Suzy Kalter Gershman and
Debra Chester Kalter, M.D.

Introduction

I welcome you to my shop, and to my country, and if you come here in person I welcome you in person. I have been in this place twenty years now. For fifty-three years I have been collecting this art and doing this work. I know the most about Mexican folk art because I have been doing it the longest.

People come to me and ask me "Where did you get this? Where did you find this?" I just tell them that I always purchased the indigenous things that I could find when I traveled, and that I traveled for many, many years, always collecting. That is my advice to my readers as well. Buy the beautiful indigenous things. I began back in the 1920s with partners, always traveling and collecting. We drove, and we saw everything the people made.

Everything that is here is Mexican. Many Americans come to my shop because they know we have the true spirit of Mexico right here. I find them things. Sometimes they ask for something special. Sometimes I am sad to sell it, because then a piece of my country is leaving, but I love for people to take this art to their hearts—to love it and take it home. I am happy if it is loved, if it is understood.

My daughter Pilar is here, and she is director. She knows very well what all these things are; she has learned from me. If you come here, she will tell you, and teach you about each thing, and show you our heritage.

So I welcome you to a place where you can begin to learn about all that Mexico is. Because only from a people's art do you really know who they are.

Victor Fosado
Victor's, Mexico City

I ▾ BIENVENIDAS & BIEN VENDIDOS

Welcome to Mexico

There are many parts of the United States—stretching from Texas to California—that bear witness to the fact that we are all related to the Mexican people, if not by blood or language, then at least by culture, by art, by architecture, by food and drink. But go south of the border, down Mexico way, and you'll find a foreign country—and a people who may seem foreign to those who did not grow up in the American Southwest.

Mexico is the closest foreign destination to the United States, the most exotic neighborhood we can claim nearby—just cross a river and you are in another world. Cross a river to an Indian and Spanish colonial heritage, to a way of life dramatically different from ours at home. The United States was founded on the notion that there had to be a better way of doing things, that the past could be changed in favor of the future. Mexico stands as a tribute to the past, looking over her shoulder for ancient traditions to show the way into her future.

The Mexico the tourist sees is a stratified society. In many cases, to see the real Mexico, to meet the real people and buy the real buys, you must look past the surface layers presented to you and dig deeper, until you find the real thing.

So take the buses, *amigos;* pull on your khakis and your crepe-sole shoes. You want resorts so fancy they seem worthy of the grand prize from a game show? Mexico has them.

You want dress-up fancy to the tune of Europe? Mexico City has it. But if you want to be transported to another time in another place, get off the beaten track and dig a little deeper. Mexico is inexpensive, unique, colorful, and yes, filled with shopping bargains.

A Brief History of Shopping in Mexico

Part of your reason for visiting Mexico is surely to shop. There's a tradition of many centuries behind you. After all, what was Hernán Cortés doing in town if not shopping?

Although Christopher Columbus is said to have known about Mexico (as early as 1502 he was perusing canoes filled with goods brought to the Caribbean from the Yucatán), it was not until 1519 that Cortés landed in what is now Veracruz and began his march on land, across the country to where Mexico City now stands. This was no supermarket expedition— Cortés burned his ships so that there was no way to return. It took him about two years to make his way to Teotihuacán, so the Spanish colonial period is traditionally dated from 1521. Yet the looting and the craving for local goods began the day Spanish boots set down on Mexican soil. And while Cortés introduced many Spanish arts and crafts to the country, he was really on a buying trip for the king of Spain. After all, this was before Bloomingdale's . . . and El Corte Inglés.

All that is available to buy in Mexico today stems from the fateful confrontation and conflagration of Montezuma's Indian and Cortés's Spanish heritages. As luck would have it, Cortés did not actually take out of Mexico as much as he brought in. The synthesis arising from the clash of the two cultures now provides the best opportunity for a shopping spree. If you've traveled to Spain, the mother country, you recognize the names of cities, the shapes of town plazas, the churches, and the tiles. Yet all these Spanish traditions have been reinterpreted through local eyes over generations and centuries—they appear fresh again, and purely Mexican. But when carefully bought, Mexican products will coordinate with your Country French or Early American home furnishings and life-style because of their traditional European roots.

A Brief History of the Economic Situation

OK, OK, so you're not that much into business, and you thought this was a shopping book. Right. But to understand why Mexico is such a good country for the shopper these days, you need to know that once upon a time (and not that very long ago) Mexico was a rich and stable country crawling with wealthy oilmen. Then, in the early 1980s, the oil business crashed, leaving the *peso* in a mess and virtually wiping out the Mexican middle class. People who were immensely wealthy found themselves barely able to hang on; many left Mexico and started new lives and new careers—often in the United States.

What remains are all the trimmings that go with money—gorgeous hotels, fine restaurants, nice shops—but few locals who can afford them. All these goodies are there for tourists who can greedily watch the financial pages and check out just how much further their dollar will go on an almost daily basis. A hotel room that goes for $300 a night in Paris costs only

$100 a night in Mexico City. A car and driver—
English-speaking—costs at most $15 an hour.
Only the $1 Coca-Colas are expensive—but
you can even beat that game: Simply buy soft
drinks in the supermarket.

The poor people of Mexico have always
been poor. But at last you have come to a
country where you can do something for them.
We keep our pockets filled with 100-*peso*
coins—100 *pesos* will buy a loaf of bread or a
fancy roll—and we dole out our coins to anyone who asks. (One to a customer, however.)
We are able to take . . . but we are also able to
give.

The Moscow Rule of Shopping

T he Moscow Rule of Shopping is one of
our most basic rules, and has little to do
with shopping in Moscow, so pay attention. Now then. The average shopper in
his pursuit of the ideal bargain may not buy an
item when he first sees it for sale, because he
is convinced that later on in his travels he will
find the same item (or an even better version)
for much less money. This is a standard thought
process for a person who lives in a capitalist
country . . . and a worthy thought, indicative
of a crafty shopper. But for someone who lives
in an Iron Curtain country, it is a ludicrous
way of shopping. Everyone there lives by only
one shopping rule: Buy it when you see it,
because if you hesitate, it will be gone. And
you will never see it again. Hence the name of
our international rule of shopping. And when
in Mexico, do as the Muscovites.

But then, since you really aren't in Moscow,
and just want to make sure you get to buy
what you want, examine the article you desire
carefully, and ask yourself these questions:

1. Is this a touristy item I am bound to find all over town? If yes, keep looking.

2. Is this a regional item that is made only in this part of the country, so that once I leave here my chances of finding another diminish significantly? Buy within the day, before you leave the region.

3. Is this an item I can't live without, even if I am overpaying tremendously? Buy it now.

4. Is this a handcrafted item that is likely to be one of a kind because the artist is standing right here before me? Or is this a mass-produced handicraft of which literally hundreds of thousands are made all over the country? If the artist is there in person (and you aren't prey to a scam in which someone insists he is the artist and you are too naive to know better), buy, and make sure you get it signed.

5. Is the shop I am buying from a reputable one that can authenticate the piece or vouch for its durability? Where do they stand on repairs and warranties? If something goes wrong, do I have some recourse, or am I simply stuck? It sometimes pays to overpay for a certain item just to have the store stand behind it.

The Leningrad Rule of Cruising

If your only contact with Mexico is going to be via cruise ship, your opportunities for fine shopping are dependent on the route. Mexican Riviera cruises stop in anywhere from three to five Mexican ports and provide plenty of opportunity to shop. Western Caribbean cruises usually include Jamaica, the Caymans, and one Mexican port—you choose to spend the day in Cozumel, in Tulum (Mayan ruins), or in Cancún. But don't worry—even in that one day, you'll have ample chance to take advantage of some of Mexico's shopping pleasures. (See page 195.)

While all cruise ships do have shops on board, and some rather elaborate shops, they carry few Mexican arts and crafts. Some have silver jewelry at competitive prices—but not prices impressive enough to make you forget what's waiting on land. Perhaps the best buy we made in Mexico was in a cruise-ship shop where we happened upon David Winter miniature cottages at bargain-basement prices. Remember that most cruise ships have shops run by international retailers who bring in merchandise from around the world; your onboard shopping scores will most often be in French perfumes and English china! *Viva México,* as they say.

The City of Origin Axiom

The best buys in Mexico are going to be arts and crafts. Such items will always be best represented (in terms of selection) and least expensive in or near the city where they are made. There happens to be one Mexican exception to this rule, which is silver. Do not assume that silver is less expensive in Taxco (or in any of the other so-called Silver Cities: San Miguel de Allende, Querétaro, or Guanajuato) than anywhere else. In fact, it may be more expensive there because of the high volume of tourists. On all other craft items, however, try to go to the source.

The major crafts cities are Oaxaca, Guadalajara, and San Miguel de Allende. You can plan to travel to any of these cities, or you will usually find examples of their crafts in markets in many other Mexican cities. We give you an overnight tour of San Miguel (see page 187). There are always crafts shops (many of them state-run) that feature goods from all the areas, and things in Mexico are generally so inexpensive that perhaps you don't care if you get the best price or not. If you do care, learn what regions specialize in what type of art form, and buy it in the markets of that city or region.

For example:

Oaxaca: Black pottery and carved wooden animals
Tlaquepaque: Pottery and glass
Puebla: Tiles
Olinalá: Pin-dot lacquer work
Mérida: Hammocks and henequen rugs
Pátzcuaro: Pottery
Tijuana: Liquor
Toluca: Wool, pottery, baskets
Michoacán: Black lacquer
Guatemala: Weaving

Mexican Sports

Some people come to Mexico for the fishing. Entire portions of the country are famous for their fishies and their deep blue sea.

Some people come to snorkel. Cozumel is known to have one of the best reefs in the Caribbean. And Xel-há offers all the beauties of the deep to landlubbers who want to peer into the shallow waters and see swimming, glimmering beauties.

Some people come to Mexico for the dig—the archaeology, the ruins, the lost cities, the pyramids. They study little booklets, learn to decipher Mayan writings, and can tell time on the ancient clock.

Yes, you can do all these things, and they are worthy accomplishments. But don't overlook shopping as a sport. Particularly at night.

You can shop the arcades of your luxury hotel. You can shop on your ship or on the pier. You can make it to the *mercado* first thing in the morning, or to the mall at midday when everybody else may be closed. But the true sporting life is the nighttime *paseo*—when everyone goes out to dinner, to walk, to see, to be seen ... and to shop casually. When the sun goes down, the vendors come out. While stores in some communities are open until 9 P.M., it is the street life that comes alive, with the calls of the merchants ("Hey, pretty lady, I take American dollars"), the waltz of the merchandise, and the thrill of the chase.

Traditionally, the *paseo* occurs in the *Zócalo* (town plaza) on Sundays after church. The families go for a walk, nodding at their friends, stopping to visit and gossip, showing off their fine clothes and their fine children. Teens make eyes at each other as the parade goes around. The tourist version of this ritual takes place when the sun goes down and the air cools off. Since it's dark, sporting opportunities are limited, and couples turn their attention to their evening meal and some shopping before heading off to the disco ... or a midnight stroll along the moonlit beach.

During the *paseo* couples shop together, and men are most often apt to buy a trinket for the lady. It is also the time when the man of the family shows how much of a man he is as he attempts to do some big-time bargaining. It is a *macho* time, a silly time, a shopping time as only the Mexicans can offer. *¡Ole!*

Buyer Beware

There is much to buy in Mexico, and it is usually well priced. What you have in your hands is a book all about it. While certain items are must-buys, others take some consideration. So before you get going, look out for a few traps:

PERFUMES & COSMETICS: Think twice about buying French perfumes in border towns, or anywhere in Mexico for that matter. When we were kids, our mother often bought her bottle of Joy here, and was thrilled with the price. Yet we have since discovered that the fragrance sold in Mexico is rarely the exact one you can buy in France. It may be mixed from concentrate, it may be American, it may be watered down, or it may come from the Caribbean. It might also be made through a licensing agreement—which means the product was actually made in Mexico (see page 39)—or it might be a total fake. We have bought cosmetics in the duty-frees or on the airplanes and ships we travel on, but Mexico itself is not really the place to stock up on perfumes.

READY-TO-WEAR: Unless you are buying inexpensive clothes for a specific purpose, there's little reason to buy ready-to-wear in Mexico. It is usually not even as well made as American garments. There are exceptions to this rule, especially if you get into couture or designer goods. If you are looking for knock-around clothes to wear while you travel and don't care what happens to them in the long run, buy Mexican. If you are looking for long-lasting classics, wait until you get home.

BOOZE: Check up on your state laws. Coming from Texas, we are aware of the fact that you can bring more liquor across the border (into Texas) if you are a nonresident than if you are a resident. (Show a driver's license to prove state residency.) Border states seem to have different regulations, and we remind you that while there are federal standards, each state does have the last word on this subject. Liquor is an excellent buy in Mexico, especially if you stick to local brands—rums, tequilas, and liqueurs. Expect to save at least 50% off the U.S. price for things like Kahlua (a coffee liqueur) or tequila. You can buy international brands in the duty-free shops at the usual savings; we saved about 25% on a bottle of Grand Marnier purchased at the big duty-free in Mexico City. We hate schlepping the weight of the liquor around—to say nothing of the liability—so we only bring back one bottle per trip, usually Bacardi Añejo, an aged rum that is not available in the United States or the Caribbean, which those with palates more refined than ours claim to be superior. But if we were driving out of Texas (since we are no longer Texas residents), you'd better believe we would each have our four bottles in tow.

SILVER: Generally speaking, sterling silver is half price in Mexico, but watch U.S. prices and sales—it can get competitive. Also remember that silver tableware (flatware and serving pieces) comes into the United States duty-free, but silver jewelry for resale does not. (For personal use is OK.) There are silver buys to be made (see page 87), but not every purchase is a sterling one.

Chains of Love

A s you shop around Mexico you'll soon note that the same stores keep popping up in every big city, every mall, and every resort city you come to. Often the stores look identical, and after a while you feel that you've already been there. A small sampler:

GUCCI: All the Gucci shops are nicely built, although they are not identical. Some are a little more swank than others. The merchandise is the same—it is based on Gucci designs and uses Gucci hardware, but it's made in Mexico. Prices are high on some items, moderate on others. The luggage is gorgeous and costs about one-half the U.S. price. A Mexican-made Gucci handbag for $300 is not a bargain, so be prepared with U.S. prices on Gucci if you are a serious shopper. Gucci manufactured in the United States may be of better quality.

DOMIT: Perhaps the fanciest men's fashion store in Mexico, featuring both business attire and sportswear. They carry licensed goods of many big names as well as their own label. Quality is usually superior.

GUESS: You guessed right if you're thinking jeans and Mr. Marciano. Prices are high by local standards, but are lower than in the United States.

POLO/RALPH LAUREN: These are not fakes, folks. Ralph has authorized this Mexican company to produce his clothing for men, women, and children. The designs are the same, but often the fabrics are not. Prices are 30% to 50% lower than in the United States. The store is usually the nicest boutique in town. Expect to pay about $25 for the famous Polo shirt. Our best buy: $40 for corduroy skirts. While these clothes are well-made by local standards, they might not pass your eagle-eyed inspection.

CALVIN KLEIN: Calvin is not involved in this operation, as Ralph Lauren is with his. With the Lauren merchandise, you can tell that a degree of control has been exercised with every intention to be the best. The Klein merchandise bears little resemblance to Calvin Klein in the States, although this is the Sport line and not the ready-to-wear. There's nothing wrong with the jeans, but many of the other items look poorly made to us. Our best buy: T-shirts embroidered with the C.K. initials for $8.

EXPLORA: This is an original shop, although it seems to have been inspired by Banana Republic. The fare is mostly T-shirts and towels, decorated with graphics of animals on the endangered species list. The graphics are sensational. The shops are generally well-stocked.

BYE-BYE: One of several big T-shirt chains that have branched into beachwear and therefore sell shorts and sweatsuits as well as Ts. Strong, bold graphics; good quality shirts. Distinguishable from the competition because there is a parrot on all Bye-Bye designs.

POCO-LOCO: The main competition to Bye-Bye, with the same basics but bearing different graphics customized to the location, like "Puerto Vallarta Beach Club," etc.

VIVA MÉXICO: Another of the many T-shirt chains you'll encounter—except that everything says *Viva México* in bold red letters.

FERRIONI: An expensive version of Poco-Loco merchandise, with a Scottie dog on it. There's sportswear in this line, which happens to be adorable although expensive.

EXPRESS: Well-priced (usually under $50), hot fashions for with-it juniors who need to look very "now." No relation to Limited Express in the United States except that the same customer—as well as an older one—will be interested.

RUBEN TORRES: One of Mexico's most famous designers for every kind of fashion. Popular with the middle class for his weekend clothes. The bright shorts and Ts are perfect for suburbia. Forget the high-fashion line; go for the gusto.

ACA JOE: A San Francisco company with financial troubles that is restructuring in the United States. Because of this there is little to no crossover between the two companies, save the name recognition. Aca Joe is one of the best stores in Mexico, and offers an outstanding line of sweats, Ts, and sports clothes that are colorful and unisex. Prices may seem a little high when compared with the other T-shirt chains, but these are quality goods. Mix and match with Ruben Torres.

SANBORNS: This is a department store that serves locals and tourists with a little of everything you might need, from books in English to maps to souvenirs. Most Sanborns shops are worth visiting (not all of them are great) and the one in downtown Mexico City is a must—it's in a building called the House of Tiles. You can always rely on Sanborns for a meal, a pharmacy, a book in English, and a clean bathroom.

GIRASOL: A very special look goes with these clothes; anyone who knows can tell you are wearing one of these designs—you get more cachet from wearing this semi–status symbol. The clothes are based on native designs that are then jazzed up in contemporary ways so they don't look like costumes. Sold in Girasol boutiques in Mexico City and other fine specialty stores in resort cities. Prices begin at $100.

ARMANDO: Along the same lines as Girasol. Armando's things are a little more bold, a little more Auntie Mame. Everything from multi-colored leather belts and one-size dresses with appliqués to beach cover-ups and resort wear. Nice for the cruise crowd. Competitive in price and design with Girasol.

2 ▾ DETAILS

Information, Please

O ne of the worst things about Mexico is the community of hustlers who have taken it upon themselves to take advantages of the tourists. The good news: Prices in Mexico are so low that even if you are cheated, you may not mind. The bad news: Once you have been cheated, you become very aware that a system exists and you—the gringo—are about to be taken time and time again, unless you possess the information (and the chutzpah) it takes to beat the system. (For more on how to bargain see page 46.)

Booking Mexico / I

T here are scads of guidebooks written about Mexico, with more being published every season. The one we find indispensable, *Travelers Guide to Mexico*, is not often sold in the United States, but is published in English and readily available in Mexico. It costs about $12. Over 300 pages long, this book includes maps, ads, and information on hotels, eateries, and shopping in every major city in Mexico. It is dated by year, and can often be found in your hotel room, with the words DO NOT TAKE THIS COPY stamped all over it. Be advised that, as with many travel books, the edition goes to press before the date on the cover. So the 1989 edition was completed in mid-1988, etc. However, the book is revised annually, and is perhaps the most up-to-date guidebook on Mexico. If you want to order it before your trip, you may send a check for $12.95 for ordinary mail (good luck), or for $18.95 for airmail, with your name and address to: *Travelers Guide to Mexico,* Box 6-1007, Mexico D.F. 06600.

We also suggest that you read Carl Franz's *The People's Guide to Mexico,* a sort of hippie version of what to expect. It happens to be easy (and fun) to read, and much more complete on the nitty-gritty, real-life matters than any other guidebook we've ever seen. It is sold in most U.S. bookstores in the travel section.

Booking Mexico / 2

We hope this isn't news to you, but here goes: The largest percentage of bookings into Mexico are done on a package basis. Therefore, the best prices for the traveler to Mexico are found through wholesalers and packagers. Your trip to Mexico may be as much as 40% cheaper if you use a packager!

Wholesalers and Packagers

It is true that anyplace in the world that you travel will be less expensive if you buy a package that includes airfare and hotel and, hopefully, some land travel arrangements, such as transfers to and from the hotel and maybe a city tour. This is particularly true in Mexico. In fact, because most of the resorts in Mexico were created by Fonatur, a government agency, a system has developed that makes it almost foolhardy to buy anything except a package. The government and the hotels offer special rates to wholesalers, who buy by the block. This way Fonatur knows how much cash is coming in, and the government and/or the hotels have no worries about occupancy. Wholesalers fill the rooms because they have already paid for them. If business is slow, they offer special promotions to fill the spaces. You gain.

Savings by booking a package are anywhere from 20% to 50%, depending on the type of airline (charter or scheduled, known in the trade as "sked") and the degree of luxury of your hotel. There are also combinations of low package rates with promotional rates that make it too cheap to stay at home. For instance, if a new hotel is opening, or a new flight route is being launched—pass the sunscreen, it's time to take off.

We have had personal experience with only two packagers, but both are biggies:

ASTI TOURS: Anne Storch Travel International, known as Asti Tours, has been booking Mexico, and only Mexico, for thirty-five years. Mrs. Storch is a wholesaler, which means she can only sell her package to you through your travel agent. (If you don't have a travel agent, ask for the name of one at Asti; they have some 6,000 agents on their lists.) You can call on her toll-free number, get all the information you need, and then book through a travel agent; but law prohibits Asti from dealing directly with the public because their prices are so low. (After all, they are wholesalers.) Asti offers all the tours and travel deals anyone could want, to any combination of cities, but Mrs. Storch stresses that her main business is in resorts. She has charter and scheduled airline packages, and land (and even food) packages, and is the only agency to offer three-

and four-night Cancún packages via charter
from New York. She says that a person who
books through her agency can expect to save
25%, but also notes that at a hotel with a rack
rate (regular rate) of $200 per night, she gets
the rate of $120 (a 40% savings). Meal plans
are sometimes available, in which you pay a
flat fee for coupons you redeem for meals. If
you just want to get an idea of the available
bargains, look for the regular Asti ad in the
Sunday Travel section of *The New York Times*.
And yes, you can get the fancy big-name hotels in an Asti package. Call toll-free: (800)
327-4390.

ASTI TOURS, 21 East 40th Street, New York
NY 10016

▼

MEXICO TRAVEL ADVISORS (MTA):
This company came to us through the Mexican tourist office. They have nine offices in
Mexico, nine in the United States, three in
Canada, and two in Europe. Like Asti, they
are wholesalers who work with travel agents
and not directly with individual travelers. They
have been in business for fifty years, offering
either one-city or multicity packages, with or
without air. While you can book a beach trip
with MTA, their best tours have themes such as
"Mexico's Religious Heritage," "The Many
Faces of Mexico," "The Colonial Art Trail,"
and the like. Call (800) 682-8687.

MEXICO TRAVEL ADVISORS, 1717 North High-
land Avenue, Los Angeles CA 90028

Hotel Chains of Mexico

I f you enjoy the ease of making all your reservations through one hotel chain and like the notion of pretty much being able to count on what you're getting in terms of a hotel room, there are a handful of big chains that service the hot spots of Mexico. While we have more specific hotel information (with price information included) in each city section of this book, these are the chains we frequent. Please be sure to ask for any special rates and deals when you call these toll-free numbers, since a hotel package or a promotional rate will be far cheaper than the regular rack rate.

HOLIDAY INNS: Holiday Inns in Mexico have a rather wide range in decor from almost fancy to very plain. In some cases, they are the most American hotel in town and therefore a blessing to the kind of traveler who expects certain amenities. They also offer one of the best bargains you can get —with their package prices (based on either three-night or seven-night occupancy) you can get a room for about $30 per person per night. There are about one dozen hotels in Mexico now. For U.S. reservations call (800) HOLIDAY.

PRESIDENTE/EL PRESIDENTE: This is a tad confusing at first, but makes perfect sense once you understand it. Up until 1985, El Presidente was a chain of superior/deluxe hotels owned by the Mexican government. Then investors bought fifteen of the thirty-seven hotels and got to work on the refurbishing. They spent $50 million on a mere seven hotels, all of which are now five-star properties located in big or resort cities. The independently owned hotels are called Presidente; the ones that are still owned by the government are called El Presidente. The seven newly done hotels are spectacular—ranging from the ultramodern Mexico City hotel (the Chapultepec) to the national landmark convent hotel in Oaxaca. Prices vary widely depending on the season and on if you get a promotional deal or not, as well as on the city you choose. Resort cities are more expensive, but even they have deals. The same room in Cancún can cost $60 per night or $170 per night. The highest price for a room in Mexico City is $85 per night, single or double. For U.S. reservations, call (800) 472-2427, which happens to be (800) GRACIAS.

SHERATON: We have been staying at Sheraton hotels in Mexico since they first started out. Sheraton has a reputation for being on top of a location, and is usually the first hotel chain to go into a new resort area. They were first in Cancún and first in Huatulco. Many of the properties have Towers sections in the hotel or adjoining the hotel where for a small amount extra (about $20 per night) you get a full breakfast and many other amenities that make the price difference worthwhile. Sheraton always offers one of the fanciest hotels in town, with all the frills Americans want and expect, without being the most expensive hotel in town. There are about a half-dozen hotels currently in the system, including one in Guatemala City. Prices vary with group rates, promotional rates, hotel, and time of year, but a double room at the María Isabel in Mexico City costs about $75 a night. Honeymoon plans are available at the five resort hotels and in Mexico City—the rate is for a couple who don't really have to be on their honeymoon, just looking for a good deal. Call (800) 325-3535 in the United States.

CAMINO REAL/WESTIN: This is only slightly confusing: The name of the Mexican division of Westin Hotels is Camino Real, and they manage properties named Camino Real as well as certain other hotels that have entirely different names—like Las Brisas, the famous Acapulco resort, and Las Hadas, the once private resort in Manzanillo that is now open to semi–jet-setters. The Camino Real hotel is always the fanciest hotel in town. There are about one dozen properties, including the fanciest hotel in Guatemala City and our secret shopping hotel in Mexico City, the Galería Plaza. Prices are high, ranging from $125 a room per night to several hundred dollars per night for a resort villa. There are packages and promotional rates available. If you must have luxury, you can't do better. For U.S. reservations call (800) 228-3000.

FIESTA AMERICANA: This is a Mexican chain that seems determined to completely take over Cancún (where they have about five hotels) and will then probably go on to increase from their current dozen hotels elsewhere. Fiesta Americana positions itself as a luxury hotel with low-to-moderate rates. They have weekly "Affordable Mexico Fiesta" promotions with a weekly room rate under $300 and add-on nights at $40 each. In Cancún, we like their Beach Club and Villas hotel with its pink Moorish splendor, but there are two even newer hotels, the Coral and the Condessa. Their Sol Caribe Hotel is the only place to be in Cozumel. Call (800) 223-2332.

Hotel Tips

Never before have we seen an entire country so anxious to fill its hotel rooms. What you have is a marketplace offering two kinds of space: resort (beaches) and urban (including places like Oaxaca). While there are hotel chains designed for the local population, there are an enormous number of hotel rooms created for tourists and priced so that locals really can't afford them. In order to fill these rooms, the hotels make deals. They deal with packagers (page 16), they deal with airlines, and they will also deal directly with the public, if you just know what to look or ask for:

▼ The season is December 15 to April 15. There are off-season and seasonal rates, as in any sunny clime. However, the first two weeks in January and the month of April are traditionally slow. Therefore some hotels lower their rates at these times. Presidente is among them.

▼ Sheraton has either Towers floors or a complete Towers building (new in Cancún) for guests who want something a little bit fancier. While these cost a bit more, ask about the extras that are "free" with the room. If there are two or more of you in the room, you will more than save the difference on breakfast alone, since all Towers rooms include a complimentary breakfast.

▼ Cruise lines have special add-on packages that apply to the hotels they work with. These rates are enormously discounted, in or out of season.

▼ When Hurricane Gilbert left Mexico with a problem, and the press went nuts making the destruction look like devastation, Mexico's hotels pulled together and lowered rates to lure tourists back to see for themselves. Watch the travel section of your newspaper and the Sunday Travel section of *The New York Times* for special deals. When rooms are going empty, deals are being made. The reason for the empty rooms could be explained in your paper. So start reading. Then start packing.

Getting There

M exican national airlines have been playing hopscotch with turmoil and crisis. Check with your travel agent to see if either Mexicana or Aeroméxico is flying, and what the status of their fares and refunds is. They often run excellent promotional rates.

American carriers also service our sisters down south. Almost all of them have some service to Mexico, although two have the bulk of the business.

Continental and Delta airlines are the most active in the U.S.-to-Mexico business—Delta bought Western Airlines' routes and services to Mexico through Los Angeles and some Southwestern U.S. cities, and is now stepping up service from the East Coast. The departure gate is always readily apparent: It's a little stucco archway.

Continental, although being pushed by Delta, still owns the East Coast business, with many flights a day from a choice of airports. With their new terminal at Newark, they push this possibility most strongly. Don't knock it; see page 45. Continental does a huge business with packagers such as Asti. And with Houston as their home base, they are also on top of the Southwestern routes.

Don't forget to look at the airline package as one of the better—and less expensive—ways of traveling in Mexico. Continental can give you any combination of Mexican cities, or a Mexico/Guatemala package, with or without Belize. Most tours are in and out of Houston (connections there are easily made with a low-cost zone-transfer price system) and include airfare, hotel, transfers, etc. Call Continental's Grand Destinations for more details, at (800) 451-0916.

You may also visit Mexico by cruise ship. The Western Riviera cruise comes in two variations—a one-week cruise departing from and returning to Los Angeles, and a one-way trip beginning in Los Angeles and ending in Acapulco (or vice versa). The Transcanal cruise route offers some Mexican ports along with several Caribbean ones as it makes its way through Panama and to San Juan or Miami/Ft. Lauderdale or New York.

There are several trains that crisscross Mexico. They are considered expensive by locals (and a steal by gringos) and are not heavily used by Mexicans, who prefer buses. Buy tickets called *Primera Especial*—mere first class won't do the trick—and stick to the touristy trains such as the *Constitucionalista,* leaving Mexico City's Buenavista Station at 7:35 A.M. headed for the Colonial Cities. Also consider the *Jarocho* to Veracruz, the *Regiomontano* to and from Nuevo Laredo, and the *Tapatio* to Guadalajara. These special trains are only about three years old, and were designed specifically to impress tourists.

Bus transportation is so incredibly inexpensive you will get tears in your eyes thinking about it: A first-class trip from Mexico City to Taxco costs about $2.50. You can take long bus trips from the United States to Mexico City (we're talking over 24 hours) or even on to Guatemala—but these are suggested only for the hearty. See page 166 for more on bus trips out of Mexico City for shopping expeditions.

Driving is popular, especially among those who live in the Southwestern border states.

We traversed Mexico in a 1963 white Dodge (fins and all), and recommend the drive to any serious shoppers who have vans or can load their vehicle with a lot of merchandise. You must buy special Mexican insurance for your car before you cross the border. There are literally dozens of shops that sell this service on the U.S. side. It costs about $12 a day; try Sanborns if you aren't impressed by any of the many billboards you pass.

Don't forget walking as a method of getting to Mexico. When we were kids in Texas, we drove to Nuevo Laredo on family day trips (bringing Uncle Rudi and Aunt Gertrude every time they were visiting from Germany), parked the car, and then, for only fifteen cents each, walked across the International Bridge to shopping heaven.

Getting Around

We have done a good bit of driving in Mexico in recent years in rented cars, but find that taxis or public transportation do the trick in most big cities. While taxis are basically cheap, few have meters (especially outside of D.F.), so the price for your trip must be arranged before you get in the taxi. If you are on a cruise, the cruise director or tour director will tell you the going price for certain destinations. This is usually a per-person price, which makes no sense if you think about it—but that's the system.

There were plenty of times when we got off the ship and paid the $2 per person and ended up where the driver wanted to take everyone (the main square, of course), not where the various people had asked to be taken. Ability to speak Spanish or to fight back is meaningless in a case like this—the driver only cares about getting back in line to take more cruise passengers. And take them he will.

In order to establish a fair price for a certain distance, it is essential to have some knowledge of local distances and rates. It is equally essential to have a good sense of humor, so that when driver A takes you two miles for $5 and driver B takes you five miles for $2, you can just throw up your arms and laugh. You can't beat the system if you are just in town for a few hours.

In Mexico City, there are specific problems you can avoid (see page 120). There, you can also take the *metro*.

Bus travel in Mexico, both city transportation and intercity transportation, is inexpensive (it costs pennies) and simple. Why pay for a taxi in Acapulco when a bus runs up and down the main drag from the cruise pier, in and out of the main shopping districts? A city bus ride in Mexico is not likely to cost more than the equivalent of fifteen cents. And that's expensive. Intercity travel is always done by bus by Mexicans; thus the entire country is united by a series of excellent bus routes. You do not need to be able to speak Spanish to successfully ride the buses in Mexico—although your conversation with fellow riders will be limited. For bus how-tos, see page 166.

Snack and Shop

Opportunities to eat well and inexpensively abound in Mexico. We are not always as careful as many travelers are, since we are here so often, but if you live in terror of becoming ill, we do have a few of Dr. Debbie's special tips for those of you who are worried about your tummies:

1. Drink bottled water, Coca-Cola, or beer. Even in communities where the water is alleged to be purified, stick to these rules.

2. No ice. Tell people that you love hot soft drinks.

3. Eat all your meals in your hotel, or in reputable hotels and restaurants. Do not eat from fast-food stands. Do not eat ice cream, ices, or milk products from a stand.

4. If that doesn't work, eat in Sanborns—almost every city has at least one branch of this department store–cum–coffee shop where you can have an American menu, low prices, and, usually, safe foods.

5. Only eat fruits you can peel yourself. Never buy a fruit (or melon) that has been cut open and is standing there, glistening in the sun. Buy the whole piece and ask the vendor to cut it for you then and there, if you care to eat in the marketplace. Or, better yet, whip out your Swiss army knife.

6. When shopping in the marketplace, you can buy foods and snack—but buy them wisely and wash them carefully before eating.

7. Don't relax your guard on the plane ride home—that food came from a Mexican kitchen.

Hours

Shopping hours in Mexico vary with the city. Resort towns and those cities with a large tourist trade usually have some form of shopping entertainment open during the afternoon siesta hours. Standard business hours in Mexico are 9 A.M. to 1 P.M. and 3 P.M. to 7 P.M. In Mexico City shops don't open until

10 A.M. In Acapulco (see page 268) the afternoon siesta is much longer—usually four hours—and stores stay open much later at night to allow for the *paseo*.

Markets open between 8 and 8:30 A.M. (or earlier), and usually close down between noon and 1 P.M. Malls usually don't close during lunch. In Mexico City, department stores are always open during lunch, as are all Sanborns stores. Mom-and-pop shops may close for the siesta, but D.F. does not close tight. Hotel shops may or may not close for the siesta.

Most stores in big cities are open all day on Saturday—meaning, they don't do half-day business. Little is open on Sunday, although there is usually a fair somewhere, or an art show.

"American Made"

M any travelers to Mexico stock up on Pepto-Bismol and assorted health and beauty goods as if they were off to the Sahara with the French Foreign Legion. Pepto-Bismol, like many other American-made goods, is readily available all over Mexico. In most cases, an "American-made" item is actually made in Mexico. It may be more expensive in Mexico than at home, but not priced out of bounds, and the familiarity of a product you know and trust is worthwhile. But *note*: some foods or products will not taste or perform the same way. All major hotels sell some health and beauty aids. Should this source fail you, go to Sanborns, which will have a wide variety of many internationally marketed pharmaceuticals (many sold over the counter, without prescription!) and a pharmacist who can assist you or call an English-speaking doctor for you.

Supermarkets

I f you want to see how middle- and upper-class Mexican people really shop, or merely want to beat the high prices in your hotel minibar, amble into the local supermarket-cum–K mart like Gigante and Aurrera, which are most often large modern structures— certainly nicer than the grocery stores in New York and Connecticut, and often as nice as the groceries in Texas and California. About one-half of the packaged goods here come from American companies, but although the packaging will look familiar, the labels are in Spanish. They also sell dry goods.

Do not buy liquor for export in a supermarket, because it will be 30% cheaper in the duty-free. If you want liquor for immediate consumption, however, the supermarket will be less expensive than your hotel.

Since supermarkets are (unfortunately) not on the usual tourist path, you may have some trouble finding one. *However, remember this tip:* There is always a big supermarket across the street from—or next door to—the many autobus terminals in Mexico City. If you are asking, in Spanish, for a supermarket, ask for a *supermercado,* not a *mercado,* or you could be directed to the local fruit and vegetable market.

Tianguis

O ur favorite word in Spanish is *tianguis,* which means market—but really means fair, or street market, or Indian market, or flea market, or giant get-together-toswap-stuff. In big cities there is a *tianguis* every day; in smaller cities there are certain market days that are famous throughout the region. There is always increased bus service on market day.

Market Days

The Secretary of Tourism has provided us with a published list of market days throughout Mexico. We must warn you that we went specially to Puebla on a Thursday because this list states that Thursday is one of the market days in Puebla and were disappointed (and shocked) to be told by the local tourist office that "Puebla is a big city. We don't have a market day like a little village."

Other than that, the list proved accurate for our investigations.

DAILY: Acámbaro, Guanajuato (except Thursday); Acayucan, Veracruz; Aguascalientes, Aguascalientes; Arriaga, Chiapas; Chetumal, Quintana Roo; Cuauhtémoc, Chiapas; Gómez Palacio, Durango; Guadalajara, Jalisco; Guasave, Sinaloa; Matehuala, San Luis Potosí; Mérida, Yucatán; Nuevo Casas Grandes, Chihuahua; Poza Rica, Veracruz; Puerto Penasco, Sonora; Querétaro, Querétaro; Saltillo, Coahuila; San Cristóbal de las Casas, Chiapas (except Sunday); San Juan de los Lagos, Jalisco; Tierra Blanca, Veracruz; Tonalá, Chiapas; Tuxtla Gutiérrez, Chiapas; Uruapan, Michoacán; Veracruz, Veracruz; Villahermosa, Tamaulipas.

MONDAY: Camargo, Chihuahua; Ixmiquilpan, Hidalgo; Izúcar de Matamoros, Puebla; León, Guanajuato; Metepec, México; Miahuatlán, Oaxaca; Moroléon, Guanajuato; Motul, Yucatán; Sayula, Hidalgo; Tepeji del Río, Hidalgo; Tepetlixpa, México; Tulancingo, Hidalgo; Xochitlán, Hidalgo; Zaachila, Oaxaca.

TUESDAY: Acatlán de Osorio, Puebla; Acatzingo, Puebla; Atlixco, Puebla; Capulhuac, México; Celaya, Guanajuato; Chiconcuac, México; Irapuato, Guanajuato; León, Guanajuato; Ozumba de Alzate, México; Pátzcuaro, Michoacán; Salamanca, Guanajuato; Santiago Tianguistenco, México; San Francisco del Rincón, Guanajuato; San Martín Texmelucan, Puebla; San Miguel de Allende, Guanajuato; Silao, Guanajuato; Tecali, Puebla; Texmelucan, Oaxaca; Tlahuelilpa, Hidalgo.

WEDNESDAY: Acaxochitlan, Hidalgo; Acolman, México; Actopán, Hidalgo; Cholula, Puebla; Ejutla, Oaxaca; Etla, Oaxaca; Huamantla, Tlaxcala; Juchitepec, México; Ocoyoacac, México; Tepoztlán, Morelos.

THURSDAY: Huejotzingo, Puebla; Morelia, Michoacán; Santiago de Anaya, Hidalgo; Taxco, Guerrero; Tecozautla, Hidalgo; Temascalapa, México; Tenancingo, México; Tenango, México; Tulancingo, Hidalgo; Valle de Bravo, México; Villa del Carbón, México; Xochimilco, D.F.

FRIDAY: Agulilla, Michoacán; Chalco, México; Jilotepec, México; Ocotlán, Jalisco; Ozumba de Alzate, México; Pátzcuaro, Michoacán; San Martín Texmelucan, Puebla; Tecali, Puebla; Tepeaca, Puebla; Teziutlán, Puebla; Tlanepantla, México; Toluca, México; Zacatlán, Puebla.

SATURDAY: Angangueo, Michoacán; Apatzingán, Michoacán; Atlixco, Puebla; Camargo, Chihuahua; Celaya, Guanajuato; Chicuautla, Hidalgo; Ciudad Mante, Tamaulipas; Concepción del Oro, Zacatecas; Cosamaloapan, Veracruz; Cotija, Michoacán; Huachinango, Puebla; Huejotzingo, Puebla; Iguala, Guerrero; Lerma, México; Manzanillo, Colima; Oaxaca, Oaxaca; Ocotlán, Jalisco; Parras, Coahuila; Sabinas, Coahuila; San Bartolo Naucalpan, México; Tecamachalco, Puebla; Tehuacán, Puebla; Tlaxcala, Tlaxcala; Xochimilco, D.F.; Zacualtipan, Hidalgo; Zimapán, Hidalgo.

SUNDAY: Acatlán, Puebla; Acaxochitlan, Hidalgo; Álamos, Sonora; Alfajayucan, Hidalgo; Almoloya de Juárez, México; Álvarado, Veracruz; Amecameca, México; Amozoc de Mota, Puebla; Angangueo, Michoacán; Apam, Hidalgo; Apatzingán, Michocán; Apizaco, Tlaxcala; Atlacomulco, Puebla; Banderilla, Veracruz; Cadereyta, Querétaro; Chiconcuac, México; Chilapa, Guerrero; Cholula, Puebla; Ciudad Hidalgo, Michoacán; Ciudad Lopez Mateos, México; Ciudad Mante, Tamaulipas; Ciudad Serdán, Puebla; Concepción del Oro, Zacatecas; Cosamaloapan, Veracruz; Cotija, Michoacán; Cuernavaca, Morelos; Cuetzalán, Puebla; Fortín, Veracruz; Fresnillo, Zacatecas; Guadalajara, Jaliso; Guanajuato, Guanajuato; Huajuápan de León, Oaxaca; Huamantla, Tlaxcala; Huichapan, Hidalgo; Iguala, Guerrero; Ixtapan de la Sal, México; Izúcar de Matamoros, Puebla; Jacala, Hidalgo; Jocotepec, Jalisco; Juchitán, Oaxaca; La Piedad, Michoacán; Luis Moya, Zacateca; Manzanillo, Colima; Martinez de la Torre, Veracruz; Metztitlán, Hidalgo; Mitla, Oaxaca; Morelia, Michoacán; Moroleón, Guanajuato; Nochixtlán, Oaxaca; Ocotlán, Jalisco; Papantla, Veracruz; Parras, Coahuila; Pátzcuaro, Michoacán; Perote, Veracruz; Puebla, Puebla; Puerto Vallarta, Jalisco; Quiroga, Michoacán; Sabinas, Coahuila; Sahuayo, Michoacán; Salamanca, Guanajuato; San Francisco del Rincón, Guanajuato; San José Purúa, Michoacán; San Juan del Río, Querétaro; San Miguel de Allende, Guanajuato; Silao, Guanajuato; Tabasco, Zacateca; Tamazunchale, San Luis Potosi; Tasquillo, Hidalgo; Taxco, Guerrero; Tehuantepec, Oaxaca; Temascalapa, México; Tenancingo, México; Tenango, México; Tepotzotlán, Morelos; Tequisquiapan, Querétaro; Tetela de Ocampo, Puebla; Texcoco, México; Teziutlán, Puebla; Tingüindin, Michoacán; Tlacolula, Oaxaca; Tlalnepantla, México; Tula, Hidalgo; Valle de Bravo, México; Villa del Carbón, México; Xicotepec, Puebla; Zacapu, Michoacán; Zacatlán, Puebla; Zacualtipán, Hidalgo; Zimpan, Hidalgo; Zitácuaro, Michoacán.

Size of Relief

I f you don't know the size of anything in metric measures, you are bound to be cheated. (See page 52.) *One tip:* Since it's unlikely that you'll want a kilo (2.2 pounds) of anything, know that you can buy things by the *mano,* which is the Spanish word for hand. If you want a handful of something, just say *"mano."* Clothing is marked with either U.S. or European sizes. (See the chart on page 279.)

Shopping Bags

W hile fancy stores have their share of slick shopping bags, in the market your purchase will be placed in a small plastic bag, usually the kind without handles. You are expected to come to the market with your own *bolsa*—bag. You can, of course, buy one at the market: Usually $1 will get you a very nice woven plastic job with two plastic handles. Giant tote bags with placket bottoms cost as much as $4 each, but they are indestructible.

A Word to the Bimbo Shoppers

We love this one. Bimbo is a Mexican brand of baked goods—sort of like Hostess in the United States. We just love the name, which is seen everywhere—on trucks, on signs, and on all of the packaging. If you are overly cautious about eating local foods, you're safe with Bimbo.

A-Pier-ances

Many cruise visitors to Mexico wonder if, when their ship comes in, and they take the tour, they will still have time to shop. Undoubtedly, the answer is yes. Almost all ship-run or -sponsored tours include time at the local tourist trap (or traps). But the best shopping may be right there at the pier. Especially if you tender into port. On return, there will be a line of shipmates waiting to return to the cruiseship. While you are standing and waiting in line, you can be assured that local vendors will come bopping by with their oranges in plastic bags, their bracelets, and their T-shirts. A quick port-by-port round-up from the cruises we've enjoyed:

Western Caribbean Route

Those going ashore at Playa del Carmen (for Tulum) are taken ashore bright and early, while those staying on board for Cozumel get an extra hour on the ship . . . they too, however, will tender in. In both ports, you will be met at the dock by the usual crowd pleasers—young boys, children, men, and women, all selling something. The biggest shocker: There is quite a retail business going on in Tulum. See page 226. Cozumel has a big international pier with shops.

Mexican Riviera Route

There's nothing happening, shoppingwise, at the pier in Los Angeles. There are phones, but no shops. In Mazatlán you dock in the middle of nowhere, in a very industrial area—if you exit through one gate you can catch the city bus (or a taxi) into town, but you will see no sign whatever of vendors. Get off the ship and onto the awaiting tram and exit through the main gate and you'll be met by a lovely stucco cruise center with about six shops and an outdoor *tianguis* consisting of some twenty-odd vendors. Puerto Vallarta requires a tender, which takes you right to the pier, where there is a huge shopping center with rows of stalls all ready to get you and take you for all you're worth. We are most charmed by Zihuatanejo, where everything is crumbling just a little bit and is exactly the way you want it to be. The whole gang will be out to greet you as your tender pulls up. In Acapulco you have several immediate choices. Few people explore the actual cruise center or know that it has a Ralph Lauren boutique in addition to the obvious duty-free shop and place for long-distance phone calls. You pass from your gangplank into the center and out the front door (which is why you don't see the Lauren shop—unless you're looking for it or go to make an international phone call), where a few more vendors are waiting with T-shirts. Most of the people waiting here are taxi drivers. But they're all here to take you shopping.

Beach Shopping

Everything you can buy in a market you can buy on the beach. If you can't come to the mountain, the mountain will most certainly come right to your beach blanket.

Club Med Shopping

It was our friend Edwina, who works at Club Med, who confessed it to us: "The French would just kill us if we didn't offer shopping." And so it is that Club Med, which is French-owned, has some of the best shopping of all its locations at its many Mexican properties. Not only can you shop at the Club, but various excursions are organized and waiting for you to just sign up and hop on board. Try:

HUATULCO: Several shopping expeditions are available to guests—take your choice of a one-hour flight to Oaxaca for incredible crafts shopping (buy this as a day tour, right there at the Club), or take the bus to Puerto Escondido.

IXTAPA: The Club is four miles out of town, but you can take advantage of a shopping trip to the malls or to Zihuatanejo . . . or do both.

CANCÚN: Take your pick of a shopping trip in Cancún City or a tour of the Hotel Zone, which includes shopping at several malls.

PLAYA BLANCA: Take daylong shopping trips to Puerto Vallarta (about two and a half hours away), or to Manzanillo.

The Paloma Picasso Principle

We have a section on buying silver (see page 87), but we know you are chomping at the bit for some solid facts and figures. So here goes—what you really wanted to know all along: The retail price of the Paloma Picasso sterling silver X pin from Tiffany & Co. is $150 (without tax); price for the Love and Kisses pin (this is the XXXOOO) is $185; and Scribbles costs $195. Call Tiffany at (800) 346-3455 for more specifics or an update on these prices.

The Putumayo Principle

One of the most difficult tasks a shopper has in Mexico is knowing the going price at home for a certain item. Help is on the way if you live in one of the six American cities where there is a Putumayo shop. Putumayo sells primarily Guatemalan imports, but also things from around the world— from Mexico to Turkey. Getting prices here will help you to know what you should be paying in the field. If there is no Putumayo nearby, try to find some shop that specializes in ethnic goods ... often a museum shop will do the trick. Once you have the U.S. prices you'll be able to decide if the item you love in Mexico is a fair deal.

Frida Freaks

Anyone half interested in the arts of Mexico is on to, or is about to be on to, Frida Kahlo and her magical mystery life. Even if you aren't big on art, and prefer instead life's little romances and soap operas, Frida's your gal. Or ghost. She is quite dead—but not in spirit. Frida was an artist who was married to Diego Rivera. She was a tad eccentric (OK, more than a tad), and her work either touches you or leaves you cold. We who admire her call ourselves Frida Freaks, and consider no shopping venture into Mexico complete without some Frida shopping. You'll find Frida merchandise at any branch of the government-owned Fonart stores, where you can buy a reproduction poster for $6 . . . or a postcard for about 50¢. Certain styles sell out faster than others, so you have to keep asking for the specific design you want.

Frauds and Fakes

You run into all kinds of problems in the counterfeit department when you begin to shop in Mexico. Some manufacturers have no respect for trademarks and no problem with producing and selling goods that they did not design. As a result, you'll see a lot of "Louis Vuitton" merchandise that neither Mr. Vuitton's relatives nor the Moët Hennessy company (which owns Louis Vuitton) would ever vouch for.

When it comes to jewelry, silver should be stamped ".925" to indicate it is sterling (see page 87), but bad boys think nothing of falsifying these stamps. Silver bracelets for $1 each, no matter what they say, are not sterling. Always buy jewelry from a reputable dealer if you expect it to be real.

In the art department, it is generally acknowledged that most precolonial relics that come to market these days are frauds. Since it's illegal to bring them out of Mexico, don't waste time scheming how to get the whole thing home.

Some good news: The Ralph Lauren, Fila, Ellesse, and Gucci items you find for sale happen to be real, not fake. But they are made in Mexico.

The Mexican-made pharmaceuticals you may be tempted to buy can have any number of problems with them. Avoid them unless absolutely necessary, and for heaven's sake, don't stock up on birth-control pills just because they are cheaper here. Unless, of course, you think unplanned parenthood is going to be fun.

Licensed to Kill

James Bond may be licensed to kill. Mexican makers are simply licensed to produce designer goods along the same lines and patterns as the mother designer, and to sell these goods in Mexico through authorized stores. When you take a look at the quality of some of these items, you too may want to be licensed to kill—or you may feel the maker was licensed to kill the art form.

But these goods are for the most part legal. Hence all those Ralph Lauren shops are selling legitimate Ralph Lauren designs. The only catch on a license is that the goods are made in Mexico and usually say *"hecho en México"* someplace inside them. Take that *"hecho en México"* Gucci handbag to Gucci in New York and see how fast they won't repair it. The Ralph Lauren shops present some of the nicest-looking decor and best-made Mexican merchandise you'll find in the country, at approximately 30% savings. The Calvin Klein merchandise does not much resemble anything Calvin Klein (or Zack Carr) ever designed—but it's hard to knock an $8 designer T-shirt. The Gucci merchandise cuts a wide swath between great and disgusting. Some of it is so terribly made that we don't care how legal it is, it's not worth the money. Gucci is also expensive: $60 for a wallet is not cheap. There are Gucci factory outlets in the United States where the prices may be comparable to those in Mexico and the merchandise is much better made. Likewise, the Guess jeans are pretty expensive, but cost less than they do in the United States. *One last tip:* If you buy licensed goods that are made in Mexico, you owe it to yourself to buy them with your American Express Card, or any credit card that offers you purchase protection (see page 56).

U.S. Customs and Duties

The United States has special laws for trade with neighboring countries, so there is a slight relaxation of the laws and increase in duty-free allowances for travelers to Mexico. The most significant difference is that the 48-hour requirement is waived. Usually, a U.S. citizen must be out of the country for forty-eight hours in order to qualify for a tax exemption—one duty-free allowance of $400 is allowed to each citizen every thirty days. However, it is totally legal to cross the U.S.-Mexico border for part of a day, load up, and then go home. But you must keep to a total of $400 or less in that time period.

Furthermore, most of what you buy in Mexico will fall under the GSP (Generalized System of Preferences) regulations. The United States allows certain noncompetitive items to enter the country without duty. *Noncompetitive* is the key word here; if you are wondering if an item is GSP-protected or not, try to think if something like it is made in the United States.

In alphabetical order, items protected by GSP laws include: baskets, candy, chess (and game sets), furniture, furs, guitars (musical instruments), leather goods in clothing (but not shoes or boots), paper goods (including artificial flowers and *piñatas*), perfumes (Mexican licenses), picture frames, pottery and china (where the china is valued at $12 or less a place setting), silver (table and flatware, not jewelry for resale, although jewelry for personal use is OK), toys (except dolls), and wood carvings.

To put this in most general terms: Arts and crafts are duty-free.

For specific information, call the U.S. Customs Service (Department of the Treasury) Travel Information line in Washington, D.C., at (202) 566-8195. If you are a businessperson or garmento bringing back samples or inquiring about piecework laws, call (202) 566-6232, a special hot line to help clarify the new laws regarding merchandise that is assembled (but not made) in Mexico. Hours are 8:30 A.M. to 8 P.M.

You may already know that there is no duty on genuine antiques (those items that are over 100 years old and come with a certificate of origin) and works of art.

Protected Items

Endangered animals are protected by both Mexico and the United States—other species endangered from the Mexican point of view include rare books and antiquities of national importance. While that little Mayan piece of red clay you bought on the trip is probably a fake, it's illegal to take it out of Mexico if it is real. Anything that dates from before colonial times (1520, give or take a year) cannot be taken out of Mexico!

Shipping Them Home

We have a very simple rule when it comes to mailing something home from Mexico: Don't do it. The mail is bad; things disappear or get broken; things happen. You can take delivery—this is the age of miracles—but we don't really like to ship from Mexico.

Schlepping Them Home

What we like to do is schlepp. We never travel without extra duffel bags and tote bags, and we pass on to you the lesson of the bus station. If you stand in the bus stations of Mexico City you will note that 95% of the people arriving are carrying egg boxes—cartons about 12 by

18 inches in size and clearly marked *"huevos,"* or with pictures of chickens and often the word *Fragile*. Is it omelet time in the big city, or what? Well, it seems that everyone transports goods in egg cartons. So when in Rome, and all that. Egg cartons carry a lot. Furthermore, they can be spliced together to form one large box.

If you are a serious shopper, you already travel with your scissors, your bubble wrap, and your brown plastic packing tape (expensive in Mexico). If you don't normally travel with these items, consider beginning to do so now.

Once you have packed all your treasures, you'll want them to fly home with you on the airplane. We've only flown two different airlines to Mexico, and have two dramatically different songs to sing. At Pan Am in Mexico City, on departure to the United States, the airline was strict about carry-ons (just one) and about allowing only two pieces of checked baggage. Everything else had to be declared excess baggage and paid for—at $31 per bag. This included a *piñata*! (We are outraged that anyone would charge for a *piñata,* since they weigh less than a pound.) At Continental, they allow 2 pieces of luggage as carry-on (bless their hearts), the *piñata* went free; the carry-on situation for all passengers was almost hilarious— the airline is very generous in what you can take on board. The best news of all: Additional baggage charges are only $20 for each bag weighing 70 lbs. or less, up to three per passenger.

If you are planning on doing a lot of shopping, or on buying odd-sized pieces, call the various airlines you are considering and get their policies and prices for additional baggage. This alone may help you choose the airline you want to do business with.

Welcome Home

With GSP laws being what they are, it is unlikely that you will go over your $400 duty-free allowance. However, if you do, Uncle Sam expects you to pay a flat 10% rate on the next $1,000 worth of merchandise. In other words, for the simple price of $100 you can bring in $1,400 worth of goods legally.

When you return home overland, however, you may find that making sure you've paid the right amount of duty is not what the border guards are most interested in. They want to know if you are carrying drugs. Of course you are not. Should you have prescription medicines with you, make sure they are in the properly labeled pharmacy containers. Naturally, when crossing borders you should be dressed for success—those with too casual clothing and backpack manners are often hassled far more than those who play the part of the dutiful (in all senses of the word) tourist.

When asked if you are carrying any foods, fruits, or vegetables, you should already know not to bring these things into the United States. However, you may be amused to know that it is legal to bring in vanilla, although some states will tax it as a liquor because of its high alcohol content. You are allowed to bring peanuts and garlic across the border—*ristras* of garlic are a standard item sold in most border towns.

Do not bring home any new pets without knowing exactly what the laws are (most likely they aren't in your favor); it is highly illegal to bring back that pretty little bird you bought in the market . . . even though you could get a fortune for it in the big city.

And for those of you who are driving into Texas (from Mexico) for the first time, yes, you'll pass through guards and inspections on the U.S. side of the river. . . . But guess what, guys: A few miles north of town (any town) they are waiting for you again. Welcome home.

Welcome Home to Newark

The more we travel to Mexico, and the more people we meet (shoppers all), the more we hear about different ports of return. Houston, they say, is the worst—long lines and tough customs officials. Los Angeles can be rough also. The breeze, as we hear it, is to come into Newark International Airport, where traffic is less, lines aren't bad, and the customs officials are downright friendly. We've met a few buyers who deal in arts and crafts for their businesses who say they always take the nonstop Continental flights in and out of Newark. From their lips to your passport. Welcome home.

3▾MONEY MATTERS

How to Bargain Like a Pro

B eating the system takes time, patience, and energy. You may not be interested. The more you know, the more you realize there is to learn. It's a never-ending struggle to stay on top of the system. So we're going to point you in the right direction and share a few of our shopper's tips with you. But if you want to bail out at any time and relax (and maybe be taken), we understand. It's a gringo's privilege.

Speaking Spanish

T his is probably true all over the world (it's undoubtedly true all over the world), but we were never in a position to truly appreciate it: If you speak the native language, you will not be taken.

Ideally, you speak like a native and have a great accent. In case you don't, remember a few things: A great accent is the most important thing—it's how you say it, not what you say. Speaking rapidly and with authority also counts for a lot—don't worry about grammar, or proper verb tense, or stopping to ask what something means. . . . Chatter on at the speed of a sizzling taco. Proper hand motions, gestures, and expressions are important—you can speak few words but pull these international gestures off properly and be taken more seriously. If you can act as if you know what you are doing (and saying), and pull it off, you will come out a winner. You can be taken seriously, or merely be taken.

Chutzpah

C*hutzpah* is Yiddish for nerve or moxie ... and if we have to define it for you, it's probably too late for you to get it. If you have the spirit of your convictions etched in your soul and the nerve to stand by them, you will be successful in all aspects of Mexican life. If you let those you are dealing with understand that you know what the deal is, and what is fair, you will not be taken advantage of. This is not so simple as it may at first seem, because you need two things in your favor: a willingness to fight for your rights and a knowledge of what is fair in the marketplace.

The last time we were in Mexico City, we sank into the car that drove us away from the city to the airport, and agreed that we were happy to leave Mexico City for a while: We were tired of fighting with taxi drivers. If you have no nerve, no chutzpah, no interest in bargaining, or haggling, or fighting for your rights, you just might not enjoy your stay in Mexico. (Stick to a cruise!)

How to Bargain Like a Gringo

T he basic premise is that there're two different price structures in the retail world. This is true not only in Mexico but in every place where there is a market, and most notably in every place where the people doing business with each other are from different cultures. Facts are facts. Gringos must speak excellent Spanish in order to not be taken. High-school Spanish will get you past first base and will serve you rather well in getting around, but in the heat of hard and fast bargaining it is usually not good enough—unless you are also a marvelous actor.

So here you are, a gringo, no doubt about it. You have probably heard that half the asking price is the so-called fair price. Don't depend on that rule, folks, because it's wrong. We wish there was a hard, fast law about all this, but it really is touch and go, depending on the market and who you are dealing with. In markets where you are a tourist and are considered fair game, the right price for any given item may be 10% to 25% of the asking price. In an Indian market, where they've never seen a gringo before, you may not even get 10% off the asking price.

So let's take this from the top:

1. Size up the marketplace. If you are on a cruise, in a resort city, at the stalls set up by the ruins . . . anywhere that has a steady flow of tourists: Forget it. This is Gyp City. Don't fall in love with anything; consider half the asking price to be the higher boundary of the real price, and negotiate from that strength. Consider that half is outrageously high! If they ask $100, the most you want to pay is $40—so you want to offer $20. Let them laugh. Or let them come back with a counteroffer. If you are in an authentic market, particularly an Indian market, don't be surprised at two amazing facts: Prices are so low that you are happy to pay the asking price (and more), and the bargaining is minimal.

2. Base your bargaining on quantity whenever possible. If you're at the stage when all the

silver earrings you've seen begin to look alike, and you figure you want to buy four or five pair (they do make the perfect gift), do so at one shop. The more you buy from one vendor, the greater your chance of a discount.

3. Realize that even though you feel that you are always supposed to bargain, there are many occasions when bargaining is unwarranted. Either the vendor simply won't budge on the price or the asking price is so ridiculously low that the pennies saved are a joke and you cannot stoop to play the game. We were in the market in Toluca one bright morning and were grabbing up the pottery bargains. Coffee mugs are sold there by the dozen—and the price quoted is always by the dozen—so when the vendor asked for $3 for the entire dozen it was, well, impossible to pretend that was just too much money.

And then we raise our coffee mug in salute to the gentleman in one of Mexico City's finer markets who quoted a high asking price for a product.

"¡No me diga!" (Don't tell me!) we said with genuine alarm in absolutely faultless Spanish.

"Sí, lo digo," he answered forthrightly. (Yes, I say it.)

And do you know what? We paid the asking price.

So, one of the first rules of bargaining is to establish if there will be any bargaining.

4. The best rule is never to express how much you love something. You'll do excellent bargaining if you work in a team with a partner. One plays good guy, the other plays bad guy. Good guys says, "Isn't that carving wonderful?" Bad guy says, "I don't know. How much is it? It's a little crooked." This is all done with the bad guy making the proper facial and hand gestures to con-

vey the message that she is not impressed.
Even if the vendor cannot understand one
word of what's been said in English, she
will understand all gestures and motions.

5. Ask prices early in the game to decide if
you are going to play. It is rude to bargain
ferociously for something and then not buy
it. Establish from the vendor's asking price
if you are serious or not. If you say "Thanks"
and proceed to walk away after the opening gambit, the seller will say "How much
you give me?" You can now make a coun-
teroffer or look him straight in the face and
say sincerely, "I'm not that interested, thank
you." If you make it clear that you really
aren't going to buy and don't want to waste
his time, you will be left alone. A hand
gesture much like a stop gesture will also
cut short any further bargaining.

6. If you are just looking and don't want to
be bothered by vendors who are trying to
deal and bargain, say simply *"Solo mirando."*
That means "Only looking." Or make a
gesture with your right hand in which your
index and middle fingers make the V sign
and you then raise them to your eyes and
pull them away from your face into midair in
a way that indicates you are just looking.

7. Once you have found a vendor you want to
deal with, begin the bargaining process of
offers and counteroffers. It helps tremendously if you can bargain in Spanish and
can say things like *"No soy turista"* (I'm
not a tourist.) Say this with scorn, empha-
sizing the word *turista* as if a tourist was a
terrible thing, beneath contempt.

8. Know exactly how much you are willing to
pay for something before you begin to bargain. It helps if you can generally establish
the going price for a particular category of
merchandise, so you know when you are
approaching the fair price. For a pair of

heavy, well-made, well-designed silver earrings, for example, $25 is more or less the going price. If you're hitting around $22, you're doing well. If you get below $20, you're doing very well. Unfortunately, you can't always know the price to aim for, and must either allow yourself to buy something you love—and possibly be taken—or shop around a lot to establish the going price. Whenever possible, ask fellow gringos what they paid for a certain item to help learn the market prices for yourself. Understand, however, that each city has slightly different prices for the same items, depending on the amount of tourist traffic.

9. Never be rude in your negotiations. Don't insult the seller or his merchandise. If a vendor asks you to make an offer on merchandise that you have no interest in, it is perfectly acceptable to say "I will not insult you with an offer." Even if someone offers you merchandise for free, just smile and keep on going. If you don't want it, act like you don't want it. Period. If you waffle, it's over.

Scams and Deals

I f your mother told you, as ours told us, that you get what you pay for—she was right. But she was referring to life in the United States. In Mexico, you often get what you are foolish enough to buy. Use your head at all times in a bargaining transaction. Beware of some of these popular scams:

The Size Switcheroo

If you don't want to be taken, you had better learn a little bit of metric measurement and how to visualize these quantities. We were once shopping one of the vendors near a cruise pier and priced a liter bottle of vanilla. The vendor asked for $20 per liter. We happen to know that a liter of real vanilla should cost no more than $13–$15. The salesman asked us how much we wanted to pay. No more than $10, we said. "OK," he said, "deal." He quickly began wrapping a bottle of vanilla, a size much smaller than a liter (750 ml). Keep your eyes on the merchandise at all times, and know what size you should be getting.

The Dollar Boo-Boo

Prices in Mexican *pesos* are correctly written with a "$" sign. Thus a price tag would properly read "$26,000." This means it costs less than twelve American dollars. Since there are so many zeroes to figure in, and because everyone knows the deal when they are Mexican, some crafty retailers try to confuse tourists by writing the prices in an abbreviated form. Thus the above *peso* price would be written $26. You see this $26 price tag and assume the price is in American dollars. If you are in a border town, this is an easy assumption, since many stores do use American dollars here. You think, "Oh my heavens, $26 for that!" and you walk away, or decide to bargain down the price. The salesgirl begins to chat with you. "How much is that item?" you ask, referring to the one you thought cost $26. "It's $13," she tells you. Delighted at either her mistake or your bargaining powers, you buy the item—maybe even paying in U.S. dollars.

In actuality, you have just been cheated, especially if you paid in U.S. dollars. The bottom line is: Don't assume any prices are in U.S. dollars; ask. Never misread a *peso* price with the $ signature to mean a price is in U.S. dollars. And never accept a store's rate of exchange without questioning it.

The Sale Scam

In some shops, especially those in resorts and in border towns, the prices are calculated in American dollars. They were calculated at the beginning of the season when all the price tags were written up. Lo and behold, the *peso* sank and the dollar prices are no longer competitive. Rather than change all the price tags—a tedious job at best—the shop will scrawl across the windows the magic word "SALE," and will offer you 20% off the marked price on anything you buy. You have just been had. The "sale" price is actually the real price out there on the street where *pesos* are a way of life. You haven't saved one dime.

The "I Change Money" Scam

This is a popular scam for taxi drivers who speak English and act as parttime guides for tourists in town for part of a day on a cruise ship. Because these guys speak English and rent out by the hour, tourists flock to them, trust them, and consider them a buffer between the real world and their world. Some time in the course of the day, probably at the *mercado,* when you think everything is going great because you have the driver/guide bargaining for you in Spanish, you run out of money. "I change money," says your guide, who quickly makes a transaction for you from his back pocket. He changes the money at 2,000 *pesos* to the dollar, which you accept because you have no choice and because you are figuring prices at that rate anyway. The lovely day comes to a close, and you are deposited back at the pier to catch your ship. You pay the driver the agreed-upon amount and perhaps a tip, or he says to you, "Something for me?" Embarrassed, you add a few bucks to the pile. You should be embarrassed; you have already tipped him quite well and probably don't realize it! If you changed money at 2,000 *pesos* to the dollar with him, you have already been sport enough.

Kid Shopper Scams

Many vendors are kids. You probably think it is impossible to be cheated by a kid. Wrong.

Also please note that your kids will love to buy from kid vendors. Even without speaking the same language, kids seem to have an immediate bond. Your child will quite willingly overpay for anything, in order to buy from a peer.

Kickback Scams

If your taxi driver or tour driver takes you to a certain shop along the way, you better believe he is getting a kickback. If you pick up a brochure for a shop from a person standing in front of that shop, or at your hotel, and find your way into that shop, the person who gave you the card will get a percentage of what you buy. It is open season on tourists in Mexico— you are expected to pay inflated prices so that various kickbacks and bribes can be paid out along the way.

It is impossible to completely beat this system, unless you speak Spanish and shop in markets on your own. If you realize that you are going to shop in a tourist trap and that someone is going to get a kickback, at least try to give that kickback to the person you deem most needy.

Miniscams

A few more scams, which are far more small-time and will probably make you laugh more than they will make you angry:

Open Sesame Scam

You are about to step into/out of a taxi. Before you can reach the handle, a small child rushes up and opens the door for you. You are now expected to give him 100 *pesos*. Congratulations.

No Change Scam

No one in Mexico likes to carry around weighty coins, so don't be surprised if after arriving at your destination, or your bargained price, the driver (or vendor) cannot give you proper change. You'll lose no more than 1,000 *pesos* on this deal (less than 50¢) ... and it's most likely that you'll lose less, but you will lose nonetheless. Congratulations.

Cash vs. Plastic

It is virtually impossible to bargain in a market without cash. Furthermore, make sure your cash is in small bills. No one, but no one, in a market will know what to do when you present him with a beautiful purple 50,000-*peso* note.

However, if you are shopping outside of a

market, and particularly if you are in a fancy store, you will do better by using your credit card, for two very specific reasons: You'll get a better rate of exchange (most credit-card companies give the bank rate for the day your transaction goes through their offices), and you will have the benefits of the card's protection plan.

While American Express pioneered Purchase Protection™ and Buyer's Assurance™—two different types of insurance for shoppers—there are now copycat versions of these policies attached to many credit cards. Before you go on a shopping spree, find out if your cards are covered. American Express members are automatically covered no matter what color their card. Bankcards are covered on an individual basis by the bank itself—check with your issuing bank about types of coverage and whether you must register your purchase to qualify. (American Express does not require registration; bankcards may.)

If the item you buy using the American Express card is lost or stolen within ninety days of purchase, the credit card company will cover the amount of the loss not covered by your personal insurance policy. If you have no insurance, the card policy acts as insurance. If the item you buy breaks, the card's warranty program will pay for either a repair or a replacement or will simply refund your money. While you will not be buying electronics in Mexico (you shouldn't be!), the warranty on anything you buy with such a card will be automatically doubled or extended.

To make all this perfectly clear, let's talk about the infamous Gucci handbag. We bought this handbag at the Gucci shop in the María Isabel Sheraton in Mexico City, where the store manager seemed to be having a special clearance sale just for us. One of us bought a magnificent bag for approximately $63. Charge it and thank you very much; the bag was sensational and we considered it an even better bargain when we saw it advertised in a Gucci ad in *The New York Times* for $375. Alas, in the hustle and bustle of New York life, the pin that held the strap hardware together broke and disappeared forever. Gucci New York politely refused to fix the bag.

Enter American Express.

Because the bag was purchased with an American Express Card, we called the toll-free number (800-322-1277) and filled out the papers that came three days later. We enclosed two photographs of the bag—one showing the right side of the strap, with the proper hardware; the other showing the left side of the bag, *sans* hardware.

Two weeks later, a check for the full amount of the purchase arrived in the mail.

Had we paid cash, it would merely have been a case of tough luck!

If you are buying merchandise made in Mexico, where the workmanship may not be of the quality that you hoped for, and if the purchase is a sizable one, you would be foolish not to use a protected credit card.

Changing Money

Yes, of course it is better to change money in banks than at hotels. But we have found, in Mexico especially, that the difference is so incredibly small that it is not worth trekking to the bank just for the exchange. If you're there anyway, great. But don't sweat it otherwise. Remember that a bank will charge a service charge every time you change money. A hotel will have a less favorable rate, but will not have a service charge.

American Dollars

E verybody in Mexico loves American dollars —a welcome treat to travelers who have found the dollar unappreciated in Europe. Often prices are written in American dollars; many people—especially street merchants—will try to negotiate in American dollars. This is fine, especially if it's easier for you. *Just one word of caution:* Know and agree on the rate of exchange. Whip out a calculator if you need to. Most people who ask for dollars work on the exchange rate of 2,000 *pesos* to one dollar. It's easy to follow this mathematically, and prices can quickly be computed: If you're looking at the *peso* price (as written without the three zeroes), cut it in half for the dollar price. However, you are cheating yourself if you allow this rate of exchange. Before you do any deals in any currency, know the exchange rate at the bank!

It Is Better to Give Than to Receive

W hen we were kids we thought the worst part about going to Mexico was the enormous number of poor people who begged for money in the streets. In recent years, the situation has improved somewhat, especially in the border towns. But it is unrealistic to think that you will travel to Mexico without seeing, or being touched by, the needy.

Our policy is to allow a small percentage of our budget for this additional financial expense. Change is heavy and basically worthless to you: Enjoy giving it away. Don't overpay in stores or markets, as this will offend a vendor's pride. But if someone on the street is asking, you can genuinely give.

On your last day in town, if you are wondering what to do with that leftover change, or those small bills, consider handing them out on the street to the kids ... or donating them to the first church you see.

The Twenty Dollar Trick

The object of the money game in Mexico is to spend all your *pesos* before you leave, as you will get a miserable rate of exchange if you want to convert them back to dollars, and you won't want to hang on to them for a future trip to Mexico because the *peso* keeps losing ground. What to do?

Stay on top of the game by using your credit card whenever possible, and by having some of your traveler's checks in $20 denominations. Thus, our plan is to cash a $100 traveler's check on our first day in town and, as we go, to judge how much we are spending, so that toward the end of the trip we are filling in with $20 checks. If you are leaving Mexico City and have successfully spent all your *pesos*, cashing one last $20 check should get you right on the plane: The taxi to the airport costs $15, and tips will eat the other $5. You pay the departure tax in U.S. dollars, so the problem of excess *pesos* is eliminated.

The Bite

Travelers (and shoppers) in Mexico should know a little bit about *la Mordida,* which translates as "the Bite," and in the real world means "the Bribe." Whether you want to park in an illegal parking space, check extra pieces of baggage, or pay with a personal check when the store doesn't usually accept checks, it can all usually be arranged with a bribe. How much of a bribe is another question.

One note: Please do not try to bribe U.S. border officials if you are crossing with more than your allowance. Just pay the duty.

Exit Tax

U.S. citizens must pay the Mexican exit tax in U.S. dollars. Put aside your $10 in a hidden place, and don't spend it— even on the world's best *piñata*. While there are exchange booths in every airport, please remember that you cannot pay the tax in *pesos* (if you are an American), nor will officials take a credit card or a personal check. The shopping is great in Mexico, but not that great. Please be sure you have your exit tax money before you leave your hotel, which will be your last opportunity to do something about it.

One Last Calculating Thought

I f you don't like to whip out your calculator every few minutes, carry a conversion chart with you. These are given away free at all the better tourist traps, and on board your ship. (Check out our quick version on page 280.)

4 ▾ BUYING ARTS & CRAFTS (AN ALPHABETICAL GUIDE)

Craft Heaven

Mexico offers a stupendous range of art forms ... so many that first-time visitors are often shocked at all that is for sale and how beautiful it is. King Ferdinand and Queen Isabella would be amazed to discover that the real wealth of this country was not gold, after all. It's crafts. The farther into Mexico you travel, the better it gets. So if your idea of Mexican arts and crafts is based on a shabby *piñata* or a few Christmas ornaments brought back from a border town, you have much to learn.

We grew up with Mexican arts and crafts as part of our lives and, as a result, are particularly sensitive to the differences between the real art and all the mass-produced junk. In order to make sure you get to the good stuff and don't just buy the first *sandía* you see, we have compiled a personal dictionary (with a lot of help from Dr. Jill) to start you on the way to becoming a knowledgeable collector.

The Source

We also advise that you do your shopping as close to the source of the art form as possible. Each state of Mexico, and indeed, each region in a state, and sometimes each village, has its own special way of preparing an art form. If you can't get out to the Indian villages and markets, shop the government arts and crafts stores (like Fonart), or even Sanborns. You needn't make a pilgrimage to the colonial cities or the weaving cities to get what you want, but you do owe it to yourself to step away from the tourist traps and get a look at the authentic art and the people who produce it.

ALPACA: *Alpaca* is the name in Mexico for a combination metal that looks like silver but is more like silver plate. (It's really an alloy of nickel, copper, and zinc.) Some vendors will tell you silver plate is called *plata*—which can be confusing, since *plata* is the word for silver in Spanish. Inspect the piece for the ".925" stamp; if you see none, ask if the item is alpaca. Alpaca should be priced 30% to 50% lower than sterling.

ÁNFORA: Ánfora is the leading brand of everyday china in middle-class Mexico. They make many patterns; some are folk patterns typical of Indian and colonial styles. Because Ánfora is mass-produced, it can be bought in stores all over Mexico (and in some stores in Texas); the set can easily be added on to, and you have no worries about lead poisoning—a problem sometimes associated with Mexican pottery (see page 85). The Ánfora factory is located in Mexico City on Reyes 279, very close to the TAPO bus terminal (take the *metro* to San Lázaro, then taxi to the Ánfora factory, less than a mile away). There is an outlet store on the premises. Our favorite Ánfora pattern is blue on white, is named "Puebla," and costs around $29.95 for a five-piece place setting in Texas, where you can easily arrange shipping. It is sold in open stock from Vega's, 954 North Star Mall, San Antonio TX 78216. In Mexico it is sold at Sanborns (among other places) and costs just over $200 for a sixty-two–piece set; but no shipping can be arranged at Sanborns. *One tip*: Some market vendors sell Ánfora and try to pass it off as local pottery, since the design is a very primal one of blue on white. Check to see if it says *"Ánfora"* on the back.

ANTIQUES: Just because Mexico is alive with new crafts, don't overlook old examples . . . or even noncraft antiques. They are hard to find, but are sold in various markets or special antiques shops. Your typical Mexican antiques shop sells about one-half European merchandise (Mexico has a very large immigrant population, particularly of Europeans who escaped Hitler immediately before World War II) and one-half crafts antiques. Prices on antiques in Mexico can be shockingly low. Bring on the van, boys, it's time to load up.

AZULEJOS: *Azulejos* ("eyes of blue") are tiles. They were brought to Iberia by the Moors in the 700s, and have continued as an artistic tradition since then. As the tile painters became more specialized, regional styles crept into the Moorish designs (especially after completion of the reconquest of Iberia in 1492); the style spread through Europe, and those designs became the schools we know and love today—delft, faïence, etc. Spanish tiles of white with primarily blue or blue-and-yellow brush-stroke designs have been made for 400 years. Used as ballast in Spanish and Portuguese ships, they came to the New World. Mexican tiles are derived from the Spanish and are similarly designed, with animal figures and decorative borders. The Spanish brought the tile-making business to Mexico; the basic differences are that Mexican designs are less formal, warmer, and a little more folksy. They are less rigidly repetitive, and have looser geometrics; designs are often peppered with Indian motifs such as animals and plants of the Americas. Some traces of the original Persian and Moorish flourishes still exist. Dr. Jill bought some *Talavera de Dolores* tiles that she says look as though they could have come from Fez because of their geometric borders. As in Spain and Portugal, tiles that will form a large geometric pattern are available, as are tiles with a single motif, usually flowers, birds, or central units of geometry. Tiles with numbers are sold individually, so you can put your street number on your home; or you can have a plaque with your name and street address made to order.

Because of the abundance of red clay in Mexico, the unglazed clay tile is also popular, and has become a U.S. design staple known in the trade simply as Mexican tile or terra cotta. Both red-clay tiles and glazed *azulejos* are available in Mexico, although they are not as easily found in tourist and souvenir shops as one would expect, given their prominence in architecture.

When the Spaniards first colonized Mexico, they arrived in Veracruz, and worked two paths to the interior. One was via Puebla, to what is now Mexico City; the other was to the Silver Cities. As a result, there are two primary styles of tilemaking: *Talavera,* which originated in Puebla, and *Talavera de Delores,* from the Silver Cities, both influenced by the style of Talavera de la Reina, near Toledo in Spain.

Talavera ceramic is sturdier than most clay ceramic, and the handpainted designs reflect mostly Persian influences. It is most often white with a cobalt-blue border and multicolored flowers, squiggles, and small animals scattered in patterns across the piece. (Strictly Moorish tiles are in geometrics only; Persian designs have animals.) The *Talavera* style is readily recognizable once one has seen an example of the work.

The best tiles are handpainted and have a thick beveled or lined backside. Clink them with your finger or a pencil to hear a clear high tone—you will actually know a good tile when you hear it. Tilemakers who are proud of their wares will happily let you clink the tiles—this is an insider's trick, and will tell them you know what you are doing.

Tile manufacturers will usually ship tiles to you, since they are inordinately heavy and almost impossible to carry in quantity. If you have a car with you, just load up. Since we don't advise shipping much of anything from Mexico, make sure you deal with a reputable source if you are planning to have tiles sent. Also ask about breakage. (We overbuy by 10% to allow for breakage.) Some houses claim to have little or no breakage. If you take tiles with you, they should be individually wrapped and packed tightly in small boxes of 100 tiles each. The pages of an old phone book are ideal for wrapping tiles.

Because shipping can double the price of your tiles, you need to know prices for similar merchandise at home before you go out to the wilds of Mexico and start buying ... and praying that any package sent from Mexico finds its way to you. In the United States, tiles are most often sold by the square foot—one square foot usually equals about nine tiles. Prices can be quite moderate ... and possibly cheaper than you expected. Meanwhile, prices in Puebla are not a matter of pennies, especially on handpainted tiles. Expect to pay $2–$4 per *Talavera* tile, which can easily mean over $25 a square foot! Red-clay tiles are much cheaper, and when bought in quantity do cost pennies. Settle for *Talavera de Delores* tiles and buy in quantity at wholesale for about 10¢ per tile, in Mexico City. (Division del Norte is the wholesale tile street. Take the *metro* to Xola.)

Shopper's tip: Price tiles in your neighborhood and decide on the method of installation (it's the price of installation that can kill you, not the tiles); have measurements with you when you travel to Mexico; buy a small amount (say fifty) of small tiles, and carry them with you in your suitcase. (Yes, you can carry fifty small tiles; we've done it.) Once home, go back to your tile resource, with your Mexican gems, and find a surrounding tile that will cover the rest of your space—whether floor or counters. Plain old 4 × 4–inch solid white U.S. bathroom tiles cost no more than a quarter a tile (and often less)—so you can coordinate a cheaper tile with the Mexican tile. Almost all styles of unglazed red-clay tiles coordinate well with the glazed *azulejos*.

Another tip: Have a tape measure that measures in both inches and centimeters. When you are buying in the wholesale districts, the tiles are priced (and sold) by the square meter. There are basically ten square feet in one square meter, or 100 4 × 4–inch tiles in a square meter.

BARK PAINTINGS: *Amatyl* is the Indian word for paper; thus the name *amates* for this art form of painted designs and codices on bark that is almost as thin as paper. The bark comes in two colors (light and dark) and can be painted in one of two styles: a handwritten story decorated with figures and animals, or *historias*, which use pictures to tell the history or story of an event without words. While these are sold in many arts-and-crafts stores, they should be bought in the state of Guerrero. The market in Taxco is filled with them; you can watch the artists work as you browse.

BASKETS: Baskets (*canastas*) were the original shopping bags, and continue as a staple in the life-style of Indians and working people. While ugly nylon shopping bags proliferate in epidemic proportions, it is not hard to find a good basket. The problem for most tourists is that they didn't plan ahead to buy a basket, and feel they cannot carry one home, or must limit their shopping to small baskets. Not true. If you travel with an empty duffel bag (doesn't everyone?), you should be able to fit a rather large basket inside it. Small baskets are nice, but can be found at home for rather reasonable prices. If you're going to do this, you want not only to save money, but to come away with a spectacular trophy.

A good basket should be handwoven. The material it is made of affects the price, but it is the weaving style itself that is most important. The more intricate or elaborate the weaving, the higher the price. Regional differences account for the style of the basket and the fiber it is woven in. Baskets should not be colored or painted or worn ... although the Lerma baskets are coiled and then painted with geometrics or animals, and are popular with tourists who use them as shopping totes on the trip and then beach bags or picnic baskets when they get home. We prefer the natural look—especially if you are buying a substantial basket to work into your home decor in the United States. A well-crafted basket can take a lot of physical punishment and is sturdy enough to travel, but you still want to start out at home with a new one.

The best place to buy a basket is in an Indian market, the more remote the better. We are not talking here about tote bags made of straw or hemp that have raffia designs of little dancing sombreros on them or say *"Viva México"* in bold strokes. Inexpensive tote-bag baskets are available beside every cruise pier and at every tourist store—the fair price for a large tote bag is under $10, although the asking price is most often over $20. If you need one of those straw totes, go ahead. The subject now is serious baskets—and these should be bought from Indians. The one we brought back from the Friday market in Toluca is almost the size of a laundry basket, and has a thick braided handle and rim. It cost $18. A tremendous amount of bargaining was involved; there were many vendors with such a wide range of prices that it was virtually impossible to know why the prices were so different. But we ended up with the very first basket we priced. A similar basket would cost $50–$100 in the United States.

BRASS: Brass is a popular medium for decorative giftware for tourists; it is not that widely used by locals. Brass is also used in combination with copper, tin, or pewter in designs in a Mexican method that is called *metales casados* or "married metals"—several metals are joined together to form an object. Our strongest recollection of brass products is of the 10-inch-tall angels our mother used to buy—each angel held a candle in her head. These are made of brass and are sold in every good tourist crafts shop.

CANDY: We're not overly fond of Mexican candy, because it is incredibly sweet. But it is beautiful to look at, and has to be considered an art form. Those who are willing to risk diabetes, the loss of all fillings, and a few new cavities might want to take in the candy market at La Merced in Mexico City. Choose from chocolates, gooey pink balls sprinkled with coconut, caramelized milky chunks, and sweetened nuts.

CARVINGS: While masks are probably the most popular handcarved items tourists take home (see page 80), don't overlook other wooden carvings, particularly of animals. We bought three carved rabbits from the artist ($5 each, after hard bargaining)—a street vendor near the pier in Zihuatanejo—that continue to be one of the best finds of any trip. The work has the naïve folk style that makes it perfect in a home decorated in country style, and each piece is signed.

Carved stone is also a popular art form, as are reproductions of the Aztec calendar, which are worked into everything from gourds to slate. One of the more popular tourist souvenir items is a carved comb made in the shape of a fish and painted with flowers and bright colors.

The most sensational, and perhaps best known, of the carvings are the animal forms, some realistic, some surrealistic, in a newly stylized form begun by Manuel Jimenez in Arrasola, outside of Oaxaca. These crazy creatures range in size from the 6-inch miniature to the 2-foot *grande*. The animal—or figurine, as some of the animals are not quite distinguishable—is carved in a strong but primitive fashion from one piece of wood, painted a solid background color that is usually hot and bright, and then decorated with multicolored paints in dots, swirls, and brushstrokes that are almost New Wave. Every now and then feathers will be applied—but this is rare. Do not buy one that is not signed by the artist. The best place to buy these is in Oaxaca, but they are sold all over Mexico. Prices differ dramatically and get higher as you get farther from the source and into art galleries. The more elaborate the piece, the higher the price. Expect to pay $50–$100 for a high-quality, good-sized animal. If you are wondering how you will get it home unharmed, wrap it in newspaper and tissue and then put it in an egg-carton box, which you can get (for a small fee) at the *mercado*. The word for box is *cartón* (say "cart-tone"). Two such boxes can be taped together to form a carrying case. *Final tip from Dr. Jill:* The wood may have larvae in it, which doesn't mean you shouldn't buy the piece, but does mean that you need to know what you've got. If you see little holes in the wood, gently pound the figure into the palm of your hand or against your knee. If dust comes out, congratulations—you've got termites! But don't panic, this problem can be solved. Wrap the figure in plastic until you get home. If it's small enough, place it in the freezer (unwrapped) for a few days. If it's too large for the freezer, consult your local exterminator about injecting the holes with the proper chemicals, or call your local museum and ask if they will be kind enough to fumigate your item for you the next time they do an organic fumigation—a process that is expensive on an individual basis.

CASCARONES: Those of us from the Southwest are more familiar with this art form than most Mexicans are: these party eggs are sold in border towns and in some party shops in D.F. *Cascarones* are eggs from which the white and yolk have been drained through a small hole in the top. Once empty and washed, the eggshell is filled with colored confetti and then decorated. A small piece of china paper covers the hole where the confetti was inserted. Normally the eggs are sold by the dozen and are then cracked over the head of some unsuspecting but beloved family member ... or an attractive person of the opposite sex. You can buy these at Fiesta in San Antonio, at the Floating Gardens in Mexico City, and in most border towns.

CHRISTMAS: While some souvenir shops sell Christmas (*Navidad*) ornaments all year round, the real time to start the hunt is after the Day of the Dead, in early November. The Sonora market in Mexico City is an excellent place for ornaments, although they can be found in any crafts market anywhere in Mexico and border towns are big on them. Ornaments come in all forms and mediums, although tin (painted and plain) and wood are the most popular. You can also find papier-mâché, yarn, and straw ornaments. Expect to pay from 50¢ to $1 per ornament, although the more you buy, the better the deal. The Silver Cities have a few silver ornaments, but these are specialty items for tourists, expensive and not easily found.

You'll also find a number of crèches, in various mediums, but predominantly in wood and ceramic. Beware of the soft clay ones, which break very, very easily.

CRUSHED MALACHITE: Mention crushed malachite to us and we are likely to screw up our noses and murmur *"mariposa,"* which is the word for butterfly. That's because when we were kids we were constantly being chased up pyramids by vendors who were selling very touristy pins (in the shape of a butterfly) made of silver and crushed malachite. We actually once owned these pins, back in our younger days. Hundreds of thousands of tourists probably still buy crushed malachite, either in pins or bookends, and feel that they have come away with a genuine craft item. Sanborns sells tons of this stuff. We are not crazy about this art form, and warn you that variations in price have to do with whether or not the metal is silver and whether or not the turquoisy-green bits are real malachite or not.

DAY OF THE DEAD: OK, so this is a holiday, not a craft. But it is a holiday that has its own art form. It is a true art form mostly in the rural areas, since the big cities tend to overcommercialize the holiday. It is an oversimplification to equate Halloween and the Day of the Dead, although they basically celebrate the same holiday—All Saints' Day. The Day of the Dead is a festive occasion on which people visit, tidy up, and often picnic at family gravesites, and celebrate death with remembrance and joy. Skeletons of many sizes are popular decorations, as are skulls. Miniature skeletons and furnishings are often left at the gravesites; flowers, waxworks, candles, and coffins are all part of the traditional decor. While it has a touch of the macabre to the *norteamericano,* it is a happy holiday with wonderful art forms. Most valuable for collectors are the life-size papier-mâché skeletons (called *calacas* or *calveras*) which Diego Rivera kept hanging in his studio year round. (They are still there.) You'll pay about $20 for one in Mexico, but $100 in the United States—if you can find one.

DOLLS: Our favorite dolls are made of pasteboard in molds, and then handpainted. They look as if they were made with papier-mâché, but have a flat finish. They are not soft and cuddly, but they do have a naive quality to them that we like. We found the best selection ($4 each) at La Mansión in Nuevo Laredo, if you can believe that! They are sold in markets all around Mexico, including the Sonora market in D.F. Dolls made of woven palmetto and straw are popular in other regions, but we think these have less warmth to them than the paper ones.

DYES: You may be one of the people who are quick to make fun of Mexico City and the pollution problem there without realizing that the pollution of Mexico has had a permanent effect on the crafts of the country. Because of the changes in the environment, ancient materials for making natural dyes are becoming harder and harder to find, and in some cases are dying out, you should excuse the pun. Items produced for the tourist market are usually dyed with chemical dyes, since these are inexpensive and practical. (And besides, gringos can't tell the difference.) If you want natural dyes, ask where each color came from, knowing that the cochineal insect makes various shades of red; sea snail makes bright red; fermented snail creates blue and tan; and yellow comes from moss. There is now a resurgence of interest in these ancient dyeing techniques—especially in the Oaxaca area—and those who intend to buy wool or natural fiber for their own craftworks should inquire about techniques. If you are lucky enough to acquire something with natural dyes, care for it properly and wash it with respect. In fact, avoid commercial washing products totally, and forget about hot water. Try a cold-water hand wash with Ivory soap.

EMBROIDERY: Most traditional women's garments are embroidered by the owner or her mother and/or grandmother. The style of the embroidery is related to the ethnolinguistic group, and most often to the person's station in life. Most typically the patterns embroidered are flowers, geometric motifs, animals, and people; but the kind of flower, its spacing on the blouse or top, the size of the petals, and the arrangement over fabric are all related to regional customs and styles. The most prominent styles of embroidered dresses are the Puebla style, a light cheap cotton with a chain of flowers across the shoulders and in the center of the top; and the Oaxaca style, a heavier cotton with more body, embroidered with small flowers across the yoke and down the center of the dress and with some figures, which in fine examples of the work are easily discerned by the naked eye as men and women. The two forms are startlingly different for something that is basically the same. These dresses are sold all over the American Southwest, as well as in Disneyland and Disney World, at competitive prices. . . . So make sure you've got a beauty or are really in love. Expect to pay $25–$45 for a street-length embroidered dress.

One of the nicest T-shirts available in Mexico is the one sold in souvenir shops displaying the Oaxaca-style embroidery, applied by hand to a plain white T-shirt. These are expensive—in the $25 range. Wash by hand.

It's rare, but on occasion you will find a store that sells old, used, or even antique embroidered *huipiles* (see page 78). These cost anywhere from $100 to $500, and are considered collector's items.

ENAMEL: With the Southwestern look taking over a lot of American homes (thank you, Ralph Lauren), you'll be amused to find blue-and-white splatter-style enamel cookware and plates sold in Mexican markets for pennies . . . or dollars, depending on what you are buying. Sometimes (in antiques shops) you can find genuine enamelware from the 1930s and 1940s as well.

FIREWORKS: Several Mexican holidays are celebrated with the use of fireworks, especially the feast of the Virgin of Guadalupe, a few weeks before Christmas (December 12). It is not against the law to buy fireworks in Mexico (yet), but it is against the law to bring them back to the United States. Furthermore, several tragic accidents and a large fire recently in the Merced Market in D.F. make us stress to you the only viable rule in this ancient art: Don't even think about it.

FURNITURE: Although you're off to Taxco for the silver, you'll find your hands getting moist and reaching for your wallet when you start passing all the homemade signs for colonial furniture (*muebles coloniales*). The Mexican countryside is dotted with carpenters who make headboards, tables, chairs, dining tables, and chests in traditional styles. While prices are usually low to moderate, shipping becomes expensive and practically impossible. Many border cities have furniture makers in locations that make it feasible to drive your car or van right to the door and then to a U.S. shipper, moving company, or other transport system. Your basic handcarved-with-animals-and-people-along-all-four-legs-the-back-and-the-two-arms dining-room chair (unpainted) is going to cost you $250–$350. Latticework headboards are about $75 for a twin-bed size.

Note two distinct styles: colonial reproductions, which have straight, clean lines; and baroque reproductions, which are curvy and carved, often with cherubs and flowers.

GABÁNES: A *gabán* is a wool overcoat for a man—it has open sides and a hole for the head. It is exactly what we called a *sarape* when we were kids, not knowing that a *sarape* has no hole in the center. A *gabán* may be called a *jorongo,* which means poncho. They are not worn by women.

GLASS: Traditional Mexican glass is cheap, comes in many styles, and is usually found in sapphire blue, aqua, green, and amber. In Monterrey, there are styles in red and black. It's often crackly or bubbly, and may come in two shades—for instance, a clear glass with a blue lip, or something like that. Glass headquarters are normally near Guadalajara and its suburb city of the arts, Tlaquepaque, but you will find glass everywhere, always in the same colors but not always in the same styles. We bought a pitcher in Nuevo Laredo in a shape we never saw again in any of our travels in Mexico. Glasses usually retail from $2.40–$4 each, which isn't nearly as cheap as it should be. A pitcher costs $10–$25. Pier 1, a chain of importers in the United States, often sells this same Mexican glass at more or less the same prices. Unless you can get to a factory and really deal, this might not be a bargain in a tourist shop in Mexico.

While Mexican glasswork is moderately to inexpensively priced, it's interesting to note that the Indians do not use glasses (they use ceramic or earthenware), and the craft glass business is mostly for tourists.

GOURDS: Gourds are used in the decorative arts in either lacquer crafts (etched or painted) or toys (gourds made into helicopters). In some regions pumpkins are used in the same fashion. The fruit is harvested in late summer and dries until December, when it is opened, hollowed out, and then decorated. The bowls formed by the gourds are most often used as drinking cups or serving dishes by the Indians, but are sold to tourists or as small boxes.

GUAYABERAS: The *guayabera* is the traditional shirt of the Caribbean and South America, worn by gentlemen to keep from sweltering in the sun. It is short-sleeved, has a collar, but is worn without a tie, buttons up the front, has a pocket at each side on the waist, and is worn outside the trousers. Most often the front of the shirt is tucked, pleated, embroidered or all three.

HAMMOCKS: The word is that you should buy hammocks in the Yucatán, as that is where the henequen is harvested and where the best hammocks are made. Hammocks are sold everywhere, but most often in fishing communities where the same talents used to weave nets also weave hammocks. A hammock for two people is called a *matrimonial,* and costs about double the price of a single hammock. Hammocks are sold in a variety of fibers—some dyed, most natural—and are surprisingly expensive. We paid $40 for a double after much bargaining. Singles go for about $25. We've never seen a Mexican hammock we were knocked out by (in the United States you can get the kind with the wooden poles that bear the weight better, and we think these are a better buy), but if you insist on buying one, you'll have plenty to choose from. Look at the strength of the fiber, the number of knots (they should be uniformly and closely spaced and tightly knotted), and the space between the webs to determine how well-made your hammock is and how comfortable the fiber is. Make sure you buy a natural fiber, not nylon.

HUARACHES: *Huaraches* are Mexican-style sandals (available with open or closed toe) made of woven leather and finished with soles made from tires. Thus, when shopping for a pair of shoes you may see Goodrich, Michelin, etc., on the soles. Many *huaraches* these days are made for the tourist market and have regular old crepe soles—they even come in American sizes. Don't buy your *huaraches* too big, because they do stretch in a short period of time. A good pair of *huaraches* (which should last you for several years) are made with real leather and rubber-tread soles, and are carefully stitched so that the tread does not separate from the sandal part. The more body to the shoe part, the more support for the foot. Make sure the hardware is well sewn onto the sandal and is sturdy enough to take the beating you plan to give the shoes—cheap hardware will slow you down looking for repairs. *Huaraches* can be shockingly expensive: While $25 is not unusual, we've seen them sold for $40 in the tourist shops! The real thing shouldn't cost you much more than $10–$12.

HUIPILES: The *huipil* (say "we-peal") is the blouselike shirt worn by an Indian woman. Traditionally it is made from two pieces of handloomed fabric, with a scoop neck where the seams meet and open space for the arms where the sides are not sewn together. Over the brocaded designs, which are handwoven in as the cloth is produced, there should be elaborate embroidery. The *huipil* is most often midthigh to midcalf length; it does not stop at the waist and is not usually worn inside a skirt. The styles vary from region to region—some regions have them sewn with yokes (usually embroidered), or with square necklines, some have lace insets, some have puffed sleeves. The most valuable ones have beautiful and densely packed embroidery over brocading.

Embroidered dresses of street length are also called *huipiles* by tourists and guidebooks, and are the style that most often comes to market for tourists. (Many tourists don't want to wear an authentic *huipil*.) However, these dresses are not authentic, and are produced specifically for the tourist business.

LACE: Just when we were going to tell you to be very careful about lace bought in Mexican resorts, and to warn you about machinemade lace (which always looks cheap) being passed off as handmade, we ate lunch in the restaurant of a swanky hotel and discovered all the tables were set with long, pink linen tablecloths draped elegantly to the ground. These pink cloths were topped by the same cheap, machinemade lace cloths we had theretofore thought too ugly for words. But we had to admit that the look was elegant and refined ... and clever. Lace tablecloths are most often sold in fishing villages, but almost every market has them.

LACQUER: There are two kinds of lacquerwork in Mexico: the ugly kind and the gorgeous kind. They usually come from the states of Guerrero or Michoacán, which have two different and very distinctive styles you will quickly learn to recognize. The most beautiful lacquer piece we've seen was at Victor's in Mexico City, and was antique—all the shine had worn off. Beware of eating foods, especially acidic fruits, directly off a lacquer tray. See page 85 for information about lead poisoning.

Olinalá lacquer, from the state of Guerrero, has a black or darkly colored background, and is fully decorated with flowers made of pinpoint dots. This is a relatively new art form, so don't look for colonial inspiration or antique versions. The most famous items in this style are wooden linen chests and trays in all sizes—but other items and sizes are available, including small boxes and tourist knickknacks. Michoacán-style lacquerware is almost always on a black background, with a few large central flowers painted in a style reminiscent of Polish or Ukranian folk art. When not done well, these can be garish. Excellent examples of the art form, however, are worth attention. It is harder to find good lacquer items than almost any other craft in Mexico, since the bad ones are easily and quickly produced and often sold in tourist traps.

LEATHER: You'll find leather everything in Mexico, from shoes to boots to clothing, bags, and briefcases. We searched high and low for a leather soccer ball, however, and had to go to an expensive sports specialty store where the item cost the same as in the United States. Do not assume leather is a bargain just because you are in Mexico, or because the dollar is strong here.

Most of the ready-to-wear is not made well, and does not compete with the fashion leather goods you may be used to at home. However, if you shop carefully you may find a good leather jacket (men's styles are more classic and therefore easier to like). You will certainly have no trouble finding leather boots—two-skin, flame-stitched boots cost about $65 a pair, are well made, and are a steal! You can have boots custom-made in several cities. We had a lot of trouble finding fashion handbags that met our approval, but nice briefcases and leather luggage can be found more easily. Suede and shearling coats are expensive when well-made, but may be less expensive than in the United States. The famous leather names are Aries, with boutiques in every big resort city, and Antil—a shop in the Zona Rosa in Mexico City known for coats and handbags.

We're big on handtooling—perhaps it is our Texas heritage—and had a lot of trouble finding a handtooled belt that was up to snuff. Of the hundreds, maybe thousands, of belts we touched and inspected, only one store in all of Mexico had belts we thought well-cut, well-tanned, and well-priced—we paid $10 at a shop in Taxco called Los Angeles for hand-tooled belts that would be the envy of Ralph Lauren. A true trophy. Handtooled coin purses (some come in the shape of a *huarache*) cost from $3 to $6 and make excellent gifts. Try the zipper plenty of times when you select the coin purse, as it may stick or come away from the leather. Handtooled saddles are an excellent buy in Mexico. Handtooled suitcases are to die for, if you are into this look, but begin at $300.

MASKS: Masks hold a celebrated place in the folk life of all peoples, going back to the beginnings of mankind. The masks of Mexico have their roots in the ancient civilizations, but have developed from a combination of ancient Indian traditions and superstitions and Catholic beliefs as taught in colonial times. The best masks are Indian and handmade. While papier-mâché is a popular form, more traditional masks are made from coconut shells, wood, or even bark. Masks are most often displayed in October and November as the celebration of the Day of the Dead approaches, and between Carnival (right before Lent starts) and Easter. But they are sold all year round.

There are a few dealers who specialize in only important masks that are truly works of art. Lesser masks are generally found in tourist shops, art galleries, and government-owned crafts shops. Dr. Jill warns that many masks are mass-produced—they have never been danced with, or used in ceremonies, and may come in styles that are merely decorative and without real anthropological significance.

MILAGROS: A lot of the art and artifacts you'll encounter in Mexico are related to religious themes. *Milagros* are small silver charms usually depicting a part of the body, but also in the shape of people, infants, and animals. One buys a miracle: You buy the symbol of the body part, or of the person, object, or saint who can help you, take it to the church, say a prayer of petition, and wear the object with the promise to do something in exchange for that saint's help. If you keep your promise, then your miracle should occur. But if you go to a store, you'll find plaques and boxes for sale, almost every inch of which are covered with these silver charms pressed into the flesh of the wood. These items are also called *milagros*. Sometimes the *milagro* has a theme, and all the charms will be related to the same subject. People buy the charm as an amulet and say a prayer to go with it. A presentation box may be crafted as either a votive offering or a tourist trick.

MUSICAL INSTRUMENTS: Mexico is known for its music and for the quality, as well as uniqueness, of some instruments. Serious musicians will want to hang out at the Plaza Garibaldi in downtown Mexico City to see all the *mariachis,* and perhaps talk instruments with them. A popular shop for *mariachis* is Repertorio Musical Reforma, at Paseo de la Reforma 260, not far from downtown. You can also buy handmade instruments in regular or toy size at markets and fairs.

ONYX: Onyx is a semiprecious stone, and appears in many craft items—it can be worked in jewelry, or carved into ornamental gifts, desktop items, or chess figures, or even made into pieces of fruit. Not wanting to be rude, but we are not big fans of the made-for-tourists crafts that are the usual fare, and will most likely run out of the onyx department of any store with tears of disappointment in our eyes. Expect to find everything from ashtrays to bookends to Aztec calendars. The pieces of fruit, especially when they are small and delicate, are actually charming; many of the beaded necklaces aren't bad. But rub them between your palms to see if they are dyed or natural. If the dye comes off on your palms, you've been had.

PANNIERS: In 1988 the French couture showed skirts with bustles and hip sacs they called *panniers.* Panniers are actually the baskets worn on the sides of a donkey. Since Jill Joseloff has a whole family of donkeys on her ranch in California, we spent a good bit of time looking for panniers in Mexico. Needless to say, a pannier has to have a flat side to fit next to the donkey's body. We tried five cities: No luck. In fact, most of the people we dealt with thought it enormously funny that a gringo even had a donkey. As it turns out, donkeys in Mexico wear baskets (*canastas*) that are round and are held to their bodies with a carved wooden yoke.

PAPER: Tissue paper (*papel de china* or "china paper") is made into a number of traditional folk designs. Our favorites are the tissue-paper flowers (you can make these yourself, but it isn't worth it) and the cutout tissue sheets, which are sold either singly or on strings for hanging, known as *papel picado.* It is rather hard to find non–holiday-related designs on strings (called *enramadas*), and it is a real mess to try to string the papers yourself ... unless you have plenty of ten-year-olds to help you, a lot of string, plenty of glue, and a great sense of humor.

The strings are usually hung across the ceiling or rooftops to signify a fiesta or celebration. The most intricate cutouts are from the Puebla and Veracruz areas.

PAPIER-MÂCHÉ: Just about anything comes in papier-mâché—almost–life-size sculptures of animals, little-bitty boxes, puppets, mirrors, jewelry. Most of it is painted in bright colors and glazed. We happen to be fond of the serving trays, which come in animal or fruit shapes with three-dimensional additions—bananas, a pig, a face, etc. These are so kitsch that you have to bring one home for your mother-in-law. Trays cost $12 to $15 each.

Perhaps it's the fruits and vegetables that are the most popular papier-mâché item for tourists who like to stock up on a basketful to make a kitchen or dining-room table arrangement when they return. These come in all sizes, from miniature to life-size, and cost a few dollars per piece, depending on size, intricacy, and your ability to bargain.

PEWTER: Pewter (*latón*) is called *tin* in some countries, but not in Mexico, where tin is something else and is used as an art form. Pewter is most often cast in picture frames, which we think the best buy in all of Mexico. They cost about $25 for a 5 × 7–inch size. The exact same frame can cost anywhere from $35 to $90 in the United States. (We saw frames for $90 at Pierre Deux in Beverly Hills that we didn't think were any more special than the ones we got for $25 in Mexico.) Pewter frames are usually sold in gift shops, and there may not be a lot of stock. You'll find two here and four there, but never dozens of frames in the same place. You can also do well with pewter serving bowls and trays.

PIÑATAS: Believe it or not, one of the best sellers in the entire shopping empire of Disney World is the miniature *piñata*. You can find these tiny creatures in Mexico, but not easily. They'll cost anywhere from $1 to $3 (they cost $4 at Disney) ... about the same price as a regular *piñata. Piñatas* are sold in fruit and vegetable markets, although in big cities there are stores that sell just *piñatas.* We haven't seen a good *piñata* in a border town in about a dozen years, but you can still get good ones in Mexico City. By "good" we mean large, colorful, creative, well-made, and inviting. Some *piñatas* (especially those with faces) are just plain ugly. There are two types of *piñatas:* the old-fashioned kind with an empty crockery bowl set into it, or the more modern figures of people, cartoon characters, animals, and fruits that are totally hollow. Usually the *piñata* is sold empty, and the buyer then goes to another store that sells the little toys and candies you stuff inside. Americans seem to be convinced that the *piñata* comes filled, which is wrong. Consider it a blessing that the *piñata* is sold empty, since this makes it lightweight and easy to carry home. Be sure to buy the toys while in Mexico, where they cost pennies apiece; they will cost considerably more back in the United States. We always check our *piñatas* as baggage, and have had minimal damage. For those moms who are anticandy, you can fill the *piñata* with many other things.

POTTERY: While you can buy made-for-tourists reproduction pottery that copies ancient pre-Columbian styles, what we love in Mexico is not so much the figures and figurines but the jugs, bowls, plates, and dishes for everyday life. Whether glazed or unglazed, painted or unpainted, we've rarely seen a pot we didn't like. There are regional differences in pottery styles, and there are certain pottery villages and towns; the style is named for the village or region. There's Atzonipa for green pottery, and Coyotepec (Oaxaca) for black pottery; Tonalá in Jalisco and Tzinzuntzan and Santa Fé in Michoacán are all known for slightly different types of a regional style. In some antiques shops you can also buy antique colonial pottery, mainly from Puebla. Pottery is essentially so inexpensive that you may want to overbuy to allow for breakage.

Just a few words of warning: lead poisoning. We have tried to get the last word on lead poisoning not only for you but for ourselves, since we are avid pottery collectors. We find that each expert we ask has a different opinion. Our best advice is simple: Do not buy painted pottery to serve or eat off of unless it is mass-produced, like Ánfora (see page 63). This is overdoing it, we know, but it is safe advice. More exact information seems to be: Don't eat anything acidic off a colored plate—this includes citrus fruits, salads with a vinegar dressing, etc. *And someone else's cautious tip:* Don't eat off anything with a green glaze on it. In fact, Dr. Jill makes it quite clear that anything with a green glaze on it is for display only. We display our Mexican pottery; that way we can enjoy it every day and don't have to worry about lead poisoning. We do drink from our coffee mugs (a dozen for $3), but there is no paint inside or on the rim of our mugs—it's only on the outside, where the design is.

PULSERAS: *Pulsera* is the Spanish word for bracelet, and anything that goes around the wrist can be a *pulsera.* But what you can go nuts buying in Mexico (and Guatemala) are the multicolored little woven jobs that all the kids in America seem to be wearing, trading, and trailing in their dinner. *Pulseras* are readily available—street kids will offer them to you at $1 a pop (too high). They are sold in markets, in stores, on beaches. There is a tremendous amount of difference in quality and styles, which you will learn as you study them. We bought one made of silk with a very elaborate Aztec design woven in ($4), and passed up the ones with names and zodiac signs. With hard bargaining, you should be able to get a single bracelet for around 50¢. The more you buy, the better your bargaining position. Great gifts for kids; excellent party favors for the next birthday party you host.

REBOZOS: *Rebozos* are shawls that women wear for just about everything—they can be belts, they can be baby carriers, they can be hats (you should cover your head when entering a church), . . . or anything else you are creative enough to come up with. Women of all social classes and economic means wear *rebozos;* the only differential is the fabric of which they are made. A *rebozo* is about one yard wide and two and a half yards long. It's woven in colors and has a fringe. Its value is determined by the fabric, the intricacy of the weave, and the intricacy of the fringe. Dr. Jill suggests you go to Tenancingo, an Indian village about an hour outside of Toluca, for some of the best cotton ikat *rebozos* in Mexico. Go to Santa María del Río (in the state of San Luis Potosí) for silk *rebozos* that are so fine they can be pulled through a ring, and which are sold with their own wooden carrying cases. Such a *rebozo* will cost between $300 and $400. Synthetic *rebozos* are also socially acceptable.

RETABLOS: The *retablo* is one of several forms of votive offerings—a type of folk art representing a personal thank-you to a saint for a blessing or a miracle. Traditional *retablos* are handpainted on tin and have three basic parts: a picture of the accident or tragedy; a picture of the saint who intervened, or of the miracle itself; and a handwritten note explaining it all. The note should be signed and dated. *Retablos* without dates are not nearly so valuable as those with dates; the older the *retablo*, the more valuable. The condition of the *retablo* is also significant. They are usually weathered, or bent; they may have rust stains or holes, usually because they have been nailed to walls or placed in churches in thanks. Anyone can make a *retablo;* those by children are especially sweet, but no more valuable than others. The going rate for a good *retablo* is about $75, although we did buy one for $15 once. You can buy brand-new *retablos* (probably created specifically for the tourist market), but they have little or no value. Do not pay more than $6–$10 for a brand-new *retablo*.

SANTOS: In a country where most of the population is Catholic, it is easy to find religious art in a wide range of prices and quality. There are many grades of *santos* (small statues of saints) available, from the molded plastic ones that cost about $1 to the handcarved wooden ones that can cost over $1,000. It is these expensive *santos*, handcarved, hand-painted, with gold work, deep colors, and incredibly detailed faces and elaborate costumes, that are both breathtaking and valuable. Even if you can't afford to buy such an item, try to see some. You will be touched forever.

SARAPES: Just as a woman finds myriad uses for her *rebozo,* a man can wear his *sarape* as a coat, or sit on it as a blanket. A *sarape* is perhaps the most common art form sold to tourists—these fringed blankets are sold even by boatmen at the Floating Gardens (Xochimilco) in Mexico City. If you are actually buying a *sarape* to wear, make sure that it isn't too coarse or scratchy. Most people use their *sarapes* as scatter rugs—an excellent choice—and are happy to pay $5–$8 for them. *One tip:* The fashion designer Michaele Vollbracht once did a collection of *sarapes* embroidered with sequins and paillettes. If you are a do-it-yourselfer, you can enhance the value of your *sarape* and create a beautifully personalized souvenir.

SILVER: There is gold in them thar hills, but there's a lot more silver. Cortés found it—and you will too. Aztecs valued silver more than gold; we think you'll begin to agree in no time at all. Everything you see in shops catering to tourists is either silver or a silver alloy (see *alpaca,* page 63). When you step off your cruise ship and onto the pier, local kids will shove armloads of bangles into your face, claiming they are silver. Tourist stores will have giant crates at their front entrances, filled with bangle bracelets marked $1 each. You may even be given some bracelets from a grateful shopkeeper if you buy a lot. It is unlikely that the bangles are sterling silver, even if they are stamped ".925"—the official imprint for sterling in Mexico (meaning that of 1,000 grams of metal, 925 grams are actually pure silver). If you want real silver, bite the bullet and buy it from a reputable shop, not the guys on the street. It is still very inexpensive, and represents one of the best buys in Mexico. Also check out the work of important silversmiths—such as the items produced by Tane—which is nontouristy and sensational.

Silver jewelry is designed in two styles: traditional—designs which are worn locally or have been sold to tourists for decades; and fashion—copies of the latest designs by internationally famous makers. The most blatant copies are those of the designs of Paloma Picasso, but designs from all of the big jewelers (Van Cleef, Bulgari, Cartier) are imitated with abandon. Before you buy a copy, check the weight and the way the piece is crafted. If it has hinges, see how they are made and test how they move. Look at clasps and closures. Look at finished edges of a piece and check the casting. A cheap piece is not well cast and is light in feel. . . . It may be large in size, but it will not have any heft or body to it.

Because the traditional silversmiths of Mexico are slow in getting fashion information, one of your best moves would be to go with ads or pictures from fashion magazines which show exactly what you want, then commission the piece. We've heard it said that Mexican artists hate to copy someone else's designs because they are so creative themselves and prefer to do original work. If you feel that you want a strict copy, make sure of the silversmith and his abilities before you work together.

There are several cities in the hills west of D.F. that are called the Silver Cities. They include San Miguel de Allende, Querétaro, and Guanajuato, although Taxco is the most famous. But there is an excellent selection of silver in almost every city, and you need not make a special trip to Taxco for the silver. (Prices there are no better than elsewhere, and can be higher.)

You can also buy silver (and silver-plate) belt buckles and belt tips in Taxco and various Silver Cities, as well as in "cowboy" shops in tourist locations. (Try Gaitan in Mexico City.) Silver bolas are also sold in these locations.

Silver picture frames are popular, but most of them are actually silver plate. A 5 × 7–inch or an 8 × 10–inch frame in silver plate is reasonably priced and affordable at $40–$50. A frame of this size in sterling silver would cost well over $100. Stores are often not forthcoming about what their frames are made of, until you start looking for the ".925" stamp.

STRAW: *Panícua* is the word for wheat straw, which is made into figurines, toys, religious symbols, and Christmas-tree ornaments in either flat or three-dimensional forms. Occasionally you may see a form called a *popote*, which is a painting made from straw used like mosaic tiles. This form is only used in Mexico City, and is considered a dying art.

TEQUILA: We're not sure if this product or the ability to drink it is an art form, but to be authentic you should buy the type with the worm in the bottle.

TIN: Tin (*hojalata*) is a popular medium because it can be cut from cans and scraps and decorated. *Retablos* are always painted on tin; many Christmas ornaments are made of tin. A design is cut, and sometimes folded or curled; an additional design may be stamped onto the tin and then left natural, or painted, or dyed.

Tin can cut your hand, so examine carefully. It also rusts. Copper-and-tin or copper-tin-and-brass combinations are popular.

TREES OF LIFE: The Tree of Life is a large candelabra representing the origin of life (Adam and Eve are often at the base); the various branches of the tree represent other forms of life. These trees are made of clay, come in all sizes—some are as big as a person—and are painted and decorated with figures of people and animals. They are extremely fragile, but a good piece is highly prized as folk art.

There are three styles to choose from: *Metepec,* crafted from natural brown clay and decorated with matte additions; *Izúcar de Matamoros*, designed with a white background covered with geometric shapes and figures of Adam and Eve; and *Acatlán*, made of bisque and burnished to a light shade of brown.

VANILLA: When Spanish colonials arrived, vanilla had already been cultivated in Mexico for hundreds of years. Originally, the vanilla bean grew only in Mexico and Central America. The industry was artificially expanded in the mid-1830s, when hand-pollinated vanilla orchids began to be raised in other parts of the world (mostly Tahiti and Indonesia), and Mexico lost the monopoly. You'll still find vanilla for sale in stores all over Mexico, but especially in the Yucatán. It is often sold in the liquor department of stores because of its high alcoholic content. (The vanilla is extracted from the bean and soaked in alcohol.) Meanwhile, there is a huge business in fake vanilla going on. Real vanilla is incredibly expensive and hard to come by; tonka beans taste and smell like vanilla and are often passed off in Mexico as the real thing. Now then, the plot thickens. The extract from tonka is coumarin, a blood thinner sometimes used as rat poison; it is banned in the United States. Soooo, don't go for the cheapest vanilla you can find. Don't drink the stuff; use only tiny bits, in moderation, and if you have any doubts about what you are buying: Forget it! Don't fall for expensive vanilla that is expensive because of the gringo tax; buy vanilla with guarantees. Look for a picture of a vanilla bean and the logo of the Vanilla Association. It should cost $13–$16 per liter. If it costs $2–$5 per liter, pass.

VINYL: You may not agree, but to us it's an art form, and we even collect it; so there. The colorful patterned vinyl that is part of Mexican life comes in several weights and designs—we counted over two dozen versions of bright colors splashed with garish fruits and vegetables or pine cones and poinsettias (the holiday version). Sold by the meter, vinyl usually costs $2 but can go for $4 to a gringo. Dr. Debbie buys in Panama, where she gets it for less than $1 a meter. If vinyl isn't your thing, take a look at awning fabrics and canvas— sold in solids or stripes (a little more stately) at bargain-basement prices. Check out the local street market—or any rural market—but get far from the tourist traps, since tourists don't usually buy this stuff.

VOTIVES: Votive offerings (*ex votos*) from the people to the saints or the church are a popular form of folk art. They are represented by both *milagros* (page 81) and *retablos* (page 86).

WEAVING: It wouldn't be a trip to Mexico if we didn't come home with some of the beautiful Mexican woven fabrics. You can get a doctoral degree in all the forms of weaving (Dr. Jill did). As a tourist you will most frequently see either the solid-colored, handwoven textiles, most often sold in place mat, napkin, or tablecloth form (in solid colors or with varying colors in the warp and weft that form a type of plaid or squares of color), or the more intricate handweaving on a narrower loom that produces fabric 12 inches wide, white or colored and with a second color woven in as ornamentation. These two styles represent hundreds of years of history. Women first did their weaving on a backstrap loom, rarely more than 12 inches wide. When the Spaniards arrived, they introduced the pedal loom, used for the commercial weaving done mostly by men. If you are knowledgeable about weaving, you'll note that there can be a discrepancy between the *huipil* a woman is wearing and the type of woven goods she is selling. She doesn't think a gringo can tell the difference between the good stuff and the bad stuff, so she saves her time and increases her profit by producing an inferior product. Ask to buy the shirt off her back. Some will sell, some won't.

WOOL: Weavers can go wild for wools from Mexico, but Dr. Jill says buyer beware—have your wool dry-cleaned once you are home, before you even look at it, as there are often larvae (invisible) hidden in it that will infest your creation as well as your home. Place newly bought yarn in an airtight plastic bag in your suitcase. The best place to buy wool with mohair in it is at the Toluca market, otherwise get your natural wool in San Miguel de Allende or Oaxaca. It is harder and harder to find pure wool these days, since the Japanese have bought most of Mexico's wool in giant contracts; locals are forced to use acrylics.

5 ▾ BORDER TOWNS

Shared Boundaries

I n case you didn't study Texas history with
Mrs. Nesbitt in the sixth grade, we will
remind you that the Rio Grande became
the boundary between the two parts of Mexico that separated. California (and the area
that became Arizona and New Mexico, all part
of the same land cession) was lost by Mexico
in 1848, after the Mexican War; Texas had
won its independence in 1836. Although Texicans and Mexicans fought verbally for years
over where their boundary should be, the Rio
Grande line held only after the United States
won the Mexican War, a few years after Texas
had joined the Union. The Rio Grande still
forms a natural barricade. While there are
manned stations at certain points and specific
crossing zones, there is no continuous fence or
giant gate running between the two countries,
although much of the border is fenced, and in
places may be reinforced with ditches.

There are a series of international bridges
that connect the United States and Mexico,
each with a border patrol and customs offices
on both sides. Because of the ease with which
drugs or illegal day workers can get into the
States, the borders are stringently guarded.

The Border Towns

There are actually about a dozen so-called border towns in the 1,952-mile stretch from the Gulf of Mexico to the Pacific Ocean. In most cases the U.S. city and the Mexican city do not share the same name. Working from the gulf westward, the major border towns in the United States and their neighbors on the Mexican side are: Brownsville, Tex./Matamaros; McAllen, Tex./Reynosa; Laredo, Tex./Nuevo Laredo; Eagle Pass, Tex./Piedras Negras; Del Rio, Tex./Ciudad Acuña; Presidio, Tex./Ojinaga; El Paso, Tex./Ciudad Juarez; Douglas, Ariz./Agua Prieta; Nogales, Ariz./Nogales; Calexico, Cal./Mexicali; and San Diego, Cal./Tijuana.

Best of the Border Towns

We haven't been in all of the border towns, nor do we see any reason to visit all of them. Although each has its own character and something special to offer, we are most familiar with Nuevo Laredo, since it is the closest to San Antonio, and Tijuana, which is just a few steps south of San Diego. Dr. Jill raves about Nogales (just an hour's drive south of Tucson), where you can buy craft items on either side of the border; and other friends remind us that El Paso has two nice, big shopping malls and that one of them, El Cielo, has a Ralph Lauren Factory Outlet Store right there in the mall.

Welcome to Laredo

A s you wander down the streets of Laredo, you're bound to say to yourself
"What an average town." And it is an
average, small American city (population just over 100,000) with the usual grocery
stores, malls, and strip centers. It's only when
you get close to one of the two international
bridges that you realize there is something
special about this town.

Come to think of it, that's not entirely true.
You can get a good idea that this is not a
typical American town when you're about 25
miles outside of it, where the billboards start.
They advertise everything from Mexican car
insurance to low hotel rates to (our favorite)
the toll-free phone number 1-800-BE-ALERT,
which you should dial if you suspect drug
smugglers.

Most of the tourist traffic into Laredo is
specifically geared to a half-day trip across the
border to poke around in Nuevo Laredo. Tour
buses and saavy shoppers stop for lunch on the
U.S. side and then drive or walk across the
border.

American citizens may walk across either
the New Bridge or the Old Bridge. We walk
over the Old Bridge, because if you walk over
the New Bridge you will be in the middle of
nowhere and won't appreciate the location.
Many hotels in Laredo have shuttle buses that
take you right to the bridge, to the point
where you start walking. We always carry our
passports with us, although no identification
has ever been requested. On returning, the
guard asks if you are a U.S. citizen. We have
never had tourist cards for the visits we've
been making to Nuevo Laredo for the past
twenty-five years. (No tourist card is required

for any cross-border visit of less than 72 hours.) You can drive across either bridge, but you must have Mexican car insurance, which costs about $12 per day and must be purchased outside of Laredo. By the time you get to the bridge (either one) you must already have your insurance papers.

If you take your own car into Nuevo Laredo, park at the Cadillac Bar and lock the car. Most rental-car agreements prohibit you from driving a rental car across the border.

Shopping Laredo

We don't do a lot of shopping in Laredo, but there are a few quick stops worth mentioning if you are staying around for a while:

SANBORNS: At Exit 1B off the highway, and clearly marked, Sanborns is a branch of the famous Mexican chain of department stores that are a combination of coffee shop, drugstore, and general store. In fact, throughout Mexico, Sanborns is the basic one-stop for all convenience shopping. They sell Mexican car insurance here, and you can grab a bite to eat and buy insurance all at the same time. This could be the first stop in what will become a long and happy relationship with Sanborns as you travel throughout Mexico.

SANBORNS, Exit 1B/U.S. 35 South, Laredo

▼

MALL DEL NORTE: It's not that exciting, but it is a large regional mall for the locals who lead regular lives in the shadow of the border.

MALL DEL NORTE, 5300 San Dario Drive, Laredo

RIVERDRIVE MALL: Right next door to the Howard Johnson Plaza Hotel, overlooking the scenic Rio Grande, the Riverdrive Mall is used by locals from both sides of the river. There's a J. C. Penney here as well.

RIVERDRIVE MALL, 1600 Water Street, Laredo

▼

LORO'S MARKET FIESTA: This is a big, beautiful American grocery store, with a touch of Mexican decor, a lot of Mexican foods, and a hint of French *hypermarché* flavor, as it also sells a little of everything—from videotapes to plastics, from clothes to basics. It's very large, modern, clean, and worth visiting, if only to see the giant display *piñatas* in the fruit and vegetable department. Each category of fruit (or veggie) is depicted by a *piñata* of the same fruit hanging above it. There is also a woman making fresh tortillas and a wide selection of Tex-Mex food supplies and makings. Stop here on your way home.

LORO'S MARKET FIESTA, Calton Avenue exit at U.S. 35, Laredo

Snack and Shop

You'll have no trouble finding a place to eat on the U.S. side. The main highway (U.S. 35) is filled with fast-food eateries as you approach the international bridges: There's Denny's (a coffee shop), Kentucky Fried Chicken, McDonald's, Pizza Hut, etc.

In all our years of going to Laredo, we've always eaten lunch at the exact same place, which happens to be the same place all the tour buses stop at: La Posada. La Posada is actually the fanciest motel in town, but it has a coffee shop that is perfect for this occasion. You may choose from the menu or eat the buffet, and best of all, you can park in their garage (parking validated when you eat lunch) and be a mere half block from the bridge. If you want to get into the spirit of things, try the chicken-fried steak—a Texas specialty.

Crossings

You can't miss the bridge. It has a huge sign: *"La Internacional Puente."* On the U.S. side you'll see such last-minute stops as a change booth, a tax-free shop, and the Last Chance Café. You can pay the toll of 15¢ in exact change of three nickels in a turnstile, or at the window, where exact change is not required. (*Please note:* It will cost you 20¢ to get back into the United States.) The Rio Grande, depending on the time of the year, is mostly small, brown, and crummy-looking. As you approach Mexican soil, you go down into a tunnel like the entrance to a subway, in order to get through the toll plaza for cars without being run over, and you emerge at the *Aduana* booth, the Mexican customs, where if you are a U.S. citizen you keep walking and if you are a Mexican citizen you show what you are bringing over. Welcome to Mexico. (*Bienvenidas.*)

Welcome to Nuevo Laredo

As border towns go, Nuevo Laredo falls into the category of more charming than most. But don't get carried away. This isn't exactly charming. Don't get us wrong, it's not a dump like the town of twenty years ago. The streets are relatively clean. There are no beggars; there is just the main shopping drag for *turistas*.

About a block from the bridge there is the town square (*Zócalo*) where you can sit in the bandstand, have your shoes shined, grab a horse-drawn *caleche*, or just stare at the passing parade. In no time at all, you'll be approached by the boys and men of the town who want to help you spend your money.

"You want to change money, lady?"

"You want cigarettes?"

"Information, lady, eh?"

This is the charm of old Mexico. Sort of.

What Nuevo Laredo does have is the feeling of stucco crumbling in the sunshine, a taste of what Mexico can be about. There is certainly no question, once you cross that bridge, that you are now in a totally different world. There are juice stands, shop awnings advertising Corona beer, shops bordered with *azulejos,* alleys filled with tiny tourist shops, and pastel-colored walls scribbled with graffiti that you can't read (unless you're fluent in Spanish ... and in Mexican slang), and possibly a lot of three-letter symbols you think must be somebody's initials but that happen to represent the names of the political parties.

People come to Nuevo Laredo for one of two reasons: to shop or to go to the horse races. While there is shopping off the main drag, you'll need a car for this (and Mexican insurance)—so we stick to the main walking

area right on the Mexican side of the Old
Bridge, which is called Bridge I. (The New
Bridge is called Bridge II.)

Hours

A bout 30% of the stores close for the siesta. Enough are open (in and out of the
mercado) that the siesta should not af-
fect you. Stores generally open at 9 or
9:30 A.M. and close at 6 P.M. Sunday hours are
usually 9:30 A.M. to 4 P.M. Some stores do close
on Mexican holidays, which can differ from
U.S. holidays.

The Lay of the Land

O nce you have crossed into Nuevo Laredo, you are on the main street, which
is called Guerrero. There are shops on
both sides of the street. The *Zócalo* is
on the left if your back is to the river.
If you wander one street to the right of the
main drag, there are some shops that are
rather nontouristy and where prices are slightly
better. But then, the main drag is the street
that is fun to shop. You can wander to your
heart's content, or stop by some of our favorite places. There're only about three blocks of
stores (both sides of the street), so you can't
wander too far out of town and will certainly
know when it's time to turn around and head
back.

Finds

NEW JUÁREZ MARKET: This is an enclosed minimall of about ten little shops, right off the main street to your right (if the bridge is to your back) on Calle Bravo. Why the market is named after a different Mexican border town is a mystery to all. The shopping here is not the best in town, but it gives you a quick look at what's possible. At No. 7 you can price the souvenirs you've been wanting, in order to get your first fix on local prices. And yes, they do have the stuffed frogs dressed up in little *mariachi* suits.

NEW JUÁREZ MARKET, Calle Bravo, Nuevo Laredo

▼

LA MANSIÓN: No doubt about it, this is our favorite store in Nuevo Laredo. We are willing to drive three hours just to spend one hour here. And we could certainly stay longer than an hour. Perhaps a day. La Mansión calls itself a frame factory, but they actually sell all sorts of arts and crafts. First, about the frames. For some reason we don't understand, picture frames are outrageously expensive in the United States, and the good ones are sold without glass, which means you pay extra for the glass and you have the additional burden of having it cut to fit—a task sometimes accomplished at a different resource from the one at which you bought the frame. A fancy, scrolled baroque or gilt frame of a good size costs well over $100 in the U.S. Welcome to La Mansión, where you can buy a 20 × 26–inch, gold-painted, wooden frame (with glass) for about $20. The selection of frames is immense and worth driving down for, no question about it. They will cut the glass to fit your frame right in the back right-hand corner of the store. The price of the glass is always included in the price of the frame!

If that isn't good enough, the shop is on two levels and offers an excellent selection of Mexican arts and crafts. Prices are a little bit higher than you'll find at Indian markets close to Mexico City, but hey, you are only five minutes from Texas. They sell some Louis Vuitton handbags here—the large duffel-bag purse costs $120. Frankly, we didn't come here for the Louis Vuitton. We like the shop's painted and vaulted ceiling, the terra-cotta floors, the shelves and shelves of treasures on the street level, and the furniture upstairs. The walls lining the stairs are packed solid with a display of native masks. Out back is a garden full of patio furniture and red-clay planters. If all this isn't enough, the carpenters—because this is basically a woodworking shop—have a little something for the young lady of your household: You can buy a traditional Victorian wooden dollhouse (with furniture) here—the unpainted structure costs $90. Christmas ornaments (excellent) are three for $1; lovely folk-style papier-mâché dolls are $4; Oaxaca-style carved animals begin at $48. You can get a handcarved dining room chair for $130, or a simple ladder-back chair with a rush seat for $35.

One warning: Some of the merchandise sold here comes from Indonesia and the Far East, not Mexico.

LA MANSIÓN, Guerrero 206, Nuevo Laredo

▼

MARTI'S: Marti's is and always was the fanciest store in Nuevo Laredo—a store that is part art form in its presentation of expensive but traditional arts and crafts that have been elevated from the status of mere souvenirs to that of items of fashion. This means the store is the most expensive in town, and also the most American. Their hours are more formal than other stores: Monday through Friday, 9:30 A.M. to 6:30 P.M.; Saturday, 9:30 A.M. to 7:30 P.M.; and Sunday, 9:30 A.M. to 4 P.M. They are closed on all Mexican holidays, whereas some other stores may stay open.

From the outside, Marti's is a brown stucco building set off with fancy brass letters and an entry patio with a piece of modern sculpture and an inviting awning of brown and biege. Inside, the store is cool, modern, large, and separated into various boutiques like any major department store. Everything is well-made, fancy, and virtually all is more expensive than it should be. But you know exactly what you are getting, and you pay for Marti's personal guarantee of quality, which is worth a great deal when you shop in Mexico. (Everything is authentic; return it for a refund if there's a problem.) There are several counters for silver, but also areas for leather goods, handbags, fiesta-style dresses, cotton sportswear, clothes suitable for any mild climate, sweaters, gifts, etc. Some home-furnishing items are also sold. No trip to the city is complete without a stop here, even if you're just looking.

MARTI'S, Victoria 2923, Nuevo Laredo

▼

DEUTSCH: This is where Mom used to buy her perfume. The shop is small and not crammed with merchandise, because most of the good stuff is not displayed. It is the kind of place that you might poke your head into and say "boring" and walk out again. But locals know that Mrs. Deutsch sells fine gold jewelry, gemstones, and art objects, as well as a few craft pieces of high quality. She also carries imported French perfumes. There's a small assortment of locally made goods that imitate American folk-art styles and are geared for American-style Country Look homes. And lest you think this store is too hoity-toity for you, there are $3 onyx beads.

DEUTSCH, Guerrero 320, Nuevo Laredo

▼

NUEVO MERCADO DE LA REFORMA: This is it, friends: the market. This is a relatively new market, very clean, and a tad too antiseptic for our tastes. The marketplace of our youth burned down, and was replaced by this two-level structure, which winds around in a figure eight so you can get a little lost, or not see all of the stores, if you're not aware of the pattern. There is a wrought-iron gate at the front steps, then you walk into an outdoor plaza full of tables and umbrellas and chairs. Then you can wander in, and go up and down the stairs and in and out of all of the stores. Most Texans are appalled at just how clean and civilized this market is, but tourists who were worried that Mexico might be dirty can rest assured that this place is perfect. There are about 100 stores in the market, which is more like a mall.

You can buy everything there is to buy in Mexico in this *mercado*, and at rather fair prices. Bargaining is expected, of course. The *piñata* selection is puny, but other than that you should be able to find everything you want from vanilla (750 ml for $1.50 or $2.50) to margaritas (75¢ each) to candies, nuts, and seeds (at La Vitoria) to crafts from perhaps Johnny Oaxaca, a fancy, high-end, touristy shop, or perhaps Rosalinda's Gifts or Eloy Garcia Salinas, which is practically a general store, with a little of everything (including pewter picture frames). Liquor (an excellent buy) is sold in several shops; be aware that your state residency determines how much duty-free liquor you can carry home. Texans can bring back one bottle duty-free (more than one and they must pay duty); residents of other states can bring back four bottles duty-free!

NUEVO MERCADO DE LA REFORMA, Guerrero 400, Nuevo Laredo

▼

THE SADDLESHOP: Smell the leather and go wild. This very authentic-feeling Western shop sells boots, tooled leathers, and even saddles at considerable savings. Great fun, even if you aren't buying.

THE SADDLESHOP, Guerrero 31, Nuevo Laredo

Welcome to Tijuana

T ijuana is not some silly little border town created for your shopping convenience or as a weekend getaway for Angelenos. It has one million inhabitants, and happens to be the most visited city in the world. Of all the foreign destinations Americans visit, Tijuana outranks London, Paris, and everywhere else too!

When we first entertained the notion of going to Tijuana (from Los Angeles, of course) we thought dog-and-pony shows, cheap liquor, and stuffed frogs dressed up as *mariachis* playing hokey musical instruments. This is not our favorite scene, since we grew up with Nuevo Laredo in our backyard and we've seen our fill of those little frog characters—but hey, we heard that this was the "in" city, and wanted to know if millions of visitors could be wrong. They're not. At least, not totally.

Getting There

We flew to Los Angeles as our main California port of call and spoke to no less than ten—count them, ten—car-rental agencies. None would rent vehicles to be driven into Mexico. And since we wanted not merely a half-day stroll across the border, but rather a drive-and-shop trek to Ensenada and a quick view of what Baja could be about, we insisted on a car.

We drove our rented car from L.A. to San Diego, where car-rental agencies seem less daunted by the fact that someone might want to drive across the border. We used Dollar Rent-a-Car, conveniently located near Lindbergh Airport at 2499 Pacific Highway and Laurel, just off Interstate 5. We paid $37 a day for the rental, then an additional $10 per day for U.S. insurance and another $11 per day for the mandatory Mexican insurance. Other San Diego–area rental agencies that allow cars to enter Mexico are Courtesy Car, Admiral Car, and Fulton Car. Budget lets you take the car 25 miles into Mexico, which makes for Tijuana but not for Ensenada. You can forget it at Avis, Hertz, and National.

From San Diego to Tijuana is a painless thirty minutes of well-marked highway through typically dry Southern California. Once you cross the border, however, you can see that it's a new world. No gradual shifting from one country to the next, no time to prepare or get adjusted. There is an instantaneous change in color, smell, language, and yes indeed, shopping. The road plunges through an area filled with automobile-upholstery shops offering deals no normal person could (or should) believe. Young men in the street try to wash your windows if you are foolish enough to slow down or, worse, stop. They would also be willing to sell you a pair of silver earrings, no doubt. Maybe your own.

The Lay of the Land

C ontinue driving on Third Street until you see Avenida Revolución, the main shopping drag. Only then is it safe to slow down and seek refuge in a parking garage. Street parking is possible, but we suggest otherwise.

The majority of shops for gringos line Avenida Revolución or are nearby. Since Tijuana is a duty-free city (this is more meaningful to Mexicans than to Americans), most of the larger stores carry French and American perfumes, crystal, etc. Every third shop in the area sells liquor, which we always buy last so we don't have to walk around all day carrying the weight of a bottle of booze.

Note: While the numbered streets, which cross Avenida Revolución, are officially called *calles* in the traditional Spanish form, stores that deal with tourists have anglicized their addresses to "Street," so a business card may say "Revolución between 5th and 6th streets" even though you won't find Fifth or Sixth Street on a map. You'll also notice that most stores do not have numbers, and that several shops may share the same address.

Snack and Shop

If you didn't eat on the U.S. side, you can get a perfectly safe lunch at Sanborns, which happens to be a good place to start your stroll through town anyway. Or a good place to finish up for a soft drink before you head back to the United States if you're just in town for a day trip. Locals advise those driving back across the border to leave by 4 P.M., when the lines at the borders begin to get long.

Border Bets

And speaking of getting home, you can bet that your shopping experiences in Mexico aren't over until you are on U.S. soil. While you are trapped in line in your car, waiting patiently for your turn (a two-hour wait is not uncommon), you will notice that this no-man's-land is lined with stalls selling the usual tourist curios and last-minute gifts. For those unwilling to leave their cars (smart choice), the vendors will come to you carrying plaster-of-paris painted Virgins of Guadalupe and/or spotted dalmatians, *sarapes,* stuffed animals, and artificial flowers. Last chance to get rid of unwanted *pesos.*

Note: Almost all prices in border towns are marked and quoted in U.S. dollars.

Medicinal and Culinary Arts

D r. Debbie (who is a real, live M.D.) has been alarmed by the Retin-A salespeople and the ads for drugs without prescriptions available in Mexico. Her words of wisdom on medicinal items and on foodstuff:

▼ Mexico offers some delicious food items that are hard to find in the United States but are featured in border towns. Buy: vanilla, bundles of cinnamon sticks, tamarinds, chili peppers (dried), and *cajeta*, or caramelized goat's milk, a sweet. Do not buy the white goat cheese, because it may not be pasteurized and could cause brucellosis, not an attractive shopping disease.

▼ Herbal medicines are fun to shop for and often have pretty packages, but who knows what's really in them!

▼ While it is legal to bring prescription drugs for your personal use back into the United States, we don't want you to be playing Ben Casey without a license. If you insist on this practice, which no medical doctor will condone, stick to products that you have used before and know the name of. You should not self-prescribe such medications without consulting your regular doctor! And never, never, never decide to try one you've never taken before—lest you die of an allergic reaction.

▼ Isoprinosine and Ribavirin, herpes medicines, are sold over the counter in Tijuana. Try not to get herpes while in Tijuana, and you won't need them.

▼ Anabolic steroids are sold over the counter in Tijuana, and you know what happened to Ben Johnson.

▼ Minoxidil (a drug to help prevent baldness in men) is sold over the counter in Tijuana, and should not be used without a doctor's supervision. It is contraindicated in patients with heart trouble. Do not self-prescribe!

▼ Retin-A has been successfully used to peel layers of skin from the face and provide an "instant face lift." It works much like acid, and should never be used without medical supervision. If you are determined to ignore this advice, note that there are two types sold: American-made and Mexican-made. If you insist on buying this product in Mexico, at least buy the American-made variety to be sure of the quality control, and do not go out into the sun.

Tianguis

There are several passages, alleys, flea markets, and *tianguis* on or off the main drag.

LAS PULGAS: This well-known flea market is kitty-corner to the jai alai fronton. The atmosphere is predatory, and all the variations of vendor incantations still translate to the usual "You're such a pretty girl, for you a special bargain. . . ." The only redeeming feature when we last visited was the Calvin Klein underwear. This is the low point of shopping in Tijuana, as far as we are concerned.

LAS PULGAS, Avenida Revolución between 7th and 8th streets

Finds

SANBORNS: It's part department store, part national hero to the millions of gringos who flock here because it's so Americanized they feel comfortable. This Sanborns, like all other Sanborns, sells everything you need—including postcards and maps, souvenirs, and even luggage to take back all the extras. Clean bathrooms; coffee shop.

SANBORNS, Avenida Revolución at 8th Street

▼

POLO/RALPH LAUREN: Much of Tijuana is Americanized, so it's no shock to find a Polo/Ralph Lauren shop (they are all over Mexico) or even to find it decorated in the traditional English style—there's nothing Mexican about this store at all. It is in a small complex with Ellesse and Fila and a tiny cigar shop that sells Cuban cigars. The merchandise is styled along the lines of the American collection: There are clothes for men, women, and children costing about half what they would cost in the United States because they are *"hecho en México."* A sample of prices, which by the way turned out to be a dollar or two higher than at other Lauren shops deeper in Mexico: man's Polo shirt, $25; kid's Polo, $17; lady's knit dress, $63.

POLO/RALPH LAUREN, Avenida Madero and 7th Street

▼

FILA: There are two Fila shops in Tijuana, and business is booming. Every American man in the city seems to want to buy his souvenirs here. One shop is next to Ralph's, the other is in a shopping center called Plaza Revolución, along with Guess and a few other shops. We bumped into a sale on our last visit and found tennis shorts for $7, polo shirts for $18, Fila T-shirts for $10, and socks for $4.

FILA
Avenida Madero and 7th Street
Avenida Revolución and 2nd Street

BENETTON: No *gangas* (bargains), friends. Prices are pegged to those in the United States per Benetton orders from headquarters, but the stuff is made in Mexico. However, there's a nice basket shop next door.

BENETTON, Avenida Revolución 830

LA FUENTE: One of our favorite shops in Tijuana, although the owner won't bargain or make deals, and she won't ship to the United States. Wooden statues and masks line the walls, as do *ex votos* and other religious pieces, from the seriously pious to the kind that plug in and light up. There are some Mexican glass items, although ceramics are better represented. Many of the carvings come from Guerrero and Michoacán; prices range from $20–$160. The life-size Day of the Dead papier-mâché skeletons are sold here; small gift items are abundant, and if you must buy a *mariachi* frog, now's your chance—for about $5.

LA FUENTE, Avenida Revolución 921–10

IRENE'S: Billed as a Mexican bazaar and dress shop, the store has an excellent selection of embroidered dresses in a few different lengths and in many colors. Prices from $16 to $30.

IRENE'S, Condominio Revolución 921

▼

THE GOLD LEAF: A great shop that actually sells wrought-iron furniture and metalwork—why not call it the Steel Magnolia? Ramón is the owner. He speaks perfect English and will make (and ship) custom orders for you. He also has giftwares on hand: ceramics, metal boxes, handicrafts, etc.

THE GOLD LEAF, Avenida Revolución 921–14

▼

JORGE ESPINOSA: This shop is so attractive and the silver jewelry so tastefully presented that you forget you are in Tijuana. The salespeople make a special effort to not be pushy. The style of the work is high-fashion and not at all touristy. Many pieces feel fluid, taking shapes that must have come from being poured into original molds.

JORGE ESPINOSA, Avenida Revolución 918, Shop B1 (Ciros Arcade)

▼

ROMA IMPORTS: Lladró and Lalique, with an impressive selection of Lalique home-furnishing and decorative items—doorknobs, brackets, light fixtures, etc. You can't even find these easily in Paris, so stock up now.

ROMA IMPORTS, Avenida Revolución 902

▼

HAND ART: Prices are nonnegotiable but fair, for a wide selection of embroidered linens and tablecloths, and especially for lace. (Good quality lace is actually hard to find in Mexico.)

HAND ART, Avenida Revolución 735

▼

TIJUANA CERAMIC TILE: You know we go nuts for tiles, and we are crazy enough to drive here just to load up the car. This is where we got the goods for many a tile floor in L.A. Bargain, and don't ship.

TIJUANA CERAMIC TILE, Bulevar Salinas 3

Welcome to Rosarito

Driving south from Tijuana on the toll road to Ensenada, one can make a brief detour to Rosarito, known for its ready-made and custom-made furniture. It is also a cruise port for some ships from L.A. or Catalina.

Be forewarned: Rosarito is a dusty little strip of shops, hotels, and morose horses waiting for beach riders, and not very much else. But there is at least one reason to stop if you're passing by.

The Lay of the Land

Rosarito is famous for its furniture making. However, we checked out some six shops and found only one we were really impressed with. The others offer rather standard colonial furniture of dubious quality. There also seem to be an abundance of liquor stores.

The main drag of the town is Avenida Benito Juárez. The numbering starts at the *Zócalo*, so the lower numbers are downtown. The higher the number, the farther away from downtown the address is.

Finds

INTERIORES DE MÉXICO: The one reason to get out of the car, just outside Rosarito, is this upbeat shop—a virtual oasis in the desert. Run by Christine and David Lugo, this is the place where you'll find the best selection of excellently crafted native art. Each piece is individual and emotive, especially the crude animal sculptures and masks. Most of the furniture is new, but some antique pieces are available. The style is massive and handwrought—sort of Southwestern/Yuppie meets Mexican Colonial. Some of the pieces are painted with cacti and running animal figures as well as with the usual geometric squiggles, dots, and dashes. A few religious sculptures are available. The owners will prepare custom orders and get them shipped to you within six to eight weeks. It must be said that this beautiful little shop in the middle of nowhere is not cheap! Chairs cost nearly $300, an armoire is $750, a chest $225. Small painted animals cost $16–$20. The owners also have a shop in the United States near San Diego. If you have any specific questions, you can write to them at 416 West San Ysidro Boulevard, Box 714, San Ysidro CA 92023.

INTERIORES DE MÉXICO, Avenida Benito Juárez 25500

Welcome to Ensenada

For those wishing to escape the border-town atmosphere of Tijuana for a real taste of Mexico, Ensenada is just about an hour away on a very good, albeit toll, road. The shopping doesn't really warrant additional travel down to Ensenada in terms of selection, but the shopping ambience is so much nicer that we suggest that if you've got the time you take the short drive. Ensenada is mostly a weekend excursion for those living in Southern California, or a cruise port for those on small ships or quickie cruise outings. The atmosphere here is far more relaxed than in Tijuana.

The Lay of the Land

The focal point of many a visit seems to be Hussong's Cantina, the original local saloon dating back to 1892. This is the place for beer, history, loud singing, and, of course, a T-shirt to tell the world you've been to Hussong's. Such T-shirts are available all over town in a variety of styles and designs.

Most of the shops in Ensenada sell T-shirts or curios, with some genuine folk arts.

Finds

BYE-BYE: Bye-Bye is a chain of T-shirt and beachwear shops located in every big, small, and resort city in Mexico. Their graphics are excellent and they sell the same two dozen designs in a customized form in each market city. Just next door to Hussong's, this shop has the best-made T-shirts in town.

BYE-BYE, Avenida Ruíz 105

▼

HUSSONG'S OFFICIAL STORE: Just as Carlos 'N' Charlie have their official stores, and Señor Frog has his official stores, this is Hussong's official store, with a wide selection of merchandise to prove to the world you've been here.

HUSSONG'S OFFICIAL STORE, Avenida Ruíz 105

▼

THE SHIRT SHOP: A wide selection of long- and short-sleeved Ts and tanks in the $6-to-$12 range. Superior quality and design.

THE SHIRT SHOP, Avenida Ruíz 100

▼

ARTES DON QUIXOTE: This is our favorite shop in all of Ensenada—it's crammed with both new and old Mexican crafts, furniture, and home decorations. Although more items are new, rather than antique, the look is colonial even for new items. There are large wooden frames surrounding mirrors ($295), mantelpieces complete with carved cherubs ($395), and a large armoire carved from antique wood ($595). Much is in the baroque style.

ARTES DON QUIXOTE, Avenida Lopez Mateos 503

▼

ORIGINALES BAJA: We love Mexican glass and like to buy it in Baja if we have the car with us and can schlepp it home and not worry about shipping. Here is where you can get a large selection of colored glassware in the usual shades of green, blue, aqua, and amber. Examine your choices in glassware carefully if you are a serious collector—some that we spotted look too thin to be handblown.

ORIGINALES BAJA, Calle 1, Shop 629A

▼

MITLA BAZAAR: Set back off of Avenida Lopez Mateos, the store has very authentic handicrafts and jewelry. Prices are high, because this is not the usual tourist fare, and is geared more toward those in the know.

MITLA BAZAAR, Avenida Lopez Mateos 453

▼

FONART: We're suckers for any Fonart store in Mexico. This one offers a wide variety of crafts as is the wont of this state-run arts shop. Frida Freaks buy here.

FONART, Avenida Lopez Mateos 1350

▼

ARTES BITTERLIN: A well-known, fancy version of a tourist trap, but with expensive and upper-end merchandise. The popular papier-mâché and clay figures by Sergio Bustamante are sold here. Other artists are also represented.

ARTES BITTERLIN, Avenida Lopez Mateos 1000B

▼

KIKI CURIOS: Vanilla in bottles and Cuban cigars (which cannot be brought into the U.S.), along with the typical curios and touristy items.

KIKI CURIOS, Calle 1 and Miramar

6 ▾ MEXICO CITY

Welcome to D.F.

Mexico City is the *Distrito Federal* (federal district) of the Mexican states. Just as Washington, D.C. is often called simply "D.C.," so as not to confuse it with Washington State, Mexico City is most often called "D.F.," or simply referred to as *"México"*—which can indeed be confusing. Of course, if you're going to really get into the local label, then you need to pronounce it properly: say "Day-Effay," the way insiders do.

So welcome to D.F., perhaps the largest city in the world. No one really even knows how many people live here—estimates range from twelve to twenty million. Most of these people are poor . . . from the working poor to the unbelievably poor. There is a small middle class and a small wealthy class. It's unlikely you'll meet any of these people in your travels throughout D.F. (unless you ride the *metro*). If you stick to the tourist way of life, you will be saddled with the burden of dealing with a very special group of people—those who place themselves between non–Spanish-speaking tourists and non–English-speaking locals. They are mostly tour guides and taxi drivers, and they are not actually out to get you, but they are intent on evening up the balance of trade . . . in their favor. They think you are a rich *norteamericano* who doesn't understand the meaning of life and that you won't even miss the money they are about to fleece from you. They could be right.

So welcome to D.F. with its incredible museums, its glorious university, its marvelous historic sites, and its wonderful shopping . . .

and welcome to some choices. Do you want to go to gringo style, or do you want to go native?

Getting There

You can get to Mexico City easily from any place in the world. The large international airport serves just about every airline. You may also get there by bus from the United States (a rather tedious expedition), or by train. Mexico City is only two to three hours' flying time away from several cities in the U.S. South and Southwest. Package prices for airfare and hotel will be about 20% to 40% cheaper than regular independent travel. Regular round-trip prices from New York are about half what it costs to go to Europe.

Getting Around

The pride of D.F. is its *metro,* which will easily and inexpensively get you just about anywhere you want to go. We use the *metro* system extensively . . . and alone. We have never had reason to be afraid, never been bothered in any way whatsoever. Since so many people warn you of pickpockets on the *metro,* we must repeat the warning—but this is true of any metro in the world.

The cars are clean and bright; the stations are mostly gorgeous; the map is easy to read. (Carry one with you at all times.) You can buy a *carnet* of ten tickets for about 50¢. And yes, the reason those tickets may look familiar to you is that they are indeed identical to the ones used on the Paris *métro*—the same French company built both systems.

We take the *metro* whenever possible, and have indicated *metro* stops in our store listings. If there is no stop in a listing, it is because the distance from the nearest station is too great to make this mode of transportation viable. We pick our hotels by their convenience to the *metro* line, or the *pesero* (jitney) line, and we use public transportation regularly.

You may want to take a van, called a *pesero,* although we warn you to sit close to the front or with the driver.... The smell of diesel fuel can be annoying. These vans are pale green minibuses that stop along a prescribed route; the fare is more than the subway, but usually less than $1. We have been overcharged on these vans ... a mere gringo tax. If you have to take two *peseros* to make a connection, there is no such thing as a transfer—so you pay twice. But on a beautiful day, and for a drive through Chapultepec Park, it could all be worth it.

Naturally, there are taxis in Mexico City. They are relatively inexpensive. The real system for locals is a simple one. The taxi, by law, must have a working meter. When you reach your destination, the driver uses a government-issued form—which you, too, can look at—to arrive at the fare. It should be a matter of a few dollars to get to anywhere a tourist wants to go: It should cost $5 to get from the Hotel Nikko to San Ángel, all the way across town. This is the way it works for locals, anyway.

For gringos, here's the deal:

▼ First of all, there are actually two types of taxis (those that you get at taxi booths, like at the airport, and the ones in front of your hotel) in the city, and you must know how to recognize each to even know how to deal with them.

▼ Taxi drivers feel honor-bound to cheat you with any of a number of scams.... We are considering writing a book about all those worked on us.

▼ When you depart from the airport or a bus terminal, there are taxi booths where you pay for the fare by zone and receive a chit. This is the only fair fare system in Mexico—use it; enjoy it; thank God for it. At the airport in D.F. you can even pay for your chit in U.S. dollars in case you have not yet changed money. This is the only place where you can do this officially. Never pass up the opportunity to use an authorized taxi stand—never.

▼ The taxi in front of your hotel, one of several in a line waiting for you like a buzzard, is not a regular taxi. He may have guide credentials; he may have hotel credentials. He considers himself licensed to take advantage of you. At some hotels (like the Sheraton María Isabel, bless their hearts) there are posted rates for destinations and hourly deals. The Sheraton's rates happen to be the fairest in town. Now then, say it's 6 A.M. and you're in a hurry to get to the bus station. You don't want to take your chances on the street, knowing that it could be difficult to flag down a cab at 6 A.M. So you use a cab from the hotel line. He will charge you $8 for a $3 ride. You are stuck. Say it's not the crack of dawn but a normal business day. You have luggage and are changing to another hotel (we try a lot of hotels when we visit a place); you cannot flag down a cab and manage all that luggage on your own. You must use the hotel driver; you are now stuck for a 500% overcharge. Any time you use one of the cabs in line in front of your hotel, you are overpaying.

▼ If you are just sightseeing or shopping and want a cab, flag one in the street. You must have some working knowledge of Spanish to pull this off, or know how much the ride should cost. If you do not speak Spanish, write down your destination and wave it with a bill—U.S. or Mexican—making hand motions that demonstrate that this amount is what you will pay for your particular destination, but no more (*nada más*).

▼ You may simply get in a taxi you have flagged down and tap the meter insistently. If you don't speak Spanish, this will be a lot of fun. You get to your destination. The driver will quote you a price, either off the top of his head (most likely) or after consulting the official piece of paper. Make him show you the official quote. If by chance you happened to get the one honest taxi driver in Mexico City and your fare is a matter of a dollar or two, give him another 50¢ to $1 as a tip, and inscribe him in the book of life. More likely, your driver will cheat you. You have two choices. Pay the man what he asks for. Or pay him what you think is fair and get out of the cab and keep on walking without ever looking back.

▼ One of the better deals is the driver-by-hourly-fee deal that all hotels have. This rate is usually about $10 an hour, but can be as high as $15. The driver wants to take you to as few places as possible. Traffic is mean, and he likes to sit in the car and wait for you while you oooh and aaah at the sights. We booked a driver for an hour and a half; he insisted on a two-hour minimum, then quit after one hour because he said he wasn't a chauffeur and wouldn't drive us to a lot of stores all over town. This resulted in a yelling and screaming battle that was not the kind of thing the average tourist wants to put up with. And we hired this driver from one of the fanciest hotels in town. So, if you are willing to play by their rules, you may do very well with a local driver on an hourly rate. All drivers have a shopping package or a market package. But if you want to bend the system in your favor, be prepared to fight for your rights.

▼ There are some legitimate supplements to be paid on a taxi fare—evening rates, help with your luggage, etc. Ask your hotel concierge what these are, or you can be supplemented to death.

▼ Your hotel has a flat rate from its door to the airport. This is the best deal you can get if you have luggage. It does vary from hotel to hotel. About $7–$10 is fair from one of the top luxury hotels.

▼ About tips: When using a cab with authorized rates or hotel flat-fee rates, you need not tip. They have already taken you for plenty.... Do you want to be considered a really big chump? We only tip—usually double the fare—if we find a driver who is honest and who goes by the chart and shows us the numbers.

Booking D.F./1

Your hotel will probably have a copy of *Travelers Guide to Mexico* in the room. (Don't steal it or tear pages from it.) If you don't want to buy this book on your own, read it and write down notes for each day's activities. The *American Express Guide to Mexico* is small enough to fit into a pocket or purse, and can go with you around town. There is a locally published guide called *The Guide to the Best of Everything in Mexico,* by Rudi Robins, which is supposed to be revised every two or three years. It costs about $8 in your hotel lobby, and has insider information and opinions on every subject, although the last one we bought was dreadfully out of date on addresses. Although the format is good and the book is easy to use, we don't find the author discerning enough for our taste. But if you're looking for a place to start, this guide is in English, and manages to synthesize a lot of information into an easy-to-carry guidebook. Please note that his lists of the ten best everything are not in any particular order, so that the first item mentioned might not be the best of the group.

We also like the *Trillas Tourist Guide to Mexico City,* which costs about $3 (Sanborns) and is a map-and-graph system to the city by neighborhood. It's in color, in English, and essential to the person who wants to get out on the street and explore on their own.

You will also want a map of the *metro* system, which your hotel should give you for free. It is also printed in many guidebooks.

Booking D.F./2

With the dollar as strong as it is in Mexico, you can get a hotel room for a very small amount of money. While it is possible to find a $12 hotel room, that's not what we look for on our trips. We appreciate the fact that for less than $100 a night you can have the fanciest room in Mexico City. We have stayed in all these hotels and can personally recommend them. While package deals and promotional rates are certainly possible, the standard going rate for these rooms is in the $80–$100 per night range, double or single. Please note the location of the hotel you choose, since Mexico City is a city of neighborhoods and traffic is terrible. You need to be in an area where it's convenient to get the *metro,* the bus, or a taxi or simply to walk.

SHERATON MARÍA ISABEL: We have been staying in this hotel since it was built over twenty years ago. Located right on the Paseo de la Reforma, at the edge of the Zona Rosa (the main tourist and shopping area), the Sheraton has always been one of the nicest hotels in town. It has a very fancy marble lobby, and while the rooms are less fancy, they are still nice. There are some Towers floors. The hotel has an excellent location (perhaps the best in town) and a large shopping arcade. Furthermore, Continental Airlines has its offices in the hotel, so you can change tickets around if need be. Telephone: 211-0001.

SHERATON MARÍA ISABEL, Paseo de la Reforma 325

▼

HOTEL NIKKO: Many consider this Japanese-owned hotel the fanciest in town. It has an ultramodern, space-age lobby, and very plush guest rooms, as well as all sorts of modern facilities and two levels of shopping. Their coffee shop, El Jardín, offers moderately priced meals—we rely on hotel food in Mexico on many occasions—and there are two floors of shops including a Ralph Lauren and a Cartier. You are next door to the Presidente Chapultepec, which you must also check out—it has a lovely area for drinks, a tearoom, and lots of good stores. Telephone: 203-4020.

HOTEL NIKKO, Campos Eliseos 204

▼

GALERÍA PLAZA: This hotel is our secret shopping find. It's owned and operated by Westin, which also has the Hotel Camino Real in Polanco. This is also a luxury hotel, but not the intimidating kind, and is located right smack in the middle of the Zona Rosa. It is slightly more convenient to the *metro* than the Sheraton is. The hotel has some shops of its own but is surrounded by the city's boutique area, so it's the perfect shopper's location. Telephone: 211-0014.

GALERÍA PLAZA, Hamburgo 195

Snack and Shop

We are overly cautious about where we eat in Mexico, period. When we organize each day, we practically plan around lunchtime so we never find ourselves in the position of having to "grab" something. Dr. Debbie's advice: When in doubt, eat in a luxury hotel. But we do have a few places that we can swear by:

CAFÉ DE TACUBA: One of the most famous cafés in Mexico City, this one is located in the old downtown area not far from the Bellas Artes theater, so after you see the Ballet Folklorico, you can come for an after-theater dinner. It's also good for lunch, or tea, or even a late breakfast. It's small and charming, with handpainted tiles and little tables where you can sit and enjoy homemade breads and cakes. One of the highlights of your trip. One half block from the *metro* stop.

CAFÉ DE TACUBA, Tacuba 812 (Metro: Allende)

▼

SANBORNS HOUSE OF TILES: That's us —boring, but safe. But wait, the House of Tiles Sanborns (also downtown, not far from Café Tacuba) is enchanting and a must-see anyway. So why not eat here? There's a sit-down, charmless coffee shop (any meal, any time of day, and cheap) and there is a restaurant in the central court surrounded by its vaulted ceilings and painted walls and tiles.

They are famous for their enchiladas, which to us (Texans) are infamous. But you might like them. Great rest rooms. Sanborns' hours are usually 7 A.M. to midnight, six days a week.

SANBORNS HOUSE OF TILES, Madero 2 (Metro: Bellas Artes)

▼

ANTOJERIA: A must for the shopper on the go in the Zona Rosa. This is your basic chicken-on-a-grill place. Since you can see them cooking the chicken, you don't have to worry about germs. And it's delicious. The place also has a lot of character. That means yellow wooden tables that might be chipped, red plastic chairs, whitewashed brick walls, ceiling fans, and local music. You pay at the cashier. Complete chicken dinner with the works, about $5.

ANTOJERIA, Hamburgo 154 (Metro: Insurgentes)

▼

SAN ÁNGEL INN: An expensive hacienda-style mansion with dining rooms in the exclusive San Ángel district. While it's chic to dine here any time, the best plan is to go to the Saturday market and then come here for lunch around 3 or 4 P.M. Reservations are essential (548-6746); public transportation is almost impossible. A memorable splurge.

SAN ÁNGEL INN, Palmas 30, San Ángel

▼

ANDERSON'S: We can't bypass a Carlos 'N' Charlie's restaurant of any kind. This one is the original; it's a block from the Sheraton on the Paseo de la Reforma. Always crowded, they may or may not take reservations (525-1006). We're wild for the lime steak and the caramel crepes.

ANDERSON'S, Paseo de la Reforma 400 (Metro: Insurgentes)

EL MORRAL: So you're dying for real Mexican food. Tex-Mex won't do, and you want the best, the absolutely best quesadillas in the world? Search no farther. This is the place for atmosphere and eats. It's in Coyoacán, the oldest part of town, and is not too far from San Ángel, so you can eat here after your trip to the bazaar.

EL MORRAL, Universidad 903-A

The Lay of the Land

Mexico City is a very large city, offering much to do that will fill your days and probably leave you breathless and eager to return. Actually, you're breathless because of the altitude. As others will warn you, start off slowly and never overschedule for your first day or two. A shopping marathon should not be planned until the third day, when you are more acclimated. You also want to get the feel of things a bit before you start the spending.

D.F. is very much a city of neighborhoods (see page 131). Traffic (and pollution) are mind-boggling, so each day should be planned by locations and neighborhoods. One of the best things about Mexico City is its proximity to other interesting Mexican cities—some of which are not regular tourist fare. We suggest several day trips from D.F., especially for shopping. Plan all your days in Mexico City with the understanding that come Friday, you will be going to Toluca. Although Dr. Jill says the Toluca market is too gimmicky for her taste, she's the only person we know who doesn't like it. We feel that if you're going to Mexico City on a shopping expedition, you can't possibly miss a day trip to Toluca. There's also Puebla, Taxco, etc. See our chapter on day trips for more suggestions.

Mexico City, D.F.

TO MERCADO LAGUNILLA ▲

TO TERMINAL DE AUTOBUSES DE ORIENTE ▲

TO MERCADO MERCED ▲

TO MERCADO SONORA ▲

TO CENTRAL DE AUTOBUSES DEL SUR ►

PINO SUAREZ

MONTE DE PIEDAD

Zocalo

SAN ANTONIO ABAD

Cafe Tacuba

CENTRAL
(see map)

TACUBA

GARMENTO

BOLIVAR

J. MA. IZAZAGA

AVENIDA HIDALGO

AVENIDA BENITO JUAREZ

Palacio de las Bellas Artes

ARCOS DE BELEN

BALDERAS

NINOS HEROES

GUERRERO

PUENTE DE ALVARADO

BUCARELI

PASEO DE LA REFORMA

AVENIDA CUAUHTEMOC

AVENIDA INSURGENTES

CALLE LIVERPOOL

AVENIDA

CALLE NIZA

CENTRO

TO DIVISION DEL NORTE ►

AVENIDA INSURGENTES SUR

CALLE GENOVA

ZONA ROSA
(see map)

CALLE HAMBURGO

CALLE FLORENCIA

CHAPULTEPEC

AVENIDA MELCHOR OCAMPO

Galeria Plaza

Sheraton Maria Isabel

CALLE SEVILLA

AVENIDA VICTOR HUGO

N ←

CALZADA TACUBAYA

ESCOBEDO

PASEO DE LA REFORMA

AVENIDA CONSTITUYENTES

CALZADA MARIANO

ELISEOS

AVENIDA PRESIDENTE MAZARIK

AVENIDA CAMPOS

POLANCO

Museo Nacional de Antropologia

Hotel Presidente Chapultepec

Hotel Nikko

TO SAN ANGEL INN

TO TERMINAL CENTRAL DE AUTOBUSES DEL PONIENTE

TO ANILLO PERIFERICO ▼

130

Mexico City is a big city, a business city, a get-up-and-get-'em city—so don't lie back and relax. Start shopping!

Shopping D.F.

On the whole, the shopping experience in D.F. can be considered most exciting either for its proximity to more good shopping (Toluca), for its abundance of markets (page 146), or for its abundance of those few good stores that sell everything and are so special that even if there's just a handful of them they are wholly satisfying.

While there are department stores in D.F., we don't send you to them, because they are much like department stores in the United States. And while you can buy ready-to-wear in D.F., except for Ralph Lauren or something really special, we don't think this is the place for ready-to-wear. Do buy your cowboy boots here; do stock up on silver; and open up the tote bag and get out the bubble wrap: The crafts are great here. Don't leave without a giant *piñata* for the kids. A small one will not impress. Go all out. Spend $5.

Mexico City Neighborhoods

Mexico City is officially divided into sixteen *delegaciones* (city wards), which are, in turn, subdivided into 240 neighborhoods called *colonias*, which are much like Paris's *arrondissements*. The *colonia* is often abbreviated on a business card or in an address as "Col." Our neighborhoods are not strictly divided by *colonias*. Sometimes they overlap, sometimes they are just a portion of one *colonia*. They are, more accurately, tourist shopping neighborhoods.

Polanco

Polanco is a very, very nice, quasiresidential area spotted with embassies and decorated with some swank hotels such as the Nikko, Presidente Chapultepec, and Camino Real. It is not an easy area to shop because it is broken up for use by locals who have cars—this neighborhood alone has four distinctly different shopping areas. All are upscale and enormous fun. In fact, if you just did these four areas (possible in an hour or two ... or three) and then went to a few markets, you would have a very healthy, very fresh, very positive outlook on shopping in Mexico City.

NIKKO

The shopping here is for rich American tourists and businesspeople who frequent the two luxury hotels (the Nikko and the Presidente Chapultepec). It begins indoors, since both hotels have excellent arcades. Continue outdoors to a short row of shops directly across the street from the two hotels. This "neighborhood" takes up only a city block, but each place is a winner!

CASA DE LAS ARTESANÍAS DE MICHOACÁN: It is popular in Mexico for each state to have its own arts-and-crafts store that sells regional goodies. This is the best of such stores, and one of the best stores in Mexico City, as you'll realize even before you go inside—just look at the handpainted doors! The shop sells mostly furniture and crafts, some textiles, and ready-to-wear. Michoacán, as you know, is most famous for its black lacquerwork.

The handpainted items for sale in this shop are especially beautiful. Directly across from the Nikko.

CASA DE LAS ARTESANÍAS DE MICHOACÁN, Corner of Calle Temistocle and Campos Eliseos (Metro: Auditorio)

▼

MARU ALONSO: Just bring your bags and move in here; forget the two hotels across the street. A chic, rich, tony home-decor store with clay pots, and colonial furniture, and savoir faire to spare. This is everything Mexico can be, and more.

MARU ALONSO, Campos Eliseos 199 (Metro: Auditorio)

▼

BASIL: An antiques store with the right stuff . . . including *Talavera* planters from the 18th century for $1,000 each.

BASIL, Campos Eliseos 215 Local C (Metro: Auditorio)

▼

CESAR FRANCO: A big-name designer and maker of nice ready-to-wear with high quality and high fashion guaranteed. The address represents an entire block of shops that includes Franco's and Basil, as well as a Benetton, which does not close for lunch.

CESAR FRANCO, Campos Eliseos 215 (Metro: Auditorio)

PLAZA POLANCO CENTRO COMERCIAL

This is a shopping center for locals, and is not within walking distance of any of the hotels we've listed. And it's not even that easy to get to on public transportation. It's not that exciting, and you can live without it, but there are some branch stores of licensed names you know and love, such as **CHARLES JOURDAN, POLO/ RALPH LAUREN, GODIVA** (chocolates), and **LASERRE**, as well as local big names like **ARIES** (leather goods), **EDOARDO** (jeans), etc. If there was something to swoon over at Charles Jourdan, we would tell you.

AVENIDA PRESIDENTE MASARYK

This is a main drag of Polanco that bisects Avenida Mariano Escobedo, the other main drag in Polanco—where the Hotel Camino Real is located. This wide, tree-lined avenue is packed with fancy boutiques, and is far nicer than the Zona Rosa (which also has a lot of boutiques, but is known as the touristy part of town). Everyone who is everyone has a shop here, including **ALBERT NIPON, HALSTON, ACA JOE, ARIES, ESPRIT, DOMIT, RUBEN TORRES, MARACA, EDOARDO,** etc. All these stores are in rows next to each other on both sides of the street in the 300 and 400 blocks. Take a taxi from the Nikko neighborhood. Or walk from the Hotel Camino Real. It's also possible to get there from the Polanco stop on the *metro*.

CAMINO REAL

There are stores inside the Hotel Camino Real and a few stores beside the Hotel Camino Real, most notably:

LO QUE EL VIENTO SE LLEVO: This is supposed to translate as "Gone With the Wind" but actually means "That Which the Wind Blew In." But the wind could never round up such a gorgeous collection of crafts and home furnishings, including colonial furniture, textiles, and pewter picture frames.

LO QUE EL VIENTO SE LLEVO, Victor Hugo 56 (Metro: Chapultepec)

Zona Rosa

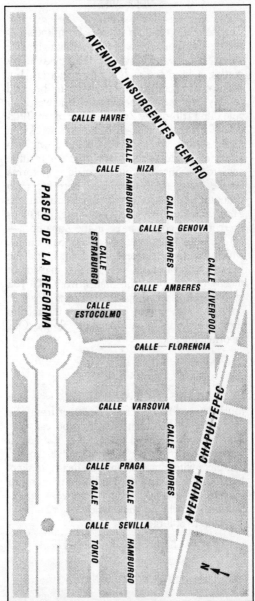

CALLE HAVRE

AVENIDA INSURGENTES CENTRO

CALLE HAMBURGO

CALLE NIZA

CALLE LONDRES

CALLE GENOVA

PASEO DE LA REFORMA

CALLE ESTRABURGO

CALLE AMBERES

CALLE LIVERPOOL

CALLE ESTOCOLMO

CALLE FLORENCIA

CALLE VARSOVIA

CALLE LONDRES

CALLE PRAGA

AVENIDA CHAPULTEPEC

CALLE

CALLE

CALLE SEVILLA

TOKIO

HAMBURGO

N

Zona Rosa

The Zona Rosa has for decades been known as
the best shopping area of town, although since
we're so honest we have to tell you that it's
getting a little seedy. It's not dangerous, but
it's not as glamorous as it used to be, and
frankly, we like Polanco better. But we don't
rule out a trip to the Zona Rosa or tea at **DUCA
D'ESTE** (Hamburgo 164B). This area works on
a grid system; you can walk up and down each
street and side street. Take a *pesero* (shuttle
van) to the Sheraton on Paseo de la Reforma
or the *metro* to Insurgentes. There are truly
thousands of shops here; take a look at the
Tianguis section of this book (page 146), as
there are two good markets in the Zona Rosa—
an antiques market at the Plaza San Ángel,
which is a shopping center of dealers, and the
Insurgentes Mercado, an indoor market of
mostly crafts. All of the chains, from **ACA JOE**
to **CARTIER**, have shops in the Zona Rosa, as
do many independents. The *metro* to Insurgentes
should get you to any of these shops. Our
favorites include:

▼

EL SARAPE MEXICANO: This is a tiny
tourist trap directly across the street from one
of the Best Western hotels, but you can bargain here and have a good time. We found
some delicately made pins of native women
complete with chickens on their heads, baskets
filled with eggs, and the kind of workmanship
that makes your eyes water. They were expensive at $3 each, but hey, what's a vacation if
not time to splurge?

EL SARAPE MEXICANO, Londres 117 A

▼

ARTESANÍAS FINAS: A good resource for embroidered dresses, flouncy Mexican-style skirts, and Oaxaca-style embroidered T-shirts, which are hard to find.

ARTESANÍAS FINAS, Londres 139

▼

FONART: Not our favorite Fonart, but a serviceable one, located in a three-story building—you must go up one flight of stairs to get to the lobby of the shop, then up another flight for textiles.

FONART, Londres 36

▼

POLO/RALPH LAUREN: One of several Ralph Lauren stores in town (there are others in Plaza Polanco and at the Hotel Nikko), this is a two-story boutique with men's, women's, and kids' clothing. The style is Ralph meets Mexico.... It's your chance to buy at 30% less than in the United States. These made-in-Mexico clothes are legit and of fairly high quality.

POLO/RALPH LAUREN, Amberes 24

▼

LEBRONZ: A wonderful resource for big, heavy furniture, pewter picture frames, and the look of the Southwest.

LEBRONZ, Amberes 1

▼

SOL ARTE: A small, spare boutique with shelves that contain some very special pieces of religious art and some gorgeous, gorgeous *santones*. About $200 for a real work of art.

SOL ARTE, Amberes 3

MULTI EXPORT: The home of the greatest inventory of papier-mâché fruits and vegetables you've ever seen. These are piled in bins in the front part of the shop. The rest of the place is crammed with arts and crafts from various states. We think about half of what's here is so ugly that you have to brace yourself, but the rest is great. A tray for $50 was much too expensive, but you will have fun looking. Allow time for browsing here, and have a ball. They are open nonstop from 9 A.M. to 8 P.M.

MULTI EXPORT, Amberes 21

▼

GIRASOL: Unique Mexican ethnic dresses that are wearable and not too costumey; they are made from gorgeous fabrics, and often appliquéd. Not inexpensive, but remarkable.

GIRASOL, Génova 39

▼

GAITAN: The silliest store in the area—this is a cowboy shop that is much fun. Upstairs is a rather standard tourist trap, but the street-level part of the store is filled with cowboy boots, leather jackets, tooled belts, handbags, briefcases, etc. Only the cowboy boots impressed us, but the store is worth a visit.

GAITAN, Hamburgo 89

▼

GUCCI: There are two shops in the Zona Rosa; the one on Niza is for wallets and small accessories. The main shop, on Hamburgo, is nice and carries a wide selection of handbags, shoes, luggage, etc. Some things seem amazingly inexpensive; others are too high even at these prices. Worth exploring if you are into status symbols.

GUCCI
Hamburgo 136
Niza 20

▼

BAZARELI ANTIQUEDADES: One of many little shops in the Plaza del Ángel antiques arcade, this shop is hard to find but well worth it. Their specialty is in *retablos*. The owner, Raymundo, is a collector and does not speak English. If you show an interest in the art form, he'll be happy to point out his best examples. Most of his *retablos* are from the 1950s, but he has a few that are in the fifty-year-old range. Prices begin at about $75. Bargain if you buy several. (Bargain for one, too.)

BAZARELI ANTIQUEDADES, Londres 161–4

▼

ACA JOE: A big, bold shop selling the stuff we know and love. It seems a bit of a surprise on this street devoted to designer shops.

ACA JOE, Amberes 19

▼

UNITS: Here's a new one! The popular chain Units (owned by J. C. Penney), which has become America's new Benetton, has a branch here in the Zona Rosa! The clothing is Mexican-made. Fun, if you're a fan of this mix-and-match, pull-on, cotton-knit look.

UNITS, Londres 132

▼

ARTE POPULAR EN MINATURA/ COLECCIÓN DE FELEGUEREZ: Just what the name says, folks. This is a tiny little shop selling tiny little miniatures and some toy soldiers.

ARTE POPULAR EN MINATURA/COLECCIÓN DE FELEGUEREZ, Hamburgo 130

▼

ZAPATERÍA VIDAL: We love both their Christian Dior line and their original designs in shoes and handbags. Very French, Italian, European, cosmopolitan, at moderate prices ... about $100 for a great handbag; $70 for a pair of shoes. Best in town.

ZAPATERÍA VIDAL, Hamburgo 134

▼

ARIES: Aries is one of the most famous, up-scale leather-goods shops in Mexico, and we are eagerly awaiting the day they manage to impress us. The quality is excellent, but unfortunately we find them lacking in style. Pop in anyway; you may find something that suits your taste.

ARIES, Florencia 14

▼

BANANA REPUBLIC: Although this is an unofficial store, and although the ready-to-wear is not of the same selection or quality as the U.S. stores and is best ignored, we have to include them because they have some of the best T-shirts in town. We consider these to be one of the best souvenir items you can buy in Mexico. They say "Mexico Safari" on them, with the usual good graphics you can depend on Banana Republic for. A good deal in an otherwise disappointing shop.

BANANA REPUBLIC, Florencia 48

TANE: One of Mexico's most famous silversmiths. We are not talking about a pair of earrings here, rather silver sculpture and important tabletop. Several branches in tony locations.

TANE
Amberes 70
Hotel Nikko
Hotel Presidente Chapultepec

Garmento D.F.

A big city like D.F. naturally has a garment center. What we're talking about here is Mexican-made ready-to-wear, most of it without labels—as if you would recognize the labels if you saw them! If you do find any big names, they are probably not licensed. But if you're looking for inexpensive clothes, or want to get into an outlet store, this is for you. The garment center is downtown, in an area where tourists would otherwise wander, so you might want to drop by. It's all located around the main street, Avenida J. M. Izazaga between Pino Suárez and Lazaro Cardenas. Take the *metro* to the stop at Pino Suárez, then walk toward Bellas Artes; it's only a matter of a few big blocks. Check out **FASHION 55** at No. 122 and **CALIFORNIA FACTORY** at No. 99. Both sell hot looks at low prices. **RUBEN TORRES** is at No. 74. By the time the street numbers get down to No. 32, it's all over. Do note that the Museum of the Charro is right here as well.

Bellas Artes

The main street of Mexico City's downtown is Avenida Juárez, which passes in front of the Alameda and some big monuments in the old section not that far from the *Zócalo*. You can walk here from the *Zócalo* (walk down Madero, which was once the fanciest downtown

Downtown Mexico City (Central)

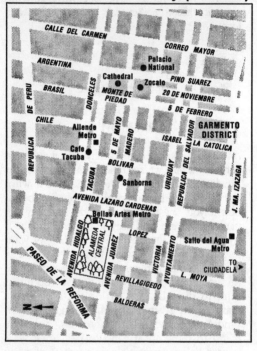

street of old Mexico City, and don't miss Sanborns House of Tiles) or simply take the *metro* to Bellas Artes and you are on the right corner for everything. This part of town was severely damaged by the 1985 earthquake, but there's still some important shopping here:

VICTOR'S: Victor Fosado is the most famous man in the Mexican folk-art world, and his shop is almost as famous. His son and daughter have continued in the business, with daughter Pilar in the shop and son Victor doing academic work. Much of the family collection of folk-art treasures is in museums already.

Victor's shop is a little hard to get to if you've never been there before, but don't be frightened. It's worth it, and you are not in any danger. The shop is actually in a set of office suites. Go upstairs (two flights) in this office building. The main shop is one room, and if you're beginning to wonder "Is this all there is?" rest assured there are some hidden rooms—one for stock and another for serious pieces for those collectors who show an interest.

A visit here is like going to a museum. Whether or not you buy is not important, although prices are reasonable and you can be sure of the quality of what you are getting. The store is open only in the afternoon, noon to 7 P.M.

VICTOR'S, Madero 10, Room 305

▼

SANBORNS HOUSE OF TILES: We rave about Sanborns on just about every page of this book, so there's not a lot new to say. Many Sanborns shops are ordinary and utilitarian. This one is special. It's in a building faced completely with *azulejos,* and has lots of arts and crafts (on two floors), as well as books in English, maps, and guidebooks, all surrounded by handpainted walls and must-see charm. Eat any meal here or just stop for coffee; good rest rooms.

SANBORNS HOUSE OF TILES, Madero 2

▼

CASART: A small, narrow gift shop, run by an agency to feature crafts. The open cases display wares you haven't seen before, as well as a good selection of china dish sets. A forty-nine–piece set of blue-and-white china, which was nice but not anything special, cost $135. They close for lunch here from 2:30 to 3:30 P.M., which is unusual.

CASART, Avenida Juárez 18

FONART: Our favorite Fonart in all of Mexico is this large downtown store, which incredibly was not destroyed in the quake of 1985—although everything around it was damaged! Large and well-displayed, the shop, run by a state-owned agency, has every form of Mexican craft. Prices are fair, and although some items cost 200% more than the street price, others were exactly the same price as at the source. The store especially appeals to the kind of shopper who just couldn't make it in the market in Toluca. Everything is very clean and easy to deal with. Excellent arty postcards. Frida merchandise. A winner.

FONART, Avenida Juárez 89

▼

MUSEO NACIONAL DE ARTES E IN-DUSTRIAS POPULARES: We aren't ashamed to admit we like Fonart, but we *love* this museum shop, which is almost a supermarket of crafts. The museum (and shop) are in a basilica with white walls and wooden beams (don't miss the tiny wrought-iron staircase in the far corner). The front chambers are also part of the store—there are some displays, and there is a corner where damaged merchandise is offered for sale (to your right as you walk in the front door); so this place has a wandering layout—but that is part of its charm. A lot of what's here can be found in any market, but the architecture and the intimacy of the place are special and you feel privileged to be shopping here. Great fun.

MUSEO NACIONAL DE ARTES E INDUSTRIAS POPULARES, Avenida Juárez 44

Shopping Centers

PERISUR: The main part of Mexico City is surrounded by a highway called the Anillo Periferico. On the southern edge, where the yuppies live, is Perisur, an American-style shopping center. You can't really get here without a car, and you may not necessarily want to get here. But this is the largest, nicest, best mall in D.F., and it does have a branch of just about every Mexican chain or designer. There is also an American Express office here.

PERISUR, Corner of Anillo Periferico Sur and Avenida Insurgentes Sur

▼

PLAZA POLANCO: Really for locals, but very upscale. See page 133.

PLAZA POLANCO, Jaimes Balmes 11

▼

PLAZA DEL ÁNGEL: A small arcade that zigs and zags under a building and has entrances on two streets (enter from Calle Londres, where it is well-marked), so you can easily enjoy this antiques center. There are about a dozen antiques shops here, and one or two dress shops. On Saturday (from 10 A.M. to 5 P.M.) additional dealers set up stalls in the walkways and in the little outdoor plaza. Very charming; worth visiting. One of the secret treasures of the Zona Rosa.

PLAZA DEL ÁNGEL, Londres 161

Tianguis and Mercados

BAZAR SABADO: Why not start out with the best one? A trip to Mexico City means scheduling yourself so that you can go to Toluca bright and early on Friday and then on to San Ángel by 10 to 11 A.M. on Saturday.

San Ángel is a rich colonial neighborhood to the south of Mexico City with a very developed fiesta atmosphere that revolves around the Bazar Sabado but is not confined to it. (Do not confuse this area with the Plaza del Ángel, which is in the Zona Rosa.) You can taxi here, but if you have a car you can not only take in the *bazar* but also stop at the San Ángel Inn on Las Palmas, the Museo Casa Estudio Diego Rivera, and the nearby suburb of Coyoacán, which is where Hernán Cortés set up housekeeping. However you get there, just get there.

The *bazar* is actually three different *tianguis*— two of which are outdoors. There is an art show in the park (Plaza San Jacinto), which is the place to spot up-and-coming artists; there is a crafts market that is a tad more expensive than need be, but so visually stimulating that you might not mind overpaying. Then there is the main show, which is inside a villa with a patio so that vendors are set up inside the house, upstairs in the house, and all around the outside. (Part of the patio is devoted to a restaurant.) The crowd here is partly tourist but mostly local yuppie and very well dressed and monied. "Elegant" is the byword of the entire affair. Most of the dealers who show in the house are regulars: There are several arts-and-crafts stalls featuring the Oaxaca-style carved animals; Feder's, the famous local glass-blower, has a booth; Girasol is sold; Matl sells the most intricate metal filigree with semi-precious stones you've ever seen in your life;

and Miguel Cortez Monsalvo sells breathtakingly beautiful *santones* that belong in a museum.

There are about 100 vendors in the house; some come from nearby cities (Taxco, Cuernavaca) for the show. Bargaining is expected, although you'll cut a better deal outside the villa than inside it. These vendors are not particularly hungry, as they know they have the best show in town. There is absolutely no touristy junk sold inside the house—it must be against the rules. We love the whole combination of the fancy stuff inside, the junkier stuff outside, and the artwork in the garden—this is a day in Mexico at its best. Hours: 10 A.M. to 7 P.M., Saturday only.

BAZAR SABADO, Plaza San Jacinto, San Ángel

▼

MERCADO INSURGENTES: Next door to the Krystal Hotel in the Zona Rosa, this market is kind of hard to spot because it is indoors; and while it has about four or five entrances, they all appear to be entrances to small tourist traps; so you may accidentally ignore them. The market is about the size of a city block, and sells some fruits and foodstuffs but mostly crafts and silver. This market is very special: It feels like a genuine local market, but it has no dead chickens. (Or live ones.) It is a sanitized *mercado* at best, but a good one that should be enjoyed. Since it's right in the Zona Rosa, don't miss it. It's also across the street from the Plaza del Ángel, the antiques market. Hours: 10 A.M. to 7 P.M.

MERCADO INSURGENTES, Londres 154 (Metro: Insurgentes)

▼

MERCED MARKET: This is the "real people" market, and it, along with the Sonora Market a block away, is our favorite in Mexico City. But beware, it gets a high dead-chicken rating. This is the real thing. There was also a terrible fire in this market (Christmas 1988) in which almost 100 people were killed; we warn you that this is the real world and fireworks (which caused the fire) are still sold here. Take the *metro* to La Merced. As you emerge into the station you'll find that you already appear to be inside the market. Every day is market day, and this place is jumping, especially in the morning hours.

The Merced Market is actually made up of several covered market areas, zillions of stalls, and a lot of outdoor vendors. It sort of runs into the Sonora Market. It's hard to know where anything starts or stops. Although you are probably not interested in the food vendors, the *piñatas* are sold inside in the food buildings, as are some dry goods and things like tin cookware and some pottery. (Wait until the Sonora Market for pottery.) The *piñata* business is a very competitive one, so shop around and bargain. It is possible to commission a *piñata*, but you need to come back for it. There are large *piñatas* here, the kind that will fill the back-seat of a VW taxi, but they are glorious and worth schlepping home. We once bought a *piñata* in the shape of a horse (and the size of a carousel pony) for $5, immediately took a taxi back to the hotel ($3), and then brought the horse home with us via Newark, where he was hand-carried by the Continental staff. Not so much as a strand was missing from his pink-and-green mane.

MERCED MARKET, Calle Rosario (Metro: Merced)

▼

SONORA MARKET: The Sonora Market is the pottery market, but it is also the *tchotchke* market. Whatever the holiday, this market sells the toys and decorations that go along with it.

For the Day of the Dead, you get your plastic skeletons here. For Christmas, you buy ornaments here. At any time of the year you can choose the toys that go inside a *piñata* (see page 84). At the back of the market is pet city. Most ceramic products are sold by the dozen—you provide your own means of carrying them home. Someone might wrap for you, but don't count on it. Much of what is available in Toluca is sold here; it costs a little more here than there, but we're talking about coffee mugs at $5 a dozen. If you are only going to one market in Mexico City, we pick this one. Despite the live pets in the rear, there are no dead chickens.

SONORA MARKET, Avenida Fray Servando Teresa de Mier (Metro: Merced)

▼

THE GREEN DOOR: This is technically a shop, but it's the size of a small warehouse, and sells enough crafts to make it a *tianguis*. It's off the beaten path, but still worth going to. Although there's no bargaining, there are no dead chickens either. In business for over fifty years, the store is set back off a parking/patio area, so you may feel a tad uncomfortable as you search for it. Walk on, you're fine. Follow signs and arrows past what looks like a shipping dock, and at last you'll see a flight of cement stairs. Go up these and you are in the warehouse. A totally safe adventure, and a good find if you don't like true markets or bargaining. The owners are importers and exporters and have a wide selection of all crafts forms. Considered a local insider's source by the embassy crowd. Not accessible by public transportation.

THE GREEN DOOR, Cedro 8, Santa María

▼

FEDER'S: This is also a shop, one that specializes in glass but has a few other crafts items. It is extremely popular despite its out-of-the-way location, and we can't figure out why. You can get a chandelier here, though. There is a wrought-iron workshop. This is a factory location; have your taxi wait for you—you'll never get another one.

FEDER'S, Lago Muritz 67

▼

LA CIUDADELA: Our friend Pat, who buys arts and crafts from Mexico and knows her stuff, likes it here a lot. This market is inside a walled patio, with covered stalls of shops; there are some artisans at work. No dead chickens. We find it contrived and touristy, without much depth to the selection. Pat says you just have to look and bargain hard. Hours: 11 A.M. to 8 P.M. Located within walking distance of Bellas Artes, but next to the Balderas *metro* stop.

LA CIUDADELA, Avenida Balderas (Metro: Balderas)

▼

CENTRO ARTESANAL BUENAVISTA: This market is an indoor affair in a giant warehouse that is painted blue on the outside; it is across the street from the Buenavista train station. It can only be described as comical. Everything in the world is sold here, and we really shouldn't knock it, but this is so sanitized and touristy (complete with tour buses parked outside) that we have trouble keeping a straight face. This shop says it's the largest market in town, and we believe them. There must be 50,000 square feet of space selling everything from patio furniture to tiles to *huaraches* to handtooled luggage ($300 for a small suitcase) to tablecloths to *huipiles*. The selection is immense; there's more on the mezzanine. This is what it would look like if K mart went into the souvenir business. You can walk the few blocks from the *metro*. They are open daily from 9 A.M. to 6 P.M. during the week and on Saturday, and on Sunday from 10 A.M. to 2 P.M.

CENTRO ARTESANAL BUENAVISTA, Aldama 187 (Metro: Revolución)

▼

THIEVES MARKET: This is essentially a local garage sale held in the street alongside the Lagunilla Market. As far as we're concerned, both are boring. The Thieves Market (which seems perfectly safe) is supposed to sell antiques, but quickly peters out. Only a small percentage of the vendors are selling anything you even want to look at, let alone buy. But on a nice day, it's kind of fun and you can chat with fellow gringos who read the same guidebook that told them this was a must-do. We're really talking a lot of vinyl soccer balls, some old issues of *National Geographic,* and maybe a few brand-new *retablos* ($6 each). Held each Sunday; gets going between 10 and 11 A.M. Take a *pesero* (marked *"La Villa"*) along Paseo de la Reforma. Go to the Floating Gardens in the afternoon. Now you are a tourist.

THIEVES MARKET, Rayón at Paseo de la Reforma

▼

SAN JUAN CURIOSITIES MARKET: We say it's not really worth the trouble to get here, but Pat disagrees! She agrees that this market is basically boring and clean, but you can deal, and the prices can't be beat. The market is in a big square building with different levels that are reached by a network of ramps and stairs, so that you go up several levels and work your way around in a square.

Although there are no dead chickens here, do note that to get here you pass through Wholesale Poultryville, and there even the tarmac on the road is stuck with chicken feathers.

The market has absolutely no charm whatsoever. But there are individual dealers selling regional crafts, and you can have a very good time here.

SAN JUAN CURIOSITIES MARKET, Corner of Ayuntamiento and Dolores (Metro: Salto del Agua)

7 ▾ HOME FURNISHINGS AND ANTIQUES

Homestyle

Those of us who live, or have lived, in the American Southwest are familiar with Mexican art and architectural influence in every aspect of our home and home furnishings. From Texas to California, with New Mexico and Arizona in between, we appreciate the tile floors we used to take for granted, the stucco walls and arches, the patios, the wrought iron, and the gentle reminder that my house is your house: *Mi casa es su casa.*

You can buy the ingredients to replicate the comforts of the Southwestern life-style in just about any city in the American Southwest. But you can buy them for less in Mexico. Southwesterners bring down the truck and load up. You might want to consider following that plan, or just start shopping around for shippers you can rely on. Thanks to the fairly easy rules regarding excess baggage, you can fly your treasures home with you on the plane (without spending a lot of cash), so you needn't worry about mail and delivery. Remember, most excess-baggage rates are figured by the piece, not by weight!

Collectibles

The most important collectibles, especially to Southwestern Americans, are handicrafts—preferably examplary antique or aged pieces. It is illegal to bring pre-Columbian treasures out of Mexico; it is illegal to remove antiquities that date from before 1520 (the start of the colonial period). Original works of Diego Rivera are considered national treasures and cannot be removed from Mexico.

Yet Americans should know that there is more to buy and collect in Mexico than crafts and pre-Columbian artifacts. And Diego Rivera works haven't come on the marketplace in Mexico for years, anyway. Mexico has a lot of collectible European antiques. You must remember that the immigration laws of the United States are strict, and that many of those who seek to enter the country are not permitted to do so. They then try Canada or Mexico. In the years immediately prior to and after World War II, masses of European immigrants tried to gain entry into the United States. Many did not succeed. They ended up in Mexico instead. Those who owned valuables brought them with them. Many of these things are still in the families that inherited them; but some have gone to sale and auction.

Europeans have been coming to Mexico steadily for well over 400 years. Their belongings often come to market in antiques stores. Even now, as the *peso*'s value fluctuates almost daily, families may be forced to sell their inherited valuables for cash.

Shipping

We wish we liked the idea of shipping from Mexico, but we don't. It's our preference to drive to Mexico with a van, load up, and drive home again, frankly. But since that isn't practical for everyone, here goes. You can ship and live happily ever after. Many people have done it. We even know people who have done it.

The variables to watch for are size of the item (the bigger the item, the less likely it will be stolen along the way), and packing—it can arrive at your doorstep just fine, thank you, but if it's broken, who cares?

We lean toward shipping furniture rather than boxes of treasures. We suggest you pack your treasures in egg boxes, which you can buy in the *mercado* for a few cents. Travel with bubble wrap, strapping tape, scissors, and heavy-duty marker. (Don't you always?) While newspaper can always be substituted for bubble wrap, strapping tape is hard to find and expensive in Mexico. Bring several rolls! Whenever possible, do your own packing—even for a shipping agent.

If you are turning the box over to an agent, make sure you have an inventory of what's inside and, ideally, a set of photos. (Always carry that instant camera with you!)

Shipping and expediting laws are in the process of changing. Previously, the government only allowed courier service on Mexican airlines. When the Mexican airlines got into financial trouble, the government began to change the laws, and in short order Federal Express and other couriers and carriers were able to carry overnight packages and freight. Our friend David, a businessman in Mexico City, sends all his business mail out by DHL Courier service, since the mail in Mexico can be iffy. This is also an excellent tip for small packages and items you care about but cannot carry with you. It won't work for a handpainted chest, but might for smaller items. If you do business with one of the courier services in the United States, ask for their international catalogue and for specific information about Mexico before you leave home. Take the appropriate forms with you, along with the bubble wrap and scissors. You can often send two pounds for about $25, which is rather reasonable considering that you know your package will be safe. Label your package with the proper words for the customs agents: "Handicrafts" or "business documents" will get you through customs just fine.

Antiques Neighborhoods

Downtown

LA GRANJA: Most people think this is the best antiques store in town. Mention to anyone that you are searching for antiques and they immediately say "Have you been to La Granja?" The store is downtown, not far from the *Zócalo*, and sells mostly European furniture—a lot of it baroque, but a little of everything—from the most incredible candlesticks you've ever seen to the portrait of the naked lady with the red veil to hang over the fireplace. Everything has been authenticated and is guaranteed. This is an insider's source that's been trusted by generations of locals.

LA GRANJA, Bolívar 16 (Metro: Salto del Agua)

▼

NATIONAL PAWNSHOP: We wish we could tell you we loved the pawnshop; we wish we could tell you we found romance and reward in the pawnshop; we wish we could tell you the pawnshop was worth your time and energy. Sorry. The place is famous, has an incredible reputation, and is astounding in its collection of junk. All the finds have already been found, since the insiders have moles who tell them exactly when something interesting comes in. Still, it is in the *Zócalo*/downtown neighborhood, and you'll be right there anyway. And, then, well, you never know if it's your lucky day. Spanish speakers only.

NATIONAL PAWNSHOP, Monte de Piedad 7 (Metro: Zócalo)

Zona Rosa

PLAZA DEL ÁNGEL: The Plaza del Ángel is hard to spot as a treasure because it is set back from the street, is over a parking garage, and kind of looks more like a motel than a national treasure. (See page 146.) But its terra-cotta–colored stucco walls should be whispering your name, and you should be listening. A short walk from the Insurgentes *metro* stop. The best time to visit is on weekends, when vendors set up stalls in the plaza and along the walkways. But during regular workdays there are several shops open, and they are worth visiting. Some are more serious than others; all are used to browsers: **BAZAR DEL SOL** (Local 21A) is a top-notch dealer for important art and antiquities of the colonial era, including many religious pieces. Formal and fine. **BAZAR SOSA** (Local 42) is the shop where we wanted to send the Mexico Ralph Lauren people. Well, you know how most of the Polo shops in the States are decorated, right? In Mexico, they aren't quite the same. But if the owners shopped here they'd have all the appropriate Ralph

Lauren touches that would turn their shops into perfect showpieces. You've got it all here—from handtooled antique saddles (wouldn't Ralph love that?) to giant portraits of family members, crystal-drop wall sconces, and brass doodads. (The owner has a second shop, more for locals, called **BAZAR SALAMANCA** at Salamanca 107 in the Condesa *colonia*.) **RAYMUNDO HERRERA** (Local 4) is already mentioned (see page 139), but he's worth mentioning again because what he has is so special. Sr. Herrera collects *retablos*, which he personally refers to as *ex votos,* should you be confused in conversation. (A *retablo* is one form of *ex voto;* see page 91.) He does not speak English, but his works speak for themselves. We found his prices high (about $75 per), but we think you can bargain with him to some extent, especially if you buy more than one item. Also, we don't want to ruin the marketplace, but we believe this is a highly collectible art form, and whatever you pay is meaningless—these babies are going to be worth more in the near future.

PLAZA DEL ÁNGEL, Londres 161 (Metro: Insurgentes)

▼

IMPERIO: Also in the Zona Rosa, this antiques dealer is one of several in a row right down the street from our usual hotel, the Galeria Plaza, so we pass it constantly and know its baroque stock rather well. Everything is very formal and fancy, and not funky enough for us. But the reputation and the goods are serious and if you are in the market for anything from a painting to a credenza with Empire lines, this is the place to begin the search.

IMPERIO, Hamburgo 149 (Metro: Insurgentes)

▼

COLONIALART: Right off Hamburgo, and a virtual stockpile of everything colonial, including large pieces of furniture. Every piece is authenticated; they speak English; you can trust them to ship. Very famous place. Yummy, yum yum.

COLONIALART, Estocolmo 37 (Metro: Insurgentes)

Antiques Markets

LAGUNILLA: Near the so-called Thieves Market, which is held on Sunday mornings. Don't bother getting there before 10 A.M. It's held in the street, off Paseo de la Reforma, and you can get there by the *pesero* that runs along the Paseo. (See page 121.) The entire Lagunilla area on Calle Allende and Calle de Vaquita is filled with little shops that sell mostly junk—from antiques to masks. Perhaps you will like these places, which certainly are atmospheric. We find them small, dark, and filled with fakes—for which exorbitant prices are asked. There is a giant gringo tax for anyone stupid enough to buy from these guys. If you speak Spanish and are really tuned into the market price, you might want to tackle it—otherwise, steer clear.

LAGUNILLA (Metro: Allende)

Furniture

DUPUIS: Gorgeous surroundings for home furnishings for the old hacienda. It's the painted furniture that we go nuts for. The colors and designs are just sensational—most are modern versions of old patterns that are either reproduced literally or slightly jazzed up. The store does not ship, but they will get you a shipping agent. This is also where to find pewter, *tchotchkes,* and picture frames. Note that on Saturday the shop opens at 11 A.M. Other days (except Sunday, when it is not open at all) it opens at 10 A.M. and closes at 7 P.M.; they are open during the siesta.

DUPUIS, Avenida de las Palmas 240 (Metro: Insurgentes)

▼

CHRISTIAN FERSEN: This is not a resource for colonial works at all, and is as different from Dupuis as night is from day and Spanish from English and all that. This is the hot decorator for the "now" look, very contemporary but not too way-out. You can buy yard goods (very well priced!), picture frames, lamps, and furniture too—although there is no reason for a gringo to buy the furniture, since you can get these styles at home. The designer has shops in several different cities; this is the main store. Possibly more important to locals, but a good source for ideas and some savings on knickknacks or fabrics.

CHRISTIAN FERSEN, Amberes 12 (Metro: Insurgentes)

▼

LEBRONZ: The first time we walked into this crowded shop we knew we were home. Or could be home. If only you could pack an armoire. The house specialty is large pieces of new furniture in the colonial style, but they also sell knickknacks and tabletop items, and some good pewter picture frames. The store will not ship, so you're on your own. You'll

probably just have to come here to look and
drool, unless you brought the van.

LEBRONZ, Amberes 1 (Metro: Insurgentes)

▼

LO QUE EL VIENTO SE LLEVO: We've
listed this store as a find (see page 134), and
mentioned it particularly to those staying at the
Hotel Camino Real, since it is next door. But if
you are making the big colonial furniture and
knickknack pilgrimage, you cannot miss this
source. Like Dupuis, this shop is in a former
home and is therefore laid out like a home,
with the merchandise put out in room sets.
There are big heavy pieces, but also small
accessories, pewter objects, and some textiles.
Saturday hours are 10 A.M. to 2 P.M.; otherwise,
the shop does not close for lunch, and is open
daily from 10 A.M. to 7 P.M.

LO QUE EL VIENTO SE LLEVO, Victor Hugo
56 (Metro: Chapultepec)

▼

MARU ALONSO: This is also a find, a
serious find. Everything from clay pots to picture frames to bed frames. Taste, elegance,
style, panache. Take a taxi to the Nikko, then
walk across the street into the shop, or run
from the *metro*. That way the store can't take
your breath away, because the running at this
high altitude already will have. This store is
part of a stretch of several excellent shops; see
Polanco shopping, page 132.

MARU ALONSO, Campos Eliseos 199 (Metro:
Auditorio)

Collectible Souvenirs

MULLER'S: We aren't big fans of onyx to begin with (unless it's black, coupled with 18K gold, and in the form of a pair of great earrings), and we think this store is a bit too bright. But if you like this stuff, and want to collect it, or to simply take home some table-top items for yourself or for gifts, this is the area's biggest dealer. We have to admit that we have seen a few onyx tables that impressed us. And the fruit can be nice. In proper doses, onyx can be very classy—and Mexican prices are not too brassy. Wear your sunglasses.

MULLER'S, Florencia 52 (Metro: Insurgentes)

▼

EUGENIO: The most famous mask shop in Mexico City, this place is a tad scary but very interesting. It is wall-to-wall masks. There are some other things, but Eugenio's is famous for the masks. His location is also good—you're downtown and near the Lagunilla shops, if you dare. Best buy for collectors, says Dr. Jill: *cristianos*—pink masks of colonials. Remember: To be valuable a mask must have been part of a complete costume, and have been worn in a dance or used in a ceremony—not specifically created for the tourist market. To show your salesperson you are not the typical gringo, ask which dance (they all have names and traditions that go with them) the mask is worn in, and by whom. If there is no immediate answer, balk. Of course, if there is an immediate answer, then you have to decide if you believe it or not. But at Eugenio's you'll get the best help and advice.

EUGENIO, Allende 84 (Metro: Allende)

TAPETES MEXICANAS: Rugs, did anyone say rugs? This shop specializes in the creative energies of the Otomi people from the state of México, who are known for their weavings. They make carpets that are somewhat reminiscent of oriental patterns, but use native colors and Mexican designs. The pieces should be made of pure wool (ask) and should last for generations. They ship. This is in the area outside of town on your way to the Bazar Sabado; it's not very accessible by *metro*, but you can get there on the *pesero* down Insurgentes (make sure you are going south!), which is a bit of a long ride, but will give you the opportunity to scope out the other interesting shops along the route. Open from 9 A.M. to 6 P.M. on weekdays, 10 A.M. to 6 P.M. on Saturday. Closed on Sunday; not closed during the siesta.

TAPETES MEXICANAS, Insurgentes Sur 2375

▼

SULLIVAN PARK ART FAIR: This is not the starving-artist kind of stuff that makes you wince with pain, but is seriously good. Many of the artists spend their Saturdays at the Bazar Sabado (see page 146) and their Sundays here. Both are worth doing! Bargain for art just as you would for anything else.

SULLIVAN PARK ART FAIR, Off Insurgentes Centro (Metro: Revolucíon)

▼

SANBORNS: We know we send you to Sanborns for everything from coffee to maps to clean toilets, but if you are collecting copies of pre-Columbian artworks, Sanborns House of Tiles has an entire room full of them. We admit that we are not moved, but many people like these clay figurines and even arrange cases of them, or display them in such a way as to convince friends and visitors that they are valuable. They are valuable from a sociocultural point of view, but not as collectibles. But who cares? They do break easily, so wrap your treasures in bubble wrap when you pack them with the T-shirts.

SANBORNS, Madero 2 (Metro: Bellas Artes)

▼

MUSEO NACIONAL DE ANTROPOLOGÍA: The famous anthropology museum is one of the very best museums in the world. It also has a good gift shop that specializes in books, stationery items, posters, postcards, and a few clay figurines—reproductions, of course. Take the *pesero* along Paseo de la Reforma.

MUSEO NACIONAL DE ANTROPOLOGÍA, Paseo de la Reforma, in Chapultepec Park

Tiles

AZULEJOS TALAVERA: This is the only tile shop we've been to in D.F., but for those who want to make a big production out of it, check out some of the other listings below. What we love about this shop is not only the tiles, but the various household and bathroom products. (We want the handpainted sink!) They have handpainted traditional tiles, they have solid colors, they have red clay, they have square tiles, they have bathroom decoratives, they have marble, they have it all! And yes, they ship. The owner is named Raymundo. Also, the neighborhood is fabulous—see Cortés's home; eat at El Morral; and shop!

AZULEJOS TALAVERA, Allende 166, Coyoacán

A few other tips from Dr. Jill: Division del Norte is Tile Street. There are dozens upon dozens of tile stores and warehouses selling interior and exterior tiles, roof tiles, sinks, the works. Find several numbers that are near each other from the phone book, or try the listings below. You don't need to go to a lot of stores. Compare prices between three to five shops and bargain like crazy. Take the metro to Xola (say "Show-la") and then a cab for the rest of the short distance. I just paid eight cents per tile for some *Talavera de Dolores* tiles for my kitchen.

See page 64 for more on how to buy tiles, and try:

AZULEJOS RIVIERA, Avenida División del Norte 1139

BANSA, Avenida División del Norte 3392

AZULEJOS COLONIALES, Avenida División del Norte 305

RECUBRIMIENTOS DEL VALLE, Avenida División del Norte 208

MAYORISTAS, S.A., Avenida División del Norte 129

8 ▼ DAY TRIPS AND TOURS

Travel Basics

Mexico City is your gateway station to the real Mexico. And to Taxco. Each corner of the city has a major bus terminal with several different lines offering various classes of service to points in that general direction. We have been warned never to travel anything but first class, which we do, so we can't tell you about second class. Since first class is so incredibly inexpensive, we don't think we'll ever find out about second class. On long trips, the buses do have bathrooms—although we've also been told to avoid these. We have used the public bathrooms in all of the bus stations and have no complaints, although ladies should always carry a package of Kleenex (or some toilet tissue) with them . . . just in case.

The concierge of your hotel should have the bus schedule at his desk. But please call the bus line anyway, or have him call for you. For some reason, we've never found two people who can agree on the schedule. If you're going to Toluca on market day, the schedule doesn't matter—there's a bus every ten minutes or so. But if you're going to Taxco, one missed bus will ruin your day.

You do not need to speak any Spanish whatsoever to ride the bus, although some high-school knowledge will make you feel more secure, and some ability to actually speak will make you popular with your bus peers. Most buses do not take reservations, so you have to get there in time to buy a ticket on the bus of your choice. The earlier you are there, the better the selection of seats. You want a seat toward the front of the bus (away from smells of toilet and diesel). Some people don't like to be over the wheels or in the very front seats—this does not bother us. Give your name at the counter when you buy your ticket with your seat choice or merely say *"¿Asiento?"* in a questioning way and let the clerk point to the preprinted seat number on your ticket. If you don't like that number, ask for *"un otro"* (another). We've waited for a second bus (ten more minutes) to get a better seat.

As you depart from Mexico City ask about the return bus. Then, upon arrival at your destination, ask again when you should return to buy tickets for your bus back—especially if this is a day trip and you have a schedule to keep to, or there aren't a ton of buses. On some day trips you must work your adventures around the bus schedules.

There is no such thing as a nonsmoking section on the bus. If you are lucky your seatmate will ask you if smoking offends you, and you may answer honestly.

On trips of several hours, the bus will make pit stops for drinks, bathrooms, and/or food at little station houses. Drink your Coke from the bottle, without ice, and have your own toilet paper in your pocket.

Travel with gum and perhaps an airline barf bag. Some roads (particularly to Taxco) are curvy; the smell of diesel may offend some. If you are prone to carsickness, sit as far forward in the bus as possible.

Diary of a Day Trip to Taxco

6:15 A.M.: We are in front of the Galería Plaza hotel in the Zona Rosa, where the sky is still a little gray and the air is slightly chilly. The taxi driver wants $8 for the ride to the station, which we know is outrageous. There are no taxis driving by, and while we know we can take the *metro,* we are too tense. If we miss the bus, our day is ruined, so we grimace and agree to pay $8 to go to Taxqueña (say "Tas-Kenya"), where the Central de Autobuses del Sur is located.

6:30 A.M.: We are in front of the bus station without any problem whatsoever. Our bus line (for first-class service) is called Estrella de Oro (Gold Star). There is no line for tickets. The bus leaves ten minutes later than the hotel concierge indicated, so we have plenty of time. It is scheduled to leave at 7:40 A.M. Why are we here so early? Better safe than sorry. We want to buy food from the vendors selling breakfast out of their car trunks, but we are not totally crazy. We go to the cafeteria instead, and get a big plate of rice for breakfast and a big package of Chiclets for the trip.

7:15 A.M.: We go outside for a look-see. We've never done this before, and are getting antsy. A bus is marked "ACAPULCO," and we wonder if this is our bus, since Taxco is on the way to Acapulco. We discuss all this (in Spanish) with the porter, who assures us that if we are going to Taxco the bus will say "TAXCO."

7:20 A.M.: We get in line with everyone else as a huge queue begins to form. We are certain that this is the gang heading off to Taxco. We soon notice the bus is going to Cocula. We get out of line.

7:35 A.M.: We are in the right line now, and are amused to see that the driver has suddenly realized he can't open the bus doors without the key. He disappears.

7:40 A.M.: The driver returns with the key: boarding begins.

7:47 A.M.: The bus is totally filled, and we move out on a three-hour trip, with a ten-minute pit stop scheduled in Cuernavaca, about an hour away. For about $2.50 we are thinking we're awfully clever. If only Mrs. Watson, our Spanish teacher, could see us now.

Welcome to Taxco

Taxco is perhaps the most famous small city in Mexico, because it is so beautiful and so well-merchandised. The town is visual poetry. It became popular after an American, William Spratling, settled there and singlehandedly turned the silver industry around, making it something special. While there are a number of so-called Silver Cities, Taxco remains the most famous.

The Lay of the Land

Taxco is located on a hillside and is closed to most vehicular traffic. The bus station is under the hill, and you must take a taxi or a *pesero* into town. There are two main shopping areas for tourists: the village itself, located in the old town, and centered around a beautiful old plaza (Plaza Bordo); and a new strip of stores right on Avenida John F. Kennedy, the road on which the bus station is located, and also the main road into town. Neither of these two shopping areas is within walking distance of the bus station. You can get a taxi or van to either destination for between $1 and $2.

We arranged our day trip in a circle so that we went from the bus station to the shopping area on Avenida John F. Kennedy, then into town, then back to Avenida John F. Kennedy, and then to the station. This costs a little more money for transportation, but by the time you go into town, you've already got an idea of what prices and selection are like in the area on Avenida John F. Kennedy. If you do all your shopping in town, you needn't return to the avenue. We're just compulsive.

Shopping in Taxco

Before we begin, *one word of warning*: You shouldn't come to Taxco just to go shopping. There isn't anything here you can't buy in Mexico City.

But once you're here, silver is the thing. When you're on vacation in Mexico there are some things you just have to do, and buying silver in Taxco is one of them. Prices are no better here than anywhere else. . . . It's just the thing to do. Our best purchase was a handtooled leather belt of such fine quality that we can't believe we didn't buy a dozen. We were attracted to a number of straw baskets, the kind with brightly colored, geometric patterns, but we resisted, since we never know what to do with them once we get home. There is more to buy here than silver.

Basically, Taxco is one giant tourist trap. You should enjoy it all and have fun. If you don't want to run into other Americans and tourists, stay out of town.

Ballpark Figures

Before you get too involved in buying, you might want to establish some ballpark figures on standard items at a few shops. Since prices change so often, we have trouble doing this for you. As a general rule, price the same thing in three stores to get an idea of the going rate—then bargain. By the time you get to Mexico, our index below may be off, but it should give you a basic idea of what we think are reasonable prices to begin bargaining from on various silver items:

Silver cuff or heavy bracelet: $100–$125
Iced-tea spoon: $25
Short necklace of mothball-size silver beads: $150
Long necklace of same silver beads: $300
Silver pillbox with semiprecious stone inset: $40
Silver napkin ring: $30
Excellent silver earrings: $40
Smaller but well-made and heavy silver earrings: $25

Snack and Shop

CIELITO LINDO: A cute eatery half a block from the plaza with painted walls, star lanterns, checkered tablecloths, and lots of charm. There's a patio area and indoor service. Americans congregate here because it's so attractive. Lunch will cost under $10 per person.

CIELITO LINDO, Zócalo

Tianguis

There is a *tianguis* in town, located on the down side of the church, down some steep cobbled steps. This is a very large market, which meanders halfway down the hill. The closer you are to town, the more touristy the items; the farther down the hill, the more "real people" the stuff. The market is a visual feast with wares hanging on lines, stacked up on tables, or laid in rows on the cobblestones. Children hawk bark paintings; old men sleep in the sun. It's very picturesque.

Finds

TALLERES DE LOS BALLESTEROS: These guys seem to actually own the silver business in town. They have several shops with different names, all with exceptional merchandise. With an appointment and proper credentials you can buy wholesale from their showroom. Otherwise, try all their stores! The merchandise is fashion-oriented: chunky and stylish, with weight and heft to it. Some combinations of brass and silver are available. These are the only earrings that have never pinched us!

TALLERES DE LOS BALLESTEROS
    Florida 21 (factory)
    Calle Celso Munoz 4 (shop)
ELENA BALLESTEROS, Avenida John F. Kennedy

▼

ANTONIO PINEDA: This is another big name in town, but we're not referring to the easily spotted main shop on the *Zócalo*. Go behind, out near the balcony overlooking the hills, back, back, back, where there are more tiny shops, for the little boutique with the very fancy work that is top of the line and far fancier than anything else in town. Antonio was trained by Spratling. Designs here are totally original and better than everyone else's. We saw a spoollike silver necklace for $255 that would have made Elsa Peretti go nuts. Sensational find.

ANTONIO PINEDA, Plaza Bordo 1 (rear)

LOS ANGELES: This shop looks like an average tourist trap. It advertises itself as a factory outlet for *huaraches* and leather goods. It is not a great shop. But it is where we found the most incredible tooled belts in all of Mexico.

LOS ANGELES, Avenida John F. Kennedy 25

▼

SEBASTIÁN: By coincidence (one we didn't realize until months later), we bought from a branch of this shop in Cancún. Here in the mother store, the selection of silver picture frames is small, but choice. They were willing to deal on silver beads. We were offered a 15% discount on our total bill. One of the biggies on the main square.

SEBASTIÁN, Plaza Bordo 5

▼

PLATERIA RANCHO ALEGRE: Enormous, huge, overwhelming space filled with silver, silver, and more silver.

PLATERIA RANCHO ALEGRE, Avenida John F. Kennedy 42

▼

PLATERIA LINDA: Another of the many silver vendors in the main square, but with a wide selection of giftwares and tabletop. We bought napkin rings here that they engraved in a half hour. We didn't like the quality of the engraving, but it was cheap.

PLATERIA LINDA, Plaza Bordo 4

Diary of a Day Trip to Puebla

7:30 A.M.: We're no longer intimidated by taxi drivers, *metro* stations at dawn, or much of anything else, and decide that we will definitely not get taken advantage of as we venture forth on another day trip—this one to Puebla. We're on our way to TAPO, the Terminal de Autobuses de Oriente at the San Lázaro *metro* stop. The rush-hour pedestrian traffic is dense, but we get out of the station at San Lázaro and move slowly onto the walkway, which leads next door to the low, modern bus station—a direct contrast to the one we used for the trip to Taxco. This place is gorgeous: modern, low-slung, marble everywhere. We've been told that the first-class bus line to take is ADO, and it takes some time to curve through the large station looking for ADO, which is off toward the right, around a corner, and in their own separate waiting area, as spiffy as a new McDonald's (complete with pink and orange seats).

8 A.M.: We discover that ADO buses leave every fifteen minutes, so we don't feel too pressured. There is a stand for *pan dulce*, which we snack on as we wait for our bus. The ticket costs about $2.

8:20 A.M.: We leave for Puebla, not knowing that some buses run right into town. We take the regular bus to the central station, which is outside of town. Live and learn. We still don't know what to say or how to get on one of the more direct buses. Perhaps the hotel concierge could have helped. . . .

10:20 A.M.: Who would have wanted to go directly to town and miss this? This is the human zoo of bus station *tianguis*—all sorts of vendors crammed right outside the station, lining the street. Everybody party! You can't help but get anxious to start shopping while you're still pulling into the station. The station itself is very large and modern, with a fair number of shops, including one that sells only religious items. After doing it all, we taxi to the *Zócalo*, and after a browse around, walk to the tourist office, which is right off the *Zócalo* at Avenida 5 Oriente 3.

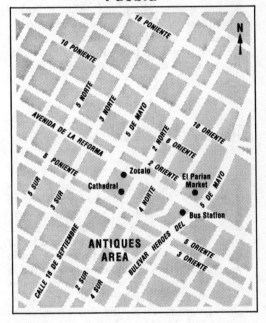

Puebla

Welcome to Puebla

Puebla is famous as the center of the *azulejo* business. We went off thinking this was going to be an incredible journey, wondering how we would schlepp back all the tiles we planned to buy. We needn't have worried. The gorgeous tiles were very expensive (several dollars each), and there were no cheap ones to be found. While the city of Puebla has its own special charm, and on an individual basis many of the buildings are remarkable, the overall look is not impressive. *Azulejos* must be searched for and discovered—they aren't lying in the streets twinkling up at you.

The Lay of the Land

Puebla's city design just doesn't hang together. As it is organized along one of those grid systems, with numbers fanning out in the four directions of the wind, you go nuts trying to figure out a layout that makes perfect sense on a map (but not in your mind). Furthermore, the city is as cold as ice to a stranger. Yes, you are in a city that is extremely real and authentic, but is not particularly gorgeous, nor are the natives overly fond of tourists. It takes a lot of exploring and patience to find the good stuff, if you wander on your own. The charm of Puebla is that it is totally real and nontouristy, and that each building downtown is a tiny gem. They are individual, and small, and personal, and when you take the time to study them you realize that they are magnificent.

Everything is in a different part of town. Little connects from one area to the next; this isn't really a town for walking around and finding little finds. Unless you know where to walk. (And, of course, that's what we're here for.) A tour is perhaps best done with a private car and driver, or with someone who really knows the city. As a day trip on your own, using the bus, you might not find this outing worthwhile.

Shopping Puebla

We came here to buy tile. After all, Puebla has been famous for its *Talavera* tiles since the 16th century. We left with two cups and a plate. At least they weren't heavy, and we consider them almost worthy of a museum. We didn't buy tiles because we like to buy $1 tiles (our top price) and we can't afford $5 tiles. Besides, the star attraction in Puebla turns out to be antiques! If only we had a van and three strong men. Well, a van anyway. While there is no reason to shop Puebla for clothing, there are a lot of things for the home here, and a diligent person would come with a truck, stay for a week, and really mine the place. If you come on a day trip, you're just going to get a small taste of what could be a great place for shopping, once you know your way around.

Please note: Talavera is a style, not the name of a factory. Every place you go, makers will sell *Talavera*. This can be very confusing, since the word *Talavera* is often in a business's name. Furthermore, please realize there are two qualities of *Talavera*. One is almost indestructible— we've seen it get hit with a hammer and remain unbroken—and is priced to match: about $35–$50 for a single plate. The other quality is also sturdy, but will not pass the hammer test. Naturally, it costs less. When pieces look identical but have vastly different prices, ask about quality. Ceramic is basically a long-lasting medium—tiles should hold up for centuries. *Talavera* tile is especially known for its strength. You pay accordingly.

Booking Puebla

All guidebooks have a page or two on Puebla. If you want a guide specific to the city, the best one we could find was at Sanborns and cost $1.50. That's the good news. The bad news is that it's in Spanish. But don't panic; the guide is so pretty you might want it anyway: *Puebla: Guía de la Ciudad*, published by El Cantador and Editorial Limusa. You'll recognize it because this is a series with the same visual identity—a fan of brightly colored pages in a small booklet. It's filled with gorgeous color pictures and snappy type as well as maps and telephone numbers (with addresses) for car rentals, banks, taxis, etc.

It is essential that you have a map of the city—or an IQ of 183 with a degree in military strategy—in order to find your way around. Although Puebla is on a grid, the street-address system is incredibly confusing to a *norteamericano* who is not used to this pattern—a pattern standard in many Mexican cities and probably a colonial tradition.

Snack and Shop

SANBORNS: The Sanborns store is not far from El Parián market or from the *Zócalo,* so you can stop here for lunch or a snack. There is a large restaurant in the central courtyard; the menu is in English (and Spanish) and prices are low to moderate. There is a buffet with the special of the day, or you can order à la carte. Good bathroom stop; also good for postcards, maps, etc.

SANBORNS, 2 Oriente 6

▼

CASA VIEJA: Leave it to us to fall in love with a Swiss restaurant in Mexico. This place is a few steps from Sanborns and is absolutely adorable. May be the highlight of the day. European-style food; low prices.

CASA VIEJA, 2 Oriente 202

Shopping Neighborhoods

Zócalo

There are stores around the edge of the *Zócalo,* as there are in all Mexican cities. These are your everyday, "real people" stores, and are not particularly interesting. There's also a post office and the tourist office—both on the far side of the *Zócalo.*

Cinco de Mayo

Branching off the top of the *Zócalo* is a pedestrian mall called Cinco de Mayo, which stretches for many blocks and is the principal shopping area for "real people." It's extremely picturesque in a true-grit way—a man selling exotic birds in a cage walks in one direction, while a woman with a passel of dead chickens under her arm walks in another. Balloon sellers parade, while a street hawker gathers a crowd around him as he points to his pet snake (very much alive and around his neck) and the herbs he has gathered on the ground and gives a tantalizing speech. (At least, everyone seems tantalized.) It's all very real and very wonderful.

Plaza los Sapos

This is the antiques area, with all the shops on one block of town, ending or beginning at the Plaza los Sapos, selling antiques—lots of big furniture pieces and some smaller items. Worth looking at:

MISTER TOAD BAZAR, Plazuela de los Sapos, 6 Sur 309
BAZAR LOS 4 HERMANOS, 6 Sur 303
BAZAR DE LOS ANGELES, 6 Sur 308
BAZAR LEOBARDO'S, 6 Sur 304
BAZAR EL CAROLINO, 3 Oriente 603 (corner 6 Sur)
EL BASURERO, 5 Oriente 402

PUEBLA / DISTRICT SHOPPING ▼ 181

District Shopping

Many of the streets in town seem to be entire districts (*barrios*) that sell basically one type of good—sort of like in Manhattan. If you walk along 18 Poniente you'll find scads of little ceramics shops and dealers, a few onyx shops and dealers, and what appears to be Pottery Row. Only one shop here is really excellent, but this seems to be the street for pottery. Now then, 20 Oriente seems to be the street for factories; an area called San Antonio is the district for wrought iron; in San José Otumba they make textiles.

If you are interested in a particular art form, have the tourist office direct you to the proper *barrio*.

Tianguis

EL PARIÁN MARKET: The main arts-and-crafts market is downtown, an easy walk from the *Zócalo*. Some of the buildings surrounding it are incredibly beautiful, with ornate baroque lines and rooftops. The market itself is a matter of several rows of stucco huts divided into units from which vendors sell their wares. A few of these vendors are craftspeople who may actually be working while you are shopping. About half the shops will close for the siesta; some will remain open nonstop. Prices in the market are high, and while you can bargain to some degree, you will generally be shocked at how expensive tile and ceramic goods are. There are the usual plates, cups, and mugs to buy, as well as a few specialty items. A few stores sell individually numbered tiles, so you can make

your own address plaque when you get home.
We're wild for the large ceramic coffee urns
and water jugs. They cost about $100 and are
well worth it, if you have some way to bring
the pot home with you. The market lacks charm
but does sell everything you came to buy and
is conveniently located.

EL PARIÁN MARKET, 8 Norte 4 Oriente

Finds

TALAVERA DE PUEBLA, S.A. DE C.V.:
This is it, folks. This is the best tile factory in
town; this is the most gorgeous building in
Mexico; this is worth the drive. Even if you
came on the bus on a day trip, this can make it
all worthwhile! We didn't buy a thing, we just
lost our minds trying to decide. We are thinking of asking for permission to be buried here.
This factory is in a villa not far from downtown (take a taxi!). The villa is completely
covered with *azulejos*. Built in traditional Spanish colonial style, it has a courtyard. You must
walk through the blue wrought-iron door into
the courtyard, across the plaza, and then into
the shop or shipping department and showroom. You may buy wholesale or retail, although to do big business you should speak
Spanish or have an interpreter. Big business
even means an appointment (telephone: 42-29-43
or 42-15-98). Everything in the world is here—
plaques, individual numbers, tiles, scenics, and
lots of pottery pieces and sets. Prices are high,
but this stuff is worth owning. They will ship,
but it will add considerably to your price. Don't
come to Puebla without visiting here! (*Note:*
Other guidebooks have listed this shop with the
name Uriarte. We have the wholesale business
card that lists the name the way we have it.)

TALAVERA DE PUEBLA, S.A. DE C.V., 4
   Poniente 911

TALAVERA DE PUEBLA: Not to be confused with the previous resource in any way, this is a shop across the street from the El Parián Market (they also have a stall at the market); the owner, Geraldo Aguilar, speaks excellent English and will happily go around banging on plates to teach you about the proper sounds they should make. He sells various qualities at various prices—plates range from $15 to $35. You can buy a complete dinner set for twelve people for about $1,000, which is not only the going price all over Mexico but a very good price for the kind of work you are getting. He will not ship to the United States, but will pack for you.

TALAVERA DE PUEBLA
  8 Norte 4 Oriente
  El Parián Market, Local 109

▼

CASA RUGERIO: Another of the more famous addresses for tiles, this maker has the factory in the back room and a shop of sorts out front. It is not glamorous, but it has some funky charm, and you know you've come to a real factory source. Ceramics are sold in the first chamber, tiles in a small back room. You can custom-order work—expect it to take about six to eight weeks for delivery. They will ship to the United States. Tiles are priced by intricacy: The simplest cost $2, the most elaborate $7 each. This is a savings of at least half (or more) of their cost in the United States. A tile equal in quality to Rugerio's $7 beauty would cost $20–$25 at an American dealer like Country Floors. Plates begin at $12 and go up to $27 for the most elaborate. The shop is open Monday through Saturday from 11:30 A.M. to 6:30 P.M.

CASA RUGERIO, 18 Poniente 111

▼

CERAMICA DE TALAVERA TECAYEUATL:
This is a large vendor in the El Parián Market.
They take credit cards and make individual
numbers for houses, as well as anything else
you might want in tile, and sell the big water
and coffee urns we love so much. There are
three different sizes of tiles. Prices seem steep
to us, but the selection is good.

CERAMICA DE TALAVERA TECAYEUATL, 8
Norte Local 93–94

▼

C R E A R T : This is one of those agency-
sponsored shops that sell crafts from the area.
There are two shops, although we like the main
one near Sanborns 500% better than the so-
called pottery one that is across from the *Zócalo*.
Creart sells all art forms, including some ceramic. There is an English-speaking clerk. If
you are walking to the El Parián Market, you'll
probably pass right by the shop at 2 Oriente,
which is the one we love, anyway. It is one of
the best shops in town.

CREART
2 Oriente 202–4
16 Septiembre 506-E (vista 7 Oriente; you
can see it from the corner of 7 Oriente)

Welcome to Toluca

A ctually we should say "Welcome to our
Toluca," which includes only the bus
station and the Friday market. Beyond
that, you don't really want to go to Toluca. We know.

Getting There

arket day in Toluca is a big day, and buses run frequently, as do tour buses and guided trips. We simply take the *metro* to Observatorio and head for the Terminal Central de Autobuses del Poniente. This is a modern bus station, but not a gorgeous one like TAPO. It has platform after platform of buses, many of which go to Toluca. When we ask at one bus, they tell us there's a twenty-minute wait for their bus, but to try TMT because they leave every ten minutes. We board immediately and take off. The bus is about three-quarters filled, and everyone seems to be going to market day; there are no other gringos on board.

As we approach town, the bus begins to make stops, and we panic. Will you know what to do? Of course you will, because we're going to tell you. Do not get off at the Carta Blanca beer factory. Do not get off at the Pfizer drug factory. Stay on the bus until it safely stops in the terminal, which you will immediately recognize because it looks like a bus terminal on Mars—it has rows of columns made from poured concrete that form sort of an inverted umbrella design. Besides, it will have taken half an hour to pull into the station because of the congestion from the market in the street. Although the market is technically across the street from the bus station, on market day the area overflows, and even the street is filled with vendors and shoppers.

Warning: This market gets a high Dead Chicken Rating. If you are not the market type, you might not like it here. Most of the chickens are alive, of course, because few people like to buy dead chickens. (You don't know how fresh they are once they are dead.) The market is mostly outdoors in good weather, so it is beautiful and not very smelly or bloody; but it is crowded, and there are women with baskets on their heads, men with turkeys (yes, live turkeys) strapped across their bodies, women pulling shopping carts filled with fowl, and men pulling 50 kilos of blankets onto their backs as they hoist them out of trucks. There are thousands of people, flies on the food, people shouting, some animal parts here and there, some sad birds in cages, and some dirty children who really don't want to go home with you, even though you think they might. Isn't it all wonderful?

Marketing Plans

There is an enclosed market, but the real fun is outdoors. There are so many areas to wander through that it is hard to find a direction or to make a plan. We just wander until we get the gist of it. . . . Then we go back and pounce. The market has trade areas, like for flowers or spices or clothes, but it all appears to be a big jumble to the untrained eye. You must bargain very hard for some items; others are so cheap you can hardly complain. The indoor portion is a much more traditional Mexican indoor market, and is boring.

The most important question of the day is how to carry what you buy. If you came in your own car (or truck), you did right and can keep loading up. If you came on the bus, you need to make choices based on what you can carry. We went to the market with a giant leather satchel (very strong) each, and then each bought a huge laundry basket, which we loaded up with goodies. That was all we could carry, and we were both so weighted down that we could not help each other. (Although

Dr. Debbie bought wool, which is lighter than pottery.)

The best buy is the pottery, which is sold by the dozen . . . unless it's big pieces like pitchers or tubs. If you buy a dozen cups, they will be strung on a piece of cord for you. You may wear this cord around your neck or over your body, bandolier-style, and the cups will do just fine. You're going to need a very hot bath when you get back to D.F., but the cups will be fine.

Snack and Shop

Since you will have to eat at the market, buy foods carefully. Cookies and fresh fruit (that you slice or peel yourself) can get you through until you return to your hotel. You may want to buy some Bimbo foods in D.F., or at the bus station, and bring them along for a picnic.

Welcome to San Miguel de Allende

San Miguel de Allende just might be one of the most magical cities in Mexico. Dr. Debbie spent a summer here apprenticed to a weaver. We consider it one of the places high on the list for retirement—if the South of France doesn't work out, San Miguel comes next. Many Americans feel the same way. The city has a large American population, and a large international population of artists. Many people who couldn't afford to be artists in the United States moved to San Miguel, where they would have less financial pressure and would be able to succeed at that which they love best. Hence the city is filled not only with shops, but with art galleries.

We met an American-Mexican artist who spends part of her year in New York City and part of the year in San Miguel; she was extremely cautious about selling her wares in her home—it is against the law for her to set up shop in Mexico (let alone in her home), so her wholesale business is done from New York. Many such artists live in San Miguel, and while they trade among themselves and have a private network, they do not and will not encourage at-home or in-studio visits from American tourists who are anxious to buy. To do this kind of shopping, you will need private recommendations and perhaps letters of introduction. Unless you are a part of the ex-pat artist scene, you must buy from the regular stores in town.

Which will be a pleasure.

The Lay of the Land

San Miguel de Allende is classified as both a colonial city and a Silver City in various descriptions and guided tours. It is a historic city that has been preserved as much as possible and is considered a national gem both by Mexicans and by tourists. You can't fly into town, so you must come by train or car or bus and take the city on its own terms, which are purely charming.

This is a city for browsing for a day or two. You can do it as a day trip from Mexico City, but you'd better be very strong, and you won't have much time for shopping. Better to come on an overnight adventure and enjoy yourself.

The *Zócalo* (Plaza de Allende) is at Calle Canal and Calle Hidalgo; Canal is the main shopping street. The railroad station is also on Canal—at the far end from the *Zócalo*. While downtown San Miguel is compact and perfect for strolling and admiring architecture (and stores), you'll have a tad more freedom if you have a car and can explore some of the more famous spas nearby and perhaps visit (or stay at) the Hacienda Taboada—a resort about fifteen minutes outside of town.

For in-town wandering, start at the *Zócalo* and take in Calle Canal, but also check out the area around the post office, one block up from the *Zócalo;* look at streets such as Mesones (don't miss the conjunction of Mesones with Calle Juárez, where the city market is located) and Zacateros—two blocks below the *Zócalo*— which is lined with crafts shops. Sunday is the biggest and best market day.

Streets are narrow and can be steep; wear your Reeboks!

Getting There

Tours to San Miguel de Allende may be bought as individual packages from Mexico City, or you can hop on a bus (the line is Tres Estrellas de Oro) from the Central de Autobuses del Norte in D.F.; or you can take the train. The bad news about the train is that it leaves at 7:30 in the morning; the good news is that it arrives by noon, so you can shop before the stores close for the siesta and then go eat a big lunch, which you will feel you deserved. The train leaves from Buenavista station (check all this again with your concierge, as all things change quickly in Mexico) and is a special tourist train (the *Constitucionalista*) that is a pleasure to ride. Few locals ride it, as it is expensive to them. You'll be thrilled with the low price (under $25).

Booking San Miguel/1

I f you want to get totally with it, check out a publication called *Juarde*, which has ads and listings for stores, restaurants, etc., devised for both locals and tourists. Available at your hotel.

Booking San Miguel/2

CASA DE SIERRA NEVADA: A renovated hacienda right downtown where you want to be, this is one of the nicer colonial-style hotels, and the only one with a swimming pool. Small, with only about thirty suites (most of the rooms are suites), this hotel exudes charm. But it doesn't take credit cards. It is a member of the Relais and Chateau family. Telephone: 20415.

CASA DE SIERRA NEVADA, Calle Hospicio 35

▼

HACIENDA TABOADA: A spa, a hotel, an old hacienda, a treat—but you need a car. Although there is van service into town, this resort is fifteen minutes away—but worth it! Telephone: 21798.

HACIENDA TABOADA, Dolores Hidalgo Highway

Shopping in San Miguel

S hopping in San Miguel is particularly fun because the city itself is so cute. The old-town, colonial nature of the architecture makes you realize that this is indeed what Walt Disney had in mind. The stores specialize in arts and crafts; the town identifies itself with the cultural, literary, and crafty. Prices are fair as compared with those in other Mexican cities. There's no lack of silver as well as serious jewelry, but also look at wrought iron (hard to put in the handbag or get through the X-ray machine at the airport) and tin.

Finds

CARMEN BECKMAN: Upscale souvenirs and arts and crafts, tabletop items, and home decor; but jewelry is the main ingredient.

CARMEN BECKMAN, Hernandez Macías 105

▼

DAVID: Fine jewelry with a fine old reputation; a craftsman who will copy from your pictures torn out of *Vogue*, or will make a custom piece just for you.

DAVID, Zacateros 53

▼

CASA MAXWELL: Owned by an artist (Robert Maxwell) and devoted to his works, as well as to important antiques, crafts, and special items chosen with a knowing eye. A snob's delight.

CASA MAXWELL, Canal 14

▼

GALERÍA ATENEA: Antiques and stuff. We are quite happy here in this old hacienda that now has all the trimmings of an art gallery with photographs, paintings, the works.

GALERÍA ATENEA, Mesones 83

▼

JULIO'S: Silver jewelry made with semi-precious stones—something not seen in every store. Across from the post office.

JULIO'S, Santo Domingo

D.F. Tour No. 1/The Folk Art Trot

1. Begin this tour at noon, so all of the stores are open. Take the *metro* to Bellas Artes and emerge right in the center of the old downtown shopping area, across the street from the famed Latin America Tower. Walk to Calle Madero (where the tower is) and look for No. 10, which is an office building. Go up the stairs to the third floor to suite 305; this is Victor Fosado's. Spend as long as you like shopping, then head back down to Calle Madero, and back across the street onto Avenida Benito Juárez, where you first came out of the *metro*.

2. Walk on the side of the street with the stores, across from Alameda Park, passing Casart, which has not closed for the siesta (unless it is after 2:30 P.M.), and going on to

Fonart, across the street at Avenida Benito Juárez 89.

3. Continue from Fonart back across Benito Juárez to the Museo de Artes e Industrias Popular, at No. 44.

4. Finish up by retracing your steps so you are almost back at Victor's on Calle Madero; but instead, turn off at Sanborns House of Tiles, at Madero 2. Use the bathroom, have your lunch in the central courtyard, park your bags at the cash register, and then shop Sanborns.

5. Taxi back to the hotel, since you will have too many packages to be comfortable on the *metro*.

D.F. Tour No. 2/See-It-All-in-a-Day Trip (Includes Art and Culture)

1. Begin as you did in Tour 1, except that you will start at 9 A.M. and will leave out Victor Fosado's, since they aren't open. Go downtown to Bellas Artes on the *metro*, visit Fonart, Casart, and the Museo de Artes e Industrias Popular, and then by 11 A.M. walk on Balderas to La Ciudadela, an enclosed market, which is about five blocks west of Juárez. Take the *metro* at Hidalgo (you can take it at Balderas—where you are—but you'll have to change twice) to Auditorio for the Nikko neighborhood. This means changing trains at Tacuba, but by now you are an old pro at this and should not have any trouble. This is a major correspondence point, well marked and easy to follow.

2. Emerge at Auditorio and cross the Paseo de la Reforma (there is a bridge); walk through

the little park and to the Hotel Nikko. If you are used to American lunchtimes, you can eat lunch now, but it's better to continue shopping. Shop the hotel stores (at both the Nikko and the Presidente), and more important the stores across the street from the hotels. In fact, start with them, then do the Nikko (with its Polo/Ralph Lauren shop) and the Presidente if you have time. At 1 P.M. almost everything will close for the siesta, so then you can eat. We eat in the Hotel Nikko at El Jardín, their coffee shop.

3. Taxi, bus, or *pesero* yourself to the Museo de Nacional Antropología e Historia, since it's probably still siesta time and the stores are closed. You could spend a lifetime in this museum; it definitely deserves a whole day. You're here now because you can't miss it, because it has a good bookstore, and because you have to kill time thoughtfully while the stores are closed. Vow to return with more time another day. At 4 P.M., grab a taxi for Avenida Presidente Masarik. Ask for Aca Joe, which every driver will know, and then wander around exploring the other boutiques for the rest of the afternoon. Don't miss Aca Joe Saldas, the outlet shop in the Aca Joe store.

4. Around 5:30 P.M., or whenever you are tired, grab a taxi for the Hotel Camino Real. Visit the shops here and on Victor Hugo (see Lo Que el Viento Se Llevo at No. 56 for certain) and then return to the Camino Real for a well-deserved drink. But only one drink, because at this altitude you can get drunk very quickly!

9▾CARIBBEAN MEXICO

Our Yucatán

Yucatán is the name of one of the states of Mexico, located in the tip of the Mexican "boot." Next door is the state of Quintana Roo, with which many Americans are familiar, either because they know this is the name of Joan Didion's daughter or because they have been to Cancún and Cozumel, which are located in this state. Below these states there is more land that is geographically connected to the boot but is not part of the country of Mexico—there's Belize, a former British colony, and Guatemala.

Many visitors to Mexico take in all of this area and call it, as we do, the Yucatán. So that while this area is not all technically in Yucatán, the generalization is popular with tourists. Don't be surprised by guidebooks or tours that suggest you "Explore the Yucatán" when most of the trip is in the state of Quintana Roo. You may also call this region (or the part of it that is in Mexico, anyway) Caribbean Mexico.

Welcome to Caribbean Mexico

The Caribbean portion of Mexico and the Central American countries beneath it are dramatically different from other parts of Mexico, mainly because of the topography. It's no wonder that cruise ships combine Jamaica, the Caymans, and some Mexican ports—they all fit together visually.

A trip to Caribbean Mexico is much more like a trip to the islands. In fact, some of the Mexican resorts are on islands. The atmosphere here is very resorty, partly because in some cities the government has come in and built up the property and welcomed resorts (Cancún); in other cases, what you have are beach communities that have for centuries responded more to the rhythm of the surf than the wristwatch.

Along the coastal areas you have beaches and resorts; in the interior you have shopping cities. It's true that shopping is a way of life in any resort area, but because of the geography of this portion of Mexico, there are some major market cities here that serve the entire boot. Mérida, the capital of Yucatán state (see page 229), is such a city, and when you get down to Guatemala, there are still more major cities and marketplaces in the interior. Yet no place is too far from another; you can stay at the beach and still make it inland to see the Mayan ruins or take in some serious shopping. Please note that we say serious, because resort shopping is not serious shopping.

The Lay of the Land

The Yucatán boot has three primary advantages over the rest of the world: gorgeous beaches (with luxury resorts to match), mysterious and fascinating ruins, and two types of shopping experiences: tourist-style in places like Cancún and Cozumel, or native-style in Mérida, Belize, or Guatemala.

As every guidebook you read will tell you, Cancún was created by a computer, which told the Mexican government where to build. Such development is popular in Mexico, where an entire government arm (Fonatur) has been created to seek and build. Cancún was their first success, then Ixtapa, and now Huatulco, which in about ten years will look just as developed as Cancún.

Cancún has a lot going for it, and for the visitor who has been experimenting with Caribbean islands, it is far more developed and sophisticated than other choices. But it's a bit too developed for us. Yet the most delicious thing about the area is its Miami Beach–like strip of hotels and resorts and the fact that three generations of the same family continue to come here en masse to enjoy these resorts. We have visited with three generations of our family and have noted that every swimming pool we soak in is filled with grandparent-and-grandkid combos, while the parents are in their beach chairs reading trashy novels. This is very much a family resort for those who seek that, a couples resort for those who want privacy, and an American resort for those who are afraid of something too native.

If you and yours seek a little adventure but still want to hunker down in the posh reaches of Cancún, remember that you are a bus ride, a drive, or a short flight or ferry from other slightly less developed sites . . . or those sites that were developed thousands of years ago. Your choice. There are shopping possibilities all around: At the pyramids little boys will run up after you, trying to sell you a silver butterfly pin; Isla Mujeres—once off the beaten track—has been opening branches of designer boutiques; Xel-Há has the nicest beachwear shopping in the area, if you'll accept a small selection but choice graphics.

Welcome to Cancún

Y ou have to love Cancún the minute you walk through the airport on arrival: no other Caribbean airport has as many shops. As you depart in a van (far cheaper than a taxi) crammed with other gringos, you'll see giant billboards tucked into the dunes, advertising the Ralph Lauren shop and other in-town stores. What's not to like?

Cancún may be commercial and glitzy and very, very American, but it welcomes you with *abrazos* (hugs) and a lot of air-conditioned malls.

Cancún on a Cruise

A few years ago some cruise ships put in at Cancún, which meant they got as close to Cancún as they could and then tendered passengers to shore. There is no pier in Cancún itself, and the waters do not provide for a close anchorage, so the tender ride was about an hour. Needless to say, this wasn't popular. Nowadays, most cruise ships stop at Playa del Carmen and offer a day tour to Cancún for those who want to visit. Unfortunately, the ship usually then moves on to Cozumel, so you are forced to pick between three different spots—Playa del Carmen, Cancún, or Cozumel. If your ship's itinerary is unclear, you just might want to have all this explained to you. Many passengers think they are going to all three cities. Good luck.

The Two Cancúns

If you are staying in one of the popular resort hotels, you are in an area called the Hotel Zone, actually a strip of land in the shape of the number 7, attached to the mainland at both ends. At the beginning of the top of the number 7 you have Cancún City, on the mainland portion of Cancún, which is where the smaller (and less expensive) hotels are, where the real people live, and where the actual town is located. As you cross onto the 7 away from Cancún City, you work your way through the famed hotel area, where a narrow strip of land with beach on both sides plays host to some of the most glorious resorts you have ever seen. At the bottom of the 7, you connect to the portion of land that leads to the airport and to Club Med.

In the beginning, when Cancún was first developed—over ten years ago—the center of the Hotel Zone was considered at the break in the number 7, where the top zigs and then plunges downward; this is an area of town known as Caracol. At this location you have your Convention Center, your main shopping areas, and the Hotel Camino Real. But as Cancún got more and more with-it, the hotels and resorts needed land and space, and southward went the tail end of the 7. At one time the Sheraton was considered at the end of the world. Now, the Ramada Renaissance is closer to the airport end of the 7, and the construction continues, so that the entire strip will someday be built up. Developers are already trying to move the so-called center of town away from the Convention Center area and farther along the neck of the 7, across the street from the Sheraton. Word on the strip is that when all is said and done, the Sheraton will be the center of the universe.

Getting Around

No matter where you stay in Cancún, you can get around inexpensively on the bus that is marked *"Zona Hotelería"* and that simply goes up and down the road along the 7, stopping at the driveway to each hotel. To catch said bus, just stand out there in the road on the correct side of the street (depends on which way you are going!) and flag the bus down. *Please note:* We had a lot of trouble getting the bus to stop for us. Maybe we didn't smile enough.

We ended up renting a car, which we did not plan on doing but which became more and more a necessity as we determined how much freedom we wanted. Car rental is rather pricey (in fact, it's downright outrageous if you insist on automatic transmission or air conditioning), but it turned out there really is a lot of driving to do in Cancún. If you want to shop a lot and go out to eat at different places, you should probably budget for a car, if not for the week then for a three-day stretch, which will allow you time to shop, take in both parts of Cancún, see some of the other hotels and resorts, and drive to the ruins of your choice.

Grandpa Sy, who has done a lot of our repeat reporting in Cancún, insists on a car and says it is impossible to relax here without one, unless you plan on never leaving your hotel.

If you plan on doing just that—staying put—you can get to the ruins, or town, or out for an afternoon by buying a tour package at your hotel. All of the hotels on the strip, and some in town, offer tours costing in the $25–$50 range for the day or half day, per person. (If there are a lot of you in your group, it could prove cheaper to rent a car.) Most of these tours are geared to get you to the sites of the ruins, such as Tulum or Chichén Itzá. There are shopping opportunities at all of the ruins.

Please note that while Cancún City has addresses and is based pretty much on a grid system, there are few addresses on the strip. It's just one long main drag named Kukulcán Boulevard (sometimes called Boulevard Cancún). Most stores are in either hotels or shopping centers, all of which have names. There are numbered markers for each kilometer as you work your way down the strip from town, and you'll soon learn that kilometer 3.5 (the address given for Plaza Nautilus, a shopping center) is rather close to Cancún City, kilometer 12 is the address of the Sheraton, and kilometer 23 is the location of the Ramada Renaissance, etc. Most directions are given by proximity to a particular hotel—"It's just past the Fiesta Americana" or some other identifying landmark. Street numbers are not usually part of an address or directions.

Booking Cancún / I

Your *Travelers Guide to Mexico,* which we recommended already (page 15), has a few pages on Cancún and a list of many of the stores and shopping centers. Since this book is updated annually, it is a solid resource. There is also a little hotel freebie that might help you—*Cancún Tips*—which is about the size of a *TV Guide* and is published twice a year. This is filled with advertising so you can get an idea of the retail scene. You may buy a hand-drawn map called *Cancún Souvenir Map* by Escudero de Sybaris, which has cute little pictures of all of the hotels and some of the shops in both Cancún City and the Hotel Zone drawn in. The version we have, however, is dated 1986, and is grossly out of date. But it does help to orient you to the basics—and let's face it, the Camino Real isn't about to move.

Booking Cancún/2

I t's hard to go wrong on a hotel choice in Cancún, since there are so many. Every chain has a hotel here; every hotel has a shopping plaza. Fiesta Americana has about five hotels here, so you can spend your vacation checking them all out. Our choices are for the right combination of luxury, price, and location. We rate hotels as inexpensive (under $100), moderate ($101–$150), and expensive (over $150). Note that all hotels are on the same street (there is only one street in the Hotel Zone) and they are all located or identified by kilometer.

SHERATON HOTEL AND TOWERS: The first time we go to any city in Mexico we always stay at a Sheraton, because we know precisely what we are getting. Nothing can possibly go wrong, and you have the perfect base from which to explore and then decide if this is the hotel of your dreams or not. It certainly fits our dreams, with three different units of various rooms. We've had an apartment with a kitchenette here, a Towers room, the works. The location is also in the hot part of town, right in the middle of much of the new stuff. Several pools (as well as the usual beach) and many sports facilities, including a small miniature golf course. Good family choice. Various promotional rates. Moderate to expensive.

SHERATON HOTEL AND TOWERS, Boulevard Kukulcán, Kilometer 12

▼

RAMADA RENAISSANCE: This swankily constructed pyramid-style hotel is the perfect combination of ritzy and glitzy, while still being humble and unpretentious. The public space is fabulous, while the rooms are very average, which keeps the rate down low. This is a great place to bring kids (they will go nuts for the pool); it's also a fine introduction to Ramada's new hotel chain with its upscale life-style and amenities delivered at below the going rate. The best swimming pool in town. Closer to the airport than others. Inexpensive.

RAMADA RENAISSANCE, Boulevard Kukulcán, Kilometer 23

▼

HOTEL CAMINO REAL: As always, the toniest hotel in town. This one is not so fancy as many of the other properties and has a very-early-1960s elegance to it that makes you feel you are in the resort your parents took you to when you were a kid. If you aren't nostalgic for those days, check out the new tower. The location is right in the heart of everything, so if you don't have a car and don't want a car, you can walk to all the shopping. Expensive.

HOTEL CAMINO REAL, Boulevard Kukulcán, Kilometer 5

Snack and Shop

While we are used to the usual resort-city hustle in which you are asked to visit a condo or time-share in exchange for a gift or a meal, we had never seen a free-meal hustle before. In Cancún, men walk up to you on the street and offer you vouchers for a free meal in a certain restaurant—one that is generally in a shopping center. We were so curious about all this that we spent about an hour looking for the place we were directed to—and never found it! There was also another hustle in which you got a free blanket just for eating in a certain restaurant, but we didn't find that one, either. We hope you're not as hungry as we were, or that you find better deals.

Note a few other deals:

Breakfast is a big meal here. All of the hotels have incredible buffets, the price of which is not normally included in the room rate, unless you are on some sort of deal or are staying in the Sheraton Towers section. We have tried them all, and our vote goes to the Sheraton's buffet. *Shoppers beware, however:* You need to be a big eater to get your money's worth. These buffets are not cheap.

Many of the restaurants are trying to attract a big breakfast business—advertisements for "American Breakfast" or "All You Can Eat Breakfast" abound all over town. Breakfast is a very competitive meal!

In any Mexican resort city we eat at least one meal at Carlos 'N' Charlie's or one of their chain eateries named things like Carlos Anderson's or Señor Frog's. You can start out in L.A. and just eat your way south. Don't miss it!

Shopping Cancún

While most people come to Cancún to relax, to party, and to partake in the many active sports, there's an awful lot of shopping going on here. The most active shopping time, especially as a couples event, is in the evening, as the sun sets. People finish up their activities for the day, shower, change clothes, and go out for a drink and some shopping, before moving on to a 9 or 10 P.M. dinner and then the disco. It's also rather hot during the day, so the after-sundown crowd are more comfortable while they shop—although all the fancy malls are air-conditioned anyway. And people seem to prefer the malls.

There seem to be two types of tourists who visit Cancún. Their shopping habits are related to their needs. Some of the crowd goes to Cancún City because it's cheap and because the state owns the beaches of Mexico. These people know they don't need a beachside hotel; they can go anywhere they want and enjoy it all. They tend to do their shopping on Avenida Tulum and in downtown Cancún City because they think that the Hotel Zone is a rip-off. The other type of tourists are more resort-oriented. They want luxury and escape, and only leave the resort to check out other resorts to see which one is nicer. These people will do their shopping in the Convention Center (they love Plaza Caracol) but may not even venture into Cancún City, because they just aren't curious enough. There is no right or wrong attitude, but with these different ways of thinking there are a lot of possibilities. The shopping comes down to the two parts of Cancún and which best suits your own personal choices.

Everyone who comes here will buy some silver and a few T-shirts. Many will buy Ralph Lauren merchandise or other Mexican-made name-brand goods. In some parts of Mexico you can recognize the tourists by the embroidered dresses they begin to wear (this happens on the cruises too), but in Cancún very few people go in for the native handiwork—at least, not for themselves. They prefer T-shirts and beachwear. (As the T-shirt industry became saturated, beachwear became the hot commodity—now you'll find shorts, pedal pushers, sweats, and running gear, all made to go with T-shirt designs sold by several different popular beachwear companies.) And Aca Joe.

Shopping Centers

PLAZA CARACOL: This is the Big Daddy of shopping centers on Cancún's resort strip. It's not the oldest, but it's the biggest and the fanciest, and it has successfully leased space to every major Mexican chain and designer convinced that this is the place to be. Shoppers are too. In fact, success breeds success, and now there are parts I and II to the mall. The place is always crawling with browsers, particularly at night when the action is enough to make you claustrophobic. There are at least 173 shops on the two levels of the mall, and several nice restaurants. It's also in the center of town, across from the Convention Center and other shopping centers—the heart of the zone. Note that the center has a strange shape and several entrances—it faces both the lagoon and the beach. Among the popular chains here are **BYE-BYE**, **ACA JOE**, **GUCCI**, **FIORUCCI**, **BENETTON**, and **EXPLORA**. For something more original, try **EL RANCHO** (sportswear), **GALERÍAS COLONIALES** (crafts and Pier1–style merchandise), **TANE** (exclusive jeweler and silversmith), and **LAS SANDÍAS** (papier-mâché). Open daily from 9 A.M. to 10 P.M. Some stores will close for the siesta (1 P.M. to 4 P.M.); should you happen to get a rain shower (there is a rainy season), this is the place to party.

PLAZA CARACOL, Across from the Convention Center, Hotel Zone

▼

EL PARIÁN: This shopping center is across the street from Plaza Caracol (toward the Convention Center), and a world away—it's older and actually dowdy in style. The highlight of the area is **VICTOR'S** for serious (and expensive) crafts. There is a **CALVIN KLEIN** shop in the strip; it is one of the worst examples of the chain in Mexico (the shop itself is unattractive, the merchandise selection sparse), although word is that a new Calvin Klein shop is coming on board. There are shops on both sides of this structure, as well as a few eateries and a small minimart where you can load up on soft drinks, snacks, beer, booze, and safe vanilla (one liter costs about $13, which is an excellent price). Hours: 9 A.M. to 10 P.M. daily.

EL PARIÁN, Convention Center, Hotel Zone

▼

PLAZA LAGUNAS: This shopping center is hard to distinguish from the jumble of shops crowded in the Plaza Caracol area. Its look is kind of jungle-meets-parking-structure. The main news here is the **ELLESSE** shop and the **OP** (Ocean Pacific) shop. The Hard Rock Café is around the back.

PLAZA LAGUNAS, Next to Plaza Caracol, Hotel Zone

▼

COSTA BLANCA: In between Plaza Caracol and Plaza Lagunas is Costa Blanca, most distinctive because of La Mansión, a fancy Mexican restaurant with floor shows and cute architecture. It's all in pink stucco, so you can tell it from the shopping centers next door and behind it. There's an art gallery or two, but not much retailing.

COSTA BLANCA, Next door to Plaza Caracol, Hotel Zone

▼

MAYFAIR GALERÍA: This one is more of the same, in the same block of real estate as Plaza Caracol and Plaza Lagunas, near the

Hard Rock Café, and across the street from the Convention Center. At last notice, it was green stucco, so you could tell it apart from the building next door, which is pink and therefore has a different name. Less memorable than others (you could miss this one totally) although **RAUL'S** stands out with well-made silver earrings. Hours: 9 A.M. to 10 P.M. daily.

MAYFAIR GALERÍA, Across from the Convention Center, Hotel Zone

▼

PLAZA NAUTILUS: This one sticks out like a sore thumb because of its adventurous architecture. Located on the lagoon side, with all the usual suspects, including a **BYE-BYE**, **DOMIT**, **EXPRESS**, **GUESS**, and **CARTIER**. This shopping center—a bit away from the others—has its own ritzy cachet and is also next door to the hot disco in town, La Boom. Plaza Nautilus is the closest strip shopping center to Cancún City, at Kilometer 3.5. It has a snazzy seashell logo and is one of the nicer places in town, competing with Plaza Caracol for rich American customers. Open 9 A.M. to 10 P.M. daily.

PLAZA NAUTILUS, Boulevard Kukulcán, Kilometer 3.5

▼

FLAMINGO PLAZA: This is our favorite of them all from the strictly architectural standpoint. We call this style "Aztec Adorable." The shops have been fitted into a semi-prefab pyramid-style strip mall overlooking the lagoon, not far from the Sheraton. Most of the stores are branches of established names such as **BYE-BYE** and **GUCCI**; there's also the usual plethora of silver shops.

FLAMINGO PLAZA, Boulevard Kukulcán, Kilometer 12

PLAZA LA FIESTA: This is not actually a shopping center, but bills itself as one; we don't want you to be totally confused. It could also be called a *tianguis;* many locals call these giant stores that sell everything indoor *tianguis.* Plaza la Fiesta is nothing more than K mart meets Cancún. Except that all it sells is tourist items. Unfortunately (to us, anyway), there is one of these in every resort city. We know we shouldn't take it so personally. It's just that we hate these giant emporiums that are so lacking in charm and bargains. The huge space is lined up aisle after aisle with sections selling certain crafts or touristy souvenirs. There's liquor, there's leather, there's dresses. Getting the picture? Meanwhile, there are swarms of people. The place is like downtown St. Thomas on the day three cruise ships come to port. A *mariachi* band plays in the front of the shop, music blares, money flashes. Perhaps this is a good place to come to see what local prices are. But we wouldn't be sorry if you chose to pass completely.

PLAZA LA FIESTA, Across from the Convention Center, Hotel Zone

Hotel Shopping

Because this is a resort community, and not everyone wants to go cruising around in the heat looking for shopping bargains, all the good hotels have their own shops. Depending on the hotel, you may get a few shops that rely mostly on postcards and Pepto-Bismol, or you may get a minimall. We enjoy these hotel stores for several reasons:

▼ It's a fun way to explore the fancier resorts and to see the hotels.

▼ The shops rarely close during the siesta.

▼ The shops in the better hotels are more upscale than the run-of-the-mill tourist traps and are a privilege to visit, especially in their air-conditioned splendor.

▼ The prices are high for the market, so you know you should pay less when you bargain elsewhere.

Check out the best and the brightest:

SHERATON HOTEL AND TOWERS: The Sheraton has three separate main buildings in the complex (this doesn't count the tennis club or pool cabanas and stuff) with shopping concentrated in the main building in a stretch outside the main lobby, going toward the pool. This means that if you walk into the main lobby and look around, you've missed the stores. You have to go outside to the stores. The best of the half-dozen or so shops is a sort of general store selling the usual resort needs but also arts and crafts at very fair prices. You could actually do all your Mexican shopping right here. The store is open until 10 P.M., so relax, enjoy your stay, and never leave the Sheraton. *Note:* Developers plan to build a shopping mall across the street from the Sheraton. So if you actually crave more shopping adventures, you'll be able to leave the Sheraton after all—just walk across the street.

SHERATON HOTEL AND TOWERS, Boulevard Kukulcán, Kilometer 12

▼

FIESTA AMERICANA CANCÚN BEACH CLUB AND VILLAS: The hotel (one of the Fiesta Americana chain, and one of several in Cancún) is made of pink stucco molded into Moorish splendor. The shopping is in two parts: inside the lobby, where there are about five or six good stores, including a very fancy silver shop, and down at the main road where there is actually a strip center. Since this is one of the most glamorous hotels in town, you should make it a point to explore the whole area.

FIESTA AMERICANA CANCÚN BEACH CLUB AND VILLAS, Boulevard Kukulcán, Kilometer 11

▼

CAMINO REAL: The best shopping location for a hotel, and smack in the center of everything, the Camino Real also has shops alongside the front entrance, in a short strip. If you go into the lobby, you'll find only the newsstand. These stores are on the street-cum-driveway, as you approach the front door.

CAMINO REAL, Boulevard Kukulcán, Kilometer 9

▼

RAMADA RENAISSANCE: This hotel has one of the best swimming pools in town, and reminds us of L.A. with its lavender stucco and Mexicano/Art Deco lobby. It's a small lobby area, more intimate than most, and it has the usual travel agency and shops. But the gift shop is excellent, with a small but classy selection of crafts. If you aren't staying here, it's worth a trip to explore the entire hotel.

RAMADA RENAISSANCE, Boulevard Kukulcán, Kilometer 23

Tianguis

KI HUIC: Located in Cancún City, this market is a mass of stalls selling the usual souvenirs. In season, we find the prices here are better than on the strip. However, out of season we actually found them to be higher! You should bargain, of course, and don't pay more than $8 for one of those blankets. ($6 is better.) We'd like to tell you this place is cute, or authentic, or a must-do. But in all honesty, it's nothing like the real thing in Mérida. Take it or leave it—only worth doing if you are already in Cancún City or are obsessed with the need to bargain and to see the local version of a tourist trap. *Note:* Many of the vendors observe the siesta and are closed in the afternoon.

KI HUIC, Avenida Tulum, Cancún City

▼

PLAZA MÉXICO: We actually like this one better than the state-sponsored Ki Huic. It doesn't pretend to be what it isn't. (It is a tourist trap and proud of it.) It's next door to the department store Pama, and being right here in Cancún City gives you much more of an I-am-not-a-gringo feeling. This is a modern structure and feels like a U.S. shopping mall, but it's kind of nice in a California way. Hours: 9 A.M. to 9 P.M. daily.

PLAZA MÉXICO, Avenida Tulum 200, Cancún City

▼

MERCADO ARTESANAL: This is your local flea market/*tianguis,* located in the Hotel Zone, right near the Convention Center. There are three buildings placed in a U shape around a central plaza with a small fountain. Each building is filled with stalls on which the usual merchandise is hanging. Asking prices are outrageously high, so that if you bargain toward the midpoint, you will still have overpaid by a long shot. Of the three *tianguis,* this one is the most fun—but you'd better know the going price, or your budget will be gone.

MERCADO ARTESANAL, Convention Center, Hotel Zone

Finds

ACA JOE: The center of the Cancún shopping universe seems to be Aca Joe, which is right inside the Plaza Caracol but has an entrance and window space directly on the street, so you can see in. It's not that this stuff is dirt cheap, but it is moderately priced and well designed. Because you're in that sporty mood, it begins to seem like a bargain. Running shorts are about $15; sweats begin at $25 but go up; colored cotton safari-style jackets are $75. One of the most popular items here and in other resort cities is the flour sack–style cotton shirt— made for men, but also worn by women—that is big and open (therefore cool) and bright white, and is printed with an advertising slogan on it, usually for beer or chilis. These cost about $25 and are the single best item to bring home to tell your friends you are with-it and cool. Since they are well designed and comfortable as well, they aren't a bad deal.

ACA JOE
  Plaza Caracol, Hotel Zone
  Avenida Tulum, Cancún City
  Airport

EXPLORA: This is another popular Mexican chain—sort of the local version of Banana Republic with more of a Galapagos feeling to it. Their specialty is well-designed T-shirts with graphics of endangered species on them. They also have some beach and jungle clothes in denim and khaki. The towels repeat the same designs that are on the T-shirts. Prices are steep: T-shirts are about $15, towels about $25.

EXPLORA, Plaza Caracol, Hotel Zone

▼

GUCCI: This store is nice and the merchandise is too, although check each piece individually to make sure it's well made. Prices are about half those in the United States. You can buy a sensational handbag for about $70. Don't miss a look at the luggage.

GUCCI
Plaza Caracol, Hotel Zone
Plaza Flamingo, Hotel Zone

▼

BALLY: A fancy store for shoes and leather goods, although obviously this is a license and not the same as Bally of Switzerland.

BALLY, Plaza Caracol, Hotel Zone

▼

EXPRESS: This is a really cute chain of women's and juniors' ready-to-wear that is extremely with-it. They usually have beautiful shops selling moderately well made clothes for beach and play—and even for real life back in the States.

EXPRESS
Plaza Nautilus, Hotel Zone
Avenida Tulum, Cancún City

POLO/RALPH LAUREN: There are two shops in town. Avoid the one in Cancún City if you can—it's just not as good, and the building itself seems to be crumbling, an attribute we admire in some Mexican buildings but not this one. Here's where you buy your Polo clothes for men, women, and children at a fraction of the U.S. price. However, they still aren't giving it away. A shirt will cost about $25.

POLO/RALPH LAUREN
  Plaza Caracol, Hotel Zone
  Avenida Tulum, Cancún City

▼

RONAY: One of Mexico's best jewelers. A little more expensive than others, and they may not bargain, but you get the top-of-the-line reputation you need for an important piece.

RONAY, Hotel Camino Real, Hotel Zone

▼

VICTOR'S: Perhaps the best place in town for serious arts and crafts, although the prices are as serious as the goods. Excellent *huipiles* and a little of everything else are sold here. Once your eye has adjusted to the good stuff, you won't mind paying for it. A true find.

VICTOR'S, El Parián, Convention Center, Hotel Zone

▼

PAMA: What can we say—we love local department stores. If you want the real thing, this is the only place to shop. They have everything from postcards to vanilla. Open from 9 A.M. to 2 P.M. and from 4 P.M. to 9 P.M. daily. Authentic and fun for real aficionados of Mexican department stores.

PAMA, Corner of avenidas Tulum and Lluvia

SEBASTIÁN: This is one of the seemingly millions of silver shops in Cancún. After looking at all of them, including those in Cancún City as well as on the strip, we decided to do business here. They were willing to bargain a little; prices are in dollars. Silver earrings ranged from $14 to $22 a pair.

SEBASTIÁN
  Plaza Caracol, Hotel Zone
  Plaza Nautilus, Hotel Zone

▼

DON COTTON: Of all the millions of beach and T-shirt places, we happen to like this shop and most of their designs, which are cute but not unusual.

DON COTTON, Plaza Caracol, Hotel Zone

▼

THE FACTORY OUTLET: Leave it to us—we've found all the seconds and botched silk-screen work from a major T-shirt company. You'll see these designs all over town, and are probably better off paying the full price for a perfect one. But if you can't resist a bargain, the prices here are about $2 less than normal. And there is a bulk rate—if you buy five you get one free. ¡Olé!

THE FACTORY OUTLET, Plaza Laguna, Hotel Zone

Welcome to Cozumel

Cozumel seems to exist solely to act as host to the Palancar Reef, which, even after the nasty blows of Hurricane Gilbert, is one of the nicest places in the world to see beautiful tropical fish. It's not a bad place to see the pretty little stores, either, and can be a very nice day trip for cruise-ship passengers. Most of the lush stuff is away from town, but it is possible to combine a shopping trip with a snorkeling trip.

Getting There

We've always been to Cozumel on a cruise ship or by the jetfoil from Playa del Carmen, but Dr. Debbie and Grandpa Sy did their part of the research by flying in and staying for a few days. They holed up at the Sol Caribe, where it's hard to get anyone away from the fancy swimming pool. We mention this because not only is this one of the best hotels in town, but it is almost directly across from the cruise pier, and sometimes your cruise line can get a day deal to use the hotel facilities.

Getting Around

While all the shopping is in two compact areas, side by side and easily managed—even on a hot day—these areas are near the jetfoil pier, and not the cruise-ship pier. You will need a taxi or a van into town if you want to shop there. Taxi prices are most often per person, and are usually quoted in dollars, especially if you are coming off a cruise ship. If you are going from town to the pier or a hotel, ask the driver the price before you get in, and make sure you both agree on the currency in which the price is to be paid. Also make sure the agreed-upon fare is for all members of your party. Don't assume you are paying $2 for the complete fare and you won't be surprised when it turns out to be $2 per person.

If you come into the main pier in the heart of downtown, you can walk everywhere and will not need any other transportation. This is where the hydrofoil from Playa del Carmen leaves you.

The Lay of the Land

The big city on Cozumel is San Miguel. It's also the only city. It's laid out on a simple grid system with one additional street—Avenida Rafael Melgar, which is the main drag along the beach that goes around the island. This street from the pier north is called, as it is on any island, the *malecón*, or seawall. The new snappy shops are along the *malecón*, all sitting in a row on one side of the street. The other shopping area, which is more Old Mexico–Meets–Cute *Turista*–style, begins at the *Zócalo*, which is where you get off the main pier or where the cruise van takes you, and continues alongside the *Zócalo* on what we like to call Fifth Avenue. The real name of this street is Calle 5, and it has a north end (*norte*) and a south end (*sur*) divided by Avenida Benito Juárez (a pedestrian street), which is where the *Zócalo* is. This part of town is far more funky, has the better part of the crafts shops, and gives you much more of the flavor of Mexico. However, the beauty of Cozumel (aside from the fishes in the sea) is that both the modern and the funky represent the true heart of all Mexico—so your one day in town will really provide you with a microcosm of the entire Mexican retail scene.

Cruising Cozumel

I f you arrive on a cruise ship, this is the big day, folks—this is Shopping Day. Shopping in the Caymans is far more expensive (as you probably already know), and in Jamaica it is, well, more native. This is where you can buy a little of everything from wearable ready-to-wear to Mexican arts and crafts. Cruise passengers, even those on tours, will have time for shopping. Although serious shoppers will spend the day on their own, since the stores close for the siesta, it will take the entire day to do it all.

Booking Cozumel

Y our *Travelers Guide to Mexico* has a section on Cozumel. The local free publication is called *Guía Que Hacer A Donde Ir* (Guide to Where You Want to Be), and has a Spanish portion and an English portion, along with the usual advertisements.

Shopping Cozumel

I f you are on a cruise ship and have to decide which port you will go to—Playa del Carmen for the Tulum all-day trip, Cancún, or Cozumel—and provided you are making this decision based solely on shopping (which under these circumstances is pretty silly, we know), we suggest you pick Cozumel. Here's why:

▼ Cancún has a bunch of shopping centers very much like what you get at home, and while it has a lot of everything, it's extremely resorty.

▼ Playa del Carmen is just downright silly (although very authentic) because all shopping there was created for tourists, and the *tianguis* at Tulum is a giant rip-off. The best of this route's shopping is actually at the small strip at Xel-Há (see p. 228) where tours also stop to see the magnificent reef—the area was totally rebuilt recently and is now clean, neat, and possessed of a small but solid gift shop offering beachwear with a nice graphic.

▼ Cozumel has its share of tourist joints, but it also has a degree of charm and is the equal (charmwise, anyway) of any Caribbean port. You can also get a better selection of crafts here and have more fun doing it than in the other cities. Yes, there is some shopping in the international terminal for cruise passengers.

Hours

D rat! Lots of places close for the siesta! Not all of them, but a fair number. Hours are basically from 9 A.M. to 1 P.M. and from 5 P.M. to 9 P.M. daily. Go back to the cruise ship for the free luncheon buffet, eat at Carlos 'N' Charlie's right there on the *malecón* (our choice), or swim in the deep blue sea.

Black Coral Shopping

All those black-coral factory outlets you see (or are taken to on your tour bus) are not real factories. Well, they are real factories, but they aren't real factory outlets. No bargains. This is Rip-off City. We don't suggest you go for black coral in a big way, since it's very hard to distinguish the real thing from black plastic, and few makers craft fashion pieces—just little touristy items. Price carefully, and if you are a serious shopper, buy from a reputable source.

What a Dive

You can dive, snorkel, or scuba in Cozumel —almost all beach areas have dive shops where you can rent the gear or get a lesson or two. There are also tours you can buy before you get to town, through your travel agent back home or through your cruise ship.

Many of the shops not only rent but sell the goods. If you're searching for the ultimate souvenir, call Tony Tate (21444) in Cozumel; he can arrange to have an underwater videotape made of your dive.

MICHELLE'S: A complete dive facility with everything you need (including insurance!) and a downright incredible selection of diving gear and sports equipment. Just walk in and be dazzled by the combos of black and neon— the fish will gather around just to see you. They also make travel arrangements, arrange tours, and rent underwater cameras. Many of their prices are in U.S. dollars. Call from the United States if you need help making plans before you arrive: (800) 328-5285, which is Go Diving Inc., a U.S. travel agent representing Michelle's.

MICHELLE'S, Calle 5 Sur, 2

Finds

CASABLANCA: Almost the first store you come to when you shop the *malecón,* Casablanca is in a white stucco villa that overlooks the sea. It has wide wooden doors, fine displays, and lots of fancy jewelry. Black coral is sold here, as well as all the gold and silver you could ever buy. Unset gems are sold with a guarantee. We only buy our gems from Hans Stern, but if you know what you are doing, you should be safe here.

CASABLANCA, Avenida Rafael Melgar 33 (Malecón at Calle 2)

▼

POCO-LOCO: This is one of those Mexican chain stores that pops up in every resort city— sort of the local equivalent of a T-shirt/Benetton store. The graphics are a little different from Bye-Bye (their main competitor) and are *de rigueur* with the tourist crowd.

POCO-LOCO, Plaza Studebaker (Malecón at Calle 2)

▼

BENETTON: It's Mexican-made, and it's expensive, so don't get carried away.

BENETTON, Plaza Studebaker (Malecón at Calle 2)

LA CONCHA: Good for arts and crafts, and half a block from the *Zócalo,* in a cute little area; see our "A Stroll Around the Square," page 225.

LA CONCHA, Corner of Calle 5 and Calle 1 Sur

▼

ROCIO ANGELICA: A great find if you love hole-in-the-wall shops, although you should bargain a tad on the price of vanilla. Home of the $5 T-shirt.

ROCIO ANGELICA, Plaza Studebaker (Malecón at Calle 2)

▼

PROCOCO: If you know us, you know we love local department stores and little grocery stores—so here's the local market with its rum, suntan lotions, perfume counter, and other necessities. It's a small department store with everything you need and some groceries. We love it. If this is too upscale for you and you want true funk, cross the street to Negociación Cozumel S.A., where no tourist has ever shopped. Prices on vanilla and booze are the same here as elsewhere.

PROCOCO, Malecón at Calle 4

▼

POLO/RALPH LAUREN: We were insulted that not everything in the store was cheap—they have the nerve to have dresses here that cost $100! You just have to realize that prices here are still 30% to 50% of what they are in the United States and not get too greedy. Then you can cope. This is one of the nicer Ralph Lauren stores you'll see in all of Mexico (yes, we have been to all of them). Two levels.

POLO/RALPH LAUREN, Avenida Rafael Melgar 11 (Malecón at Calle 4)

LOS CINCO SOLES: This is our favorite shop in town, and is the only one you need to visit if you are in a hurry. It's toward the end of the shopping part of the *malecón,* so head here first, and then work your way back to town. This is an old colonial building with salons filled with arts and crafts. Even the postcards are better here than everywhere else. It's a glorified tourist shop, but they do sell Izod shirts on the side. The selection of Mexican glass is excellent. Lots of clothes for kids. And they sell vanilla.

LOS CINCO SOLES, Avenida Rafael Melgar 27 (Malecón at Calle 8)

▼

ESPRIT: This is a license—check prices and quality before you pounce. Nice decor and OK prices, but we worry about how the clothes'll hold up in the washing machine.

ESPRIT, Avenida Rafael Melgar (Malecón at Calle 4)

▼

EXPRESS: Hip, young fashions for the with-it crowd. A major chain with a nice modern boutique in every resort city. Moderate prices.

EXPRESS, Avenida Rafael Melgar (Malecón at Calle 6)

▼

LA CASITA: Their card says it all: "The best Mexican designed clothes and carefully selected arts and crafts." They got our *pesos.* Actually, this is a fancy T-shirt shop, but who cares? A large shop with sportswear as well as Ts and many designs we never saw elsewhere.

LA CASITA, Avenida Rafael Melgar 23 (Malecón at Calle 8)

EL SOMBRERO: This one is a must if you want a laugh. Or to get a purse made from a real (once live) frog. You'll never get over this place as long as you travel. Other shoppers seem to agree, only they aren't laughing—they are buying. This place is mobbed, especially with a ship in port. Their big seller is leather airplane carry-ons, but they have other leather goods, cowboy boots, and some luggage.

EL SOMBRERO, Avenida Rafael Melgar (Malecón at Calle 6)

▼

ACA JOE: The same store they have everywhere. But if you haven't been to an Aca Joe yet, this could be your favorite store in town. No merchandise that crosses over with what they sell in the United States, by the way; but a great store nonetheless.

ACA JOE, Avenida Rafael Melgar (Malecón at Calle 6)

A Stroll Around the Square

Don't judge this area of Cozumel by the first store you see, which is likely to be **TIENDA DE SUPERSERVICIO**, sort of a tourist trap/7-Eleven store. Just ignore it and continue your stroll around the square (also called the plaza or Plaza del Sol), first on Avenida Benito Juárez, and then on both sides of Calle 5, both of which are walking streets. There are a number of T-shirt shops (**POCO-LOCO** at Avenida Benito Juárez 12), a few tourist traps, and several handicrafts stores. We found some funky pieces at **ARTIMEX** (Calle 5 Norte 9) and at the **HANDICRAFTS MARKET** (also called the *mercado*) on Calle Sur. **LA PIÑATA**

(Plaza del Sol 3) is one of the nicer tourist stores, with, yes, some *piñatas* for sale—among other things. **PAMA** (south side of the plaza) and **ORBI** (Avenida Rafael Melgar and Avenida Sur 3) are the two local department stores.

Welcome to Playa del Carmen

I f we had a store to tell you about, believe us, we'd tell. What you have here is an absolutely delightful little village whose entire wealth is based on location (location, location, location)—it's where you get the ferry to Cozumel and where the cruise ships send ashore their guests who are taking land tours. There's turquoise water and a one-block *malecón* with a few Slurpee salespeople, the *Zócalo*, and then the block behind the *Zócalo* with a strip of stall/shops selling T-shirts. There is little to rave about. But at least this place feels like Mexico. If you are a cruise passenger, it is the most authentic part of Mexico you will see all day. But other than tourist Ts and *sarapes*, there is nothing to buy.

Welcome to Tulum

O K, we'll be brutally honest. We've seen so many Mexican pyramids and ruins in our twenty-plus years of doing this that except for explaining it to the kids in the family, we'd just as soon get out of the heat.

After a quick tramp through the bushes in Tulum, and a good hard stare at the sea and one of the most breathtaking vistas at any of the ruins, we head back to the shopping area, which is set up like a *tianguis*—a series of two separate strips of corrugated tin stalls representing the finest in retailing. If you thought the ruins were something, consider the prices here—ruinous!

We don't know what to tell you cruisers who will have only this small opportunity to shop, especially for silver. (There are plenty of T-shirts in Playa del Carmen.) There is no question that the asking price on silver pieces in Tulum is more than 100% inflated and would be high for Tiffany & Co., let alone any other U.S. retailers. Unless you are willing to bargain and/or fight, and maybe walk away, or unless you want to overspend dramatically, you should not buy silver in Tulum. A chunky silver bracelet we bought in Cancún for $125 (a price well researched and bargained for) was offered for sale in Tulum for $350.

"What you pay?" asked the surly vendor.

"We pay $125," we said with conviction.

"No way."

She did not seem to even realize that what we quoted was the going price ... which we well knew after spending four days pricing this one style of bracelet.

The only thing for which you will not overpay in Tulum is the bottle of Coca-Cola (or Krystal water) you buy when you finish exploring in the ruins. After a day in the hot sun, it's one item that's worth any price!

For some reason, the other tourist items (Ts, *huipiles, sarapes*) are not so seriously overpriced as the silver. If you can get a pair of silver earrings for $25 or less, consider it a good deal.

Welcome to Xel-há

S ay "Shell Ha" and say Oooooh, all in the same breath. We happened to visit with another travel writer, who told us if she hadn't seen it with her own eyes, she wouldn't have believed it—Xel-há was cleaned up, rebuilt, and beautified in 1988, and seems to have made a stunning recovery from what many remember as a dump. It's part of many tours (especially from cruise ships), and we think it is worth doing on your own, even though we're not talking about any big-time shopping.

Xel-há is a game reserve for fish. There is a small museum here, and two snack bars where you will certainly want to sit down and have a cold beer or a Coke. Mostly what you do is look into the lagoon and see the gorgeous fish. You can snorkel if that's your thing. Many people bring their own equipment, but you can rent there. After the heat of your trek through Tulum, and the hot flashes you'll get after bargaining at the *tianguis* there, you'll want to cool down in the water. And while it would be a sin to think of this as solely a shopping stop, it just so happens to have a large and very nice shop that sells food and snack items in one half and beachwear (and souvenirs) in the other half. The real prize is that the beachwear has an excellent graphic (of some tropical fish) that is far nicer than the standard Poco-Loco or Bye-Bye stuff you find everywhere else. Silver is not sold here.

Welcome to Mérida

Mérida is the capital of the state of Yucatán, so yes, at last you are in the Yucatán. It's the main market city for not only the state but for the entire boot of Mexico, and for those as far south as Belize. Some airlines fly to Mérida not only from the Mexican interior, but from southern points in the United States. It's a fabulous big colonial city, the kind that makes your pulse beat faster if you love big cities.

Mérida is often visited as a day trip from Cancún via airplane, since it is about a five-hour drive each way, and it is not really practical as a one-day outing if you plan to drive. Since it is near Chichén Itzá, however, many people take in the two sights in one overnight trip. (There's a Holiday Inn in Mérida; it was built in 1980 and has a great location at Avenida Colon and Paseo de Montejo, in the heart of downtown.)

Mérida's colonial history includes both French and Lebanese settlers, so the city has many buildings with mansard roofs and a style of architecture not usually seen in Mexico. A lot of the buildings date to the mid-1500s (the cathedral was built in 1598, but the Montejo home—now a museum—dates to 1549); there is a large parklike plaza (*Zócalo*), and there are always a lot of people out making their *paseo*. This is a city with a large population and a lot of commerce.

Market Day in Mérida

The market, which is the real reason we come to town, is held daily. It sells everything in great volume—one of the local specialties is matlike carpets made from henequen (woven straw), called *petates*. The local honey is also touted. Don't buy any tortoiseshell—you cannot bring it back into the United States. The *huipiles* are incredible! While the market has a little of everything, local crafts are the specialty and the straw items are the best regional buy. Everything from hats to hammocks, place mats, and little fans for souvenirs is available at low, low prices. (Bargain anyway.) Near the *Zócalo*, calles 58, 60, and 62 are considered the big shopping streets, and are home to most of the branch stores, but it is the public market on the corner of calle 57 and 67 that is the draw to tourists and locals alike. The Mérida market offers the best shopping in terms of selection, authenticity, and prices in the Yucatán.

See It All; Shop It All

As a shopping tourist, however, you'll want to take in the market and perhaps some of the downtown sights. The main drag is the Paseo de Montejo, although the market is on Calle 56 at Calle 57. Most of the shopping is on Calle 60, north of the cathedral (Calle 60 at Calle 61); there are some factory outlets on Calle 59; try **JACKS** (No. 507), a maker of *guayaberas*.

Finds

GEORGIA CHARUHAUS COUTURE: Perhaps the most famous store (to gringos and locals alike) in Mérida is Georgia's, where she herself designs all the clothes. Her specialty is resort wear that's not too resorty and is sensible enough to be worn by someone over the age of twenty. She also has an art gallery and some crafts. This lady is known as the local purveyor of good taste.

GEORGIA CHARUHAUS COUTURE, Calle 55, No. 499

▼

MÉRIDA EN DOMINGO: This is the name of the Sunday festival of street vendors, etc., selling their wares and making whoopee at the *Zócalo.* Don't miss it. Bargain like mad.

MÉRIDA EN DOMINGO, Zócalo

▼

MUSEO DEL ARTE POPULAR: After you flip for the museum part, start your collection at the gift shop!

MUSEO DEL ARTE POPULAR, Calle 48 and Calle 50

10▼THE RIVIERA

Welcome to the Riviera

When we first told friends we were cruising the Mexican Riviera, they did a double take: "The what?"

So there you go. In case you didn't know, the western coastal zone of Mexico, from Baja to below, is now called the Riviera. Sometimes it's called Pacific Mexico, but cruise lines feature it as the Mexican Riviera.

Should you be cruising the Riviera, you have big choices to make, as there are two different standard Riviera cruises. One is a one-way cruise from Los Angeles to Acapulco, or vice versa. (We sailed this route with Princess.) The other cruise, offered by a larger variety of lines, is a one-week round-trip cruise from Los Angeles that goes to Puerto Vallarta. So you're going to get either three Mexican ports or five, or maybe even six, depending on the route.

Shopping the Riviera

The cruise along the Riviera is one of the best ways to shop Mexico, because you get so many choices. Short of taking specific tours to Silver Cities (Taxco, Querétaro), to colonial cities (San Miguel de Allende, Guanjuato), or to crafts cities (Oaxaca, Guadalajara), which are all located in the interior, this cruise gives you the best opportunity to buy crafts and inexpensive ready-to-wear. Remember that Acapulco doesn't really have great shopping (except for the market), and do your buying before you get there ... unless you want a made-to-order dress from Esteban.

Shopping the Ship

All cruise ships have stores on board. Our "Love Boat" had some shocking bargains: English porcelains! Who would imagine going to Mexico and finding a steal from England? Our ship (*Pacific Princess*) was rather well stocked on David Winter cottages ($25–$45 each), which someone in our family collects. We were advised to buy on the first day at sea, since the shop always sells out before the end of the cruise.

The ship's shop is also a good place to buy perfumes. Not only will prices be competitive with duty-free prices on land, but you'll know what you are getting—which is more than you can say about most perfumes bought in Mexico. Princess, as well as other lines, guarantees your purchases, so you don't have to worry about frauds or fake fragrances. They also carry some American cosmetics at about 20% off.

Cruise News

If you're on a Princess ship, you have both a cruise director and a shore-ex manager. (Some ships just have a cruise director.) It is the tour director's job to tell you what to expect in port and to help you decide if you want to take a tour or strike out on your own. He or she also has several free maps and brochures for each port, with lists of some of the better stores, and most probably a free conversion chart that show you the dollar/*peso* rates on amounts of *pesos* going up to $10 million (in case you want to buy the ship itself). Keep one of these conversion charts in your handbag or pocket for all your shopping adventures (although a calculator will do the same tricks, and even more exactly).

Your shore-ex manager (ours was Scott—hello, Scott, wherever you are) also knows the right price for a taxi or van ride to town, and more or less the right price for certain crafts. The tour director, being a guest in the country, and someone who must return each week, does not squabble over prices like we do—so consider the price he gives you on anything to be the fair, but high, price. You can often do better than this price, but the price he quotes gives you a fair idea of what the market rate is.

Cruise and Drive (and Shop)

If you are a serious shopper, you might want to give Admiral Cruise lines a jingle at (800) 327-0271. They have a Mexican Riviera cruise that allows you to bring your car onto the ship (which is technically a ferry—it once sailed in Scandinavia). When you get to port, you drive your own car. This also means you can buy a lot more and pack it in your car. Your car will be carefully inspected when it returns to the United States (so don't buy anything naughty), but this is a great method of shipping pottery and crafts if you plan to take advantage of the strong dollar in the best possible way. Admiral also has a variety of Mexican routes, many of which are different from everyone else's. They have a short hop that allows you to buy some big stuff (furniture) if you can get it in the car. See pages 114–118 for Ensenada and Rosarito ideas and tips.

Booking the Riviera/1

Fodor's has moved into regional guides, and has one for Baja and northwestern Mexico, covering terrain from Tijuana south, including Puerto Vallarta, Mazatlán, Manzanillo, and the Copper Canyon. You have to buy another book to get Acapulco, etc., but this is a good guide.

Princess (like all lines, no doubt) publishes a ports-of-call guide; theirs is in magazine form and has advertising for many of the stores as well as pretty pictures of the area.

The cities along the Riviera are covered in all pan-Mexican guidebooks. There is not much written on Huatulco yet for several reasons—it's too far south for the cruise ships to get to; it's still developing; and there isn't much there in terms of shopping.

Booking the Riviera/2

If you are booking cruise-ship passage, check for the various discounts that are offered under all sorts of plans. The cruise line itself may discount the fares in special promotions, or you can get a discount by paying for the ticket six months in advance, or by having been a passenger on the line before. There are also a few travel discount firms that sell cruise packages. Try:

THE TRAVEL COMPANY: (800) 858-5888
VACATIONS TO GO: (800) 624-7338

MOMENT'S NOTICE: (212) 486-0503, or their hot-line: (212) 750-9111
WHITE TRAVEL SERVICE: (800) 547-4790
CRUISEMASTERS: (800) 242-9444

Call several discounters (the whole list above is worth trying), because different packagers get different trips. Different packagers charge different rates for the same trips!

If you are looking for a hotel room, pack-ages will be your best bet, offered either di-rectly through the hotel of your choice or through a travel agent. (See page 16.) The Pacific coast of Mexico is most attractive to people who live on the west coast of the United States and Canada, so try an L.A.-based dis-counter if possible.

The hotel chains that have a hotel in all or almost every port city are:

WESTIN: Westin continues its tradition of offering the fanciest hotel in town. Some of the west coast properties are called Camino Real, but there are two ringers: in Acapulco, Westin now manages Las Brisas, one of the city's most famous resorts, and in Manzanillo they manage Las Hadas, which, as you may recall, began life as a private playground for the rich and famous when tin magnate Anto-nio Patillio built it along the lines of a Moorish palace. For reservations call (800) 228-3000.

SHERATON: The Sheraton in Puerto Vallarta is absolutely gorgeous. It's well located—halfway between the cruise pier and the center of town—but you cannot walk into town. In Ixtapa the hotel is across the street from the main shopping area, so you can walk. In Acapulco, the hotel shares the back side of the same hill as the famous Las Brisas, and also overlooks the bay. For reservations call (800) 325-3535.

Snack and Shop

We have two very stern rules about eating and shopping on Mexico's west coast. Here goes:

▼ Always eat on the ship or in a Carlos 'N' Charlie's.

▼ Drink warm Coca-Cola (no ice) or cold beer (no ice).

"Im-Port-ant" News

Most cruise ships offer their own tours while in port. Passengers should be delighted to note that these packages are much less expensive than similar tours on Caribbean islands and are usually a good way to see a lot in the small amount of time in port. Rest assured that all tours stop off for shopping, and that some cities (Mazatlán and Acapulco) don't have great shopping anyway, so you might as well go on the tour. The cities where you want to shop 'til you drop are Puerto Vallarta and, if you're lucky enough to get there (as not all cruise lines make this stop), Ixtapa/Zihuatanejo.

Mazatlán doesn't really have the greatest shopping, but check out the possibility that your ship offers a tour similar to one that we took while on our Princess cruise: a ride up into the hills to visit Concordia, a colonial city filled with local artisans. This tour returned to Mazatlán at the end of the day and stopped at a few touristy shops in the Golden Zone (Zona

Dorada), but also provided a better chance to get into the little villages that you so often miss while on a cruise. We're not saying this tour is to die for and that you must, must, must go on it. We're simply saying that you don't need all day in Mazatlán to get the shopping picture, and a tour is a good idea here.

As far as Acapulco is concerned, we are very opinionated. First: The shopping here is not great. Second: The place is not charming unless you get up above it and into any of the magnificent resorts. If you love down-and-dirty markets, as we do, do not miss the *mercado* in Acapulco. But be warned that this is not a very American place, and it's not for everybody. If you're here for a day, we suggest a tour. If you're here for three days, we suggest Las Brisas.

Welcome to San Pedro

Y our Mexican Riviera cruise usually begins from the international piers in the port of San Pedro, California. (Unless it begins in San Diego.) You'll be driven by motor coach from the airport directly to the pier, and won't even go into Los Angeles or drive by Disneyland (which is in Anaheim).

There is no shopping. You can make phone calls, but you can't buy anything. Of course, items are for sale on the ship, but the ship's shop can't open until after you've left San Pedro. Ports O'Call Village is two minutes away by taxi if you need a few souveniers before you sail.

Welcome to Cabo San Lucas

I f you didn't read the fine print in the ship's catalogue, now's the time to do so. Princess does not stop in Cabo southbound on the one-way cruise to Acapulco. They stop here on the one-way cruise to L.A. (from Acapulco); so if Cabo is important to you, adjust accordingly. When the ship does come into port, she is in for only about three or four hours. Most people want to see the rock formations, not shop, and the cruise-by that you get on the way down is sufficient. There is a *tianguis* right at the waterfront for pierside shoppers, but you'll get more of the same in your other ports.

Welcome to Mazatlán

W e love the way the southbound Princess cruise is designed, because if Mazatlán is your first stop, it means you'll be in the least attractive of the cities first and can know that each day will get a little bit bigger and better.

The Lay of the Land

I f your idea of shopping heaven is to buy an "I Got Drunk in Mazatlán" T-shirt, you will have ample opportunity. You can also buy ready-to-wear at the various chain stores, or crafts from several crafty dealers.

Cowboy boots are a good buy here, as are shoes—we met a man on our ship who raved about his turtle shoes. When we mentioned that we thought turtle was illegal to bring back to the United States, he shrugged and said, "Who can prove they're not alligator?" They cost him less than $200, and he thought he was a great shopper.

Actually, great shoppers know that Mazatlán has a few too many tourist traps and that Puerto Vallarta—coming up the next day on the cruise—is a better place to shop.

Oh yes, one thing: Don't be surprised if stores in the Zona Dorado (tourist area) don't have exact addresses. Some give street numbers, some give cross streets, and some just give numbers and then say "Zona Dorada," which is the area and not a street. Don't worry. Everyone knows where everything is; just ask.

Shopping Neighborhoods

There are actually four different shopping areas to Mazatlán. You can visit all four in your day in port, although you might not find them all worth your time.

The Pier

From your ship you can hop into a Disneyland-style blue-and-white tram and be taken to the front gate of the pier, where a white stucco (clean, new, modern) building trimmed with blue awaits you as your official door to Mazatlán. Here is where you can get a taxi into town, or shop the *tianguis* that is set up just outside and to the left. There are some stores inside the building, but there is a flea market outside. Clean bathrooms.

Downtown Mazatlán

Take a taxi to the *mercado* if you want to be in the heart of downtown Mazatlán, which is questionable. This area is not where the tourist shopping is located, although tourists do come here on the tours they buy from the ship. The *mercado* is divided into two parts: stalls selling souvenir items and crafts in two rows alongside the main market, but under the same roof; and then the larger space, with its ceiling fans and wrought-iron curlicues, which has areas for foodstuffs, divided into categories so that all the fruit is in one area, all the meat in another, etc. There are some dry-goods store/stalls in this larger area, and yes, one of them does sell vinyl, but the prices here (for vinyl anyway) are outrageous ($4 a meter). You will probably enjoy the market—it is very picturesque (and a kilo of tomatoes costs less than 50¢)—but this is not a great shopping neighborhood. Successful stores in this area are branches of stores that are in the Golden Zone.

Camarón Sábalo

The Zona Dorado (also called the Gold Zone) is the tourist zone, where everything is created to woo you from your dollars. The main street is Calzada Camarón Sábalo. At one time this was the main drag and a nice shopping area, and it still has a lot of the nicer stores (like **ACA JOE** and **POLO**). However, the new money has moved one block over, and if you never even walk along Camarón Sábalo, you won't be totally unhappy. (You're going to see these same chain stores in other ports and in better repair.) The street becomes more and more shabby each day as the energy goes over to the Avenida R. T. Loaiza right around the Playa Mazatlán Hotel.

Playa Mazatlán Hotel

Around the Playa Mazatlán is a two-block stretch of shop after shop after shop. Some of these are downright incredibly built with wild and wonderful architecture (**MAYA**); some of them are just plain old tourist traps. Don't miss the shops in the hotel's shopping center, which is a small strip filled with good offerings. If the Playa Mazatlán is the far end of the area, then the **CENTRO DE ARTESANÍAS** (Arts and Crafts Center) is at the beginning of this shopping strip. The entire area is not more than two or three blocks, but it is much more attractive than Camarón Sábalo. Taxi from the ship to the Centro de Artesanías, and then stroll.

Shopping Centers

El Cid is a combination mall and resort right on the main drag (Camarón Sábalo) and close to the shopping area of the Zona Dorada. This is a modern mall with branches of many chain stores (**GUESS, CALVIN KLEIN, RUBEN TORRES, SEÑOR FROG'S, GUCCI, OP, BYE-BYE**), and a fabulous artsy-craftsy store called La Carreta. (See page 245.) It is located on Camarón Sábalo about halfway between the touristy part of town and the Camino Real hotel. You can walk or cab it from the main Golden Zone.

Finds

DAGG BAZAR: We know we didn't recommend downtown with much relish, but should you find yourself there, we do have a great little store for you. This boutique is about a block from the market, on the same side of the street, and sells the usual combination of T-shirts and crafts items. Although they mostly sell clothes, their gift items are unusual and worth looking at—ceramic chilis, pewter, pottery, etc. They also sell vanilla and a little bit of silver.

DAGG BAZAR, Avenida Juárez 1702

▼

CENTRO DE ARTESANÍAS: You cannot be in Mazatlán, on approach to Mazatlán, or around Mazatlán without knowing about the Arts and Crafts Center, which must be either connected with every cruise ship in the sea or owned by one of them. It is a huge, attractive villa–cum–shopping center that has it all. They bill themselves as the largest handicrafts store in Mexico, which they quite possibly are. What they have going on here is quite impressive. Not only do they have shops, they have a theater, a few artisans at work, some little animals in cages, a place to eat—along with free drinks and happy-hour coupons, and all sorts of deals to lure you in. They intend this to be your one stop-and-shop source. Inside the villa there are some boutiques like Guess and Gucci, there is mezzanine filled with dresses, there is an outdoor *tianguis* of artisans, and there is yet another gallery for the glassware. The selection here is immense. The prices are in the high-to-moderate range. If you will not be going to a native market, this is an awfully good chance to see it all. We just hate how perfect it all is. We hate not being able to bargain. (Give us a day in Toluca!) We hate how clean it is. But many will love it here.

CENTRO DE ARTESANÍAS, Avenida R. T. Loaiza

▼

MAYA: Even if you are only in town for fifteen minutes, you have to get a good look at Maya—from outside and inside. Maya is actually an upscale tourist shop, but you have to give them the award for theatrics. The place is a miniature Mayan temple. The house specialty is leather goods: Shoes and boots are the best buys. Don't miss a peek at the ceiling; don't forget to ask for a discount. (Cruisers get 20% off.)

MAYA, Avenida R. T. Loaiza 411

▼

MERCADO VIEJO MAZATLÁN: We're not sure what's so *viejo* (old) about this market, since it looks brand-new to us, but it has a nice Mediterranean architectural style and is a pleasant shop for arts and crafts and souvenirs. While they actually sell the standard fare, it feels rustic and comfortable here, and you don't quite feel like you're being hustled. We spotted some lacquer tissue boxes the likes of which we've never seen anywhere else.

MERCADO VIEJO MAZATLÁN, Avenida R. T. Loaiza

▼

MR. INDIO: Although the name makes it sound like some curio shop from the 1950s, this is actually one of the nicest shops in town. It's large, modern, clean, and nicely furnished—

not to mention centrally air-conditioned. You can go in, sit yourself down in the central seating area, and have a free soft drink, which is served in the bottle, chilled, so you don't have to worry about the ice problem. It's a very plush store that is sort of like an art gallery and sells high-end this and that—mostly sculpture and jewelry, although there is also leather and pottery. You feel very safe buying from this store because their presentation is so American and so substantial that you assume a bond of trust.

MR. INDIO, Avenida R. T. Loaiza 311

▼

CASA ROBERTO: This is one of the best stores in town—or should we say two of the best stores? The owner has a second shop two doors down called EL TAPANCO. Both sell gift items, home items, and local crafts . . . as well as a few pieces of furniture. The Casa Roberto shop has a mezzanine with weavings, tapestries, and rugs. Prices aren't low, but the quality is high. Open 9 A.M. to 6 P.M. daily.

CASA ROBERTO, Playa Mazatlán Hotel
EL TAPANCO, Playa Mazatlán Hotel

▼

PARDO JOYEROS: A really fancy little shop with high-quality silver and gold and some gemstones. Old-fashioned wooden display cases house posh merchandise; prices are quoted in dollars.

PARDO JOYEROS, Avenida R. T. Loaiza 411

▼

LA CARRETA: The best store for pewter in town! We bought so much at La Carreta that we had to get a taxi and go back to the ship directly from the store! This is a small shop in the El Cid resort, inside the mall but along the main street, with an entrance right on the street. It's filled with well-displayed treasures. Pewter serving pieces are in the $30–$45 range; *Talavera* lamps cost about $100, picture frames about $25 each. There is some religious work for sale, and some American Country Style work. Everything in this store is fabulous! This is not on the usual tourist run, so make it a point to get here. If you pay cash, you can ask for a 10% discount. This is the single best source for pewter on the entire cruise route.

LA CARRETA, El Cid Plaza

A Stroll Down Calzada Camarón Sábalo

Calzada Camarón Sábalo is seedy and run-down and without a sidewalk, so drive by in your taxi to see if you even want to visit. If you care to do so, we're really talking about just a few blocks that will include **POLO/RALPH LAUREN** (No. 410), **EXPLORA** (No. 610) **FILA** (No. 418), **BENETTON** (No. 418), **ELLESSE** (No. 418), and **ACA JOE** (No. 503). If you stay on Camarón Sábalo a little longer, you'll get to El Cid with its mall and resort hotel, one of the nicest in Mazatlán.

Welcome to Puerto Vallarta

This will be the only guidebook you'll ever see about Puerto Vallarta that doesn't mention the name of a certain movie-star couple. Amen. She may have been born to shop, but so were we.

Puerto Vallarta is adorable! Puerto Vallarta is fabulous! Puerto Vallarta is dramatically different from Mazatlán, and from every other city in Mexico, for that matter. It's too cute to be truly authentic, but it's authentic enough to be charming.

The Lay of the Land

Without a doubt, there is too much to do (shoppingwise) in Puerto Vallarta to get it all done in the one-day visit the cruise ship allows you. All the more reason to vow to come back. (You can combine a trip to Guadalajara and Puerto Vallarta into the perfect one-week shopping holiday!)

The city is spread out on either side of the Rio Cuale, with a tiny island in the middle. One long main drag connects the cruise-ship pier to the town. A quick city tour will help you understand the layout of both parts of the town, but that will cut into your shopping time.

Puerto Vallarta

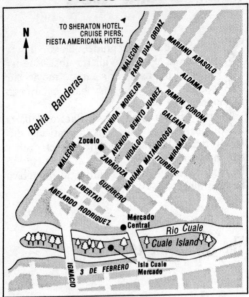

Shopping Neighborhoods

The Pier

There is a *tianguis* at the pier where you will
have time to shop independently, or between
when your tour returns and when you tender
back to the ship. You must bargain fiercely
here, but there are over two dozen shops selling everything you want to buy.

Midtown

If you can visualize the pier as Uptown (we
have a Manhattan state of mind) and the

mercado as Downtown, then the area around the Sheraton is Midtown. More precisely, the shopping area between the Sheraton and the Fiesta Americana (which is attached to a rather large mall) can be considered Midtown. This is where you can find the Centro Comercial Villa Vallarta, Plaza Genova, and newer shops in town that are just taking advantage of lower rents here as this area begins to boom.

Malecón

The *malecón* is the main drag along the seawall with shops and bistros on it, and Puerto Vallarta has a terrific *malecón*. For shoppers it begins at Plaza Malecón, a type of mall (see page 250) and ends at the bridge to Isla Cuale. This is expensive real estate, so the bigger chains and more famous stores are located here. The *malecón* is named Paseo Diaz Ordaz at one end, and Avenida Morelos at the other. The high-rent part is Paseo Diaz Ordaz.

Downtown

The grid of streets behind the *malecón* and at the edge of town, next to the two bridges, is what we call Downtown. This is the central shopping area, and the part of town where you just walk up one side of the street and down the other. This could take two days, but you get the idea. All of the streets are packed with shops. The main shopping street running parallel to the *malecón* is Avenida Benito Juárez, and the important side streets that cross it are Avenida de Iturbide, Ignacio Aldama, and Via Guerrero.

Isla Cuale

Cross over the bridge at the central *mercado* and in a minute's walk you'll be on the Isla Cuale, which is more like a park than anything else. Walk to your right through the park (there's a walkway) toward the ocean and you'll find a whole *tianguis* worth of vendors selling crafts and items similar to those for sale in the larger *mercado*. It's beautiful here, and very peaceful, and perhaps the most perfect place in the whole city—except for those stuffed armadillos that are actually for sale. (Our friend Pete says never pay more than $20 for an armadillo, and beware, their little feet are quite fragile and will break off easily.)

Shopping Centers

PLAZA GENOVA: The new mall in town, near the Centro Comercial Villa Vallarta shopping center with its own Hard Rock Café.

PLAZA GENOVA, Kilometer 1.4, Carreterra

▼

PLAZA MALECÓN: A hacienda-style mall with entry gates (and a costumed senorita to greet you) and a gazebo and bandstand in the center plaza. All around are small cute shops loaded with charm. The van from the pier usually drops everyone off here, as this is the beginning of the shopping zone on the *malecón*.

PLAZA MALECÓN, Corner Diaz Ordaz and Allende

▼

PUEBLO VIEJO: A downtown version of Plaza Malecón, without the senorita and a little less strong on the charm. A tad more touristy, but a bevy of shops right near the Isla Cuale.

PUEBLO VIEJO, Rio Cuale Bridge

CENTRO COMERCIAL VILLA VALLARTA:
The good news is that this giant center is next
door to a really nice hotel (the Fiesta Americana) so that if you are a guest and are desperate to shop, it's right here at your feet. The
bad news is that you'll have to be desperate.
Villa Vallarta just hasn't got the right stuff.
Maybe its time is coming; maybe its time is
past. The mall is new and clean in the hacienda style of architecture, but it has no soul.
But wait, don't quit on us now—it does have
one redeeming feature that makes it all worthwhile, and one amusing feature that may be
interesting to you. So there.

Amusement first: La Fiesta. If you go on a
tour, you can bet your tour bus will stop by
for a spree at La Fiesta, which is one of those
giant, 20,000-square-feet-of-supermarket–style
gringo shopping haunts that Mexicans think
tourists like. This is a warehouse of souvenirs
that is always jammed with tourists and may
appeal to you. It's even open on Sunday, 10
A.M.–5 P.M.

More appealing to us is Comercial Mexicana,
which is the grocery store next door to the
tourist trap. This is a fabulous, modern, clean,
grocery store that also sells dry goods, beach
toys, health and beauty aids, and everything
you might need—and then some. Now this is a
good find.

CENTRO COMERCIAL VILLA VALLARTA, Kilometer 1.5, Carreterra

Tianguis

CENTRO MERCADO: The Centro Mercado
happens to be a bit difficult to find, and quite
a bit of a schlepp through town (scenic as it is)
should your taxi driver unceremoniously dump

you at Plaza Malecón as ours did. He insisted the market was one block away; we didn't know he was lying. The Centro Mercado is in a corner of downtown right up against the river and the Gringo Gulch bridge over to the Isla Cuale. It's directly across from a very cute pub called La Fuente del Puente. While the market does not look promising from outside, don't despair. This one is fun. This is an indoor market where every inch of stall and wall and ceiling space is hung with merchandise. Parrots, *piñatas,* trays decorated with bananas (papier-mâché), string bags, guitars, everything. We found prices in keeping with those in the shops and in other cities—silver earrings still come out around $20 a pair (after hard bargaining); a big necklace of large silver beads is still around $300. The *mercado* building is in a strange triangular shape to accommodate the riverbank, so there are several different entrances and exits.

CENTRO MERCADO, Rio Cuale Bridge

▼

ALFARERÍA TLAQUEPAQUE: Tlaquepaque is a city near Guadalajara that is famous for its pottery and glass and crafts in general. The merchandise in this store is not necessarily from Tlaquepaque. In fact, this isn't really a store, although it does have walls. It's more like a *tianguis* or crafts flea market, and we like it better than all the others in town. You have to go out of your way to get here, but it's worth doing if you like these kinds of places. Although the store is on the main drag, it's in midtown and not in a place well known to tourists. The shop holds rack after rack and row after row of pottery and souvenir items at very good prices. If you buy a lot, try to bargain even more. But when a piece of pottery costs $1 and a large wooden spoon costs 50¢, it's hard to quibble. We love it here!

ALFARERÍA TLAQUEPAQUE, Avenida México 1100

MARINA FLEA MARKET: And God said, "Let there be Tourists." And there were tourists. And the locals saw that they were good. And the locals said, "Let there be tourist traps." And there were tourist traps. And the shopping experts saw that they were no good—unless you are desperate and don't care.

MARINA FLEA MARKET, Marina Dock

Finds

MAJOLICA: A beautiful shop selling top-of-the-line *Talavera* tiles in scenics, fountains, and individual units. The prices are very high and the shop will not ship for you. We can't imagine being able to afford the price of both the tiles and the shipping. The tiles we were in love with cost $35 per unit! The store volunteered to drive them to the airport for us.

MAJOLICA, Ramón Corona 191

EL PATIO ANTIQUES: The best store in town! This small villa has room after room of antiques with some new pottery and colonial-style gift items. Some religious work is sold; this is where we bought the *retablo* for $15! The American owner is quite knowledgeable on arts and crafts and antiques—ask her all your questions.

EL PATIO ANTIQUES, Ramón Corona 169

LA REJA: Sort of a tourist shop, but with much ambience and a huge selection of papier-mâché fruits and vegetables. Everything else is also sold here, including the usual frog *mariachis* we know you've been wondering about.

LA REJA, Avenida Benito Juárez 501

MAX: This is an excellent local sportswear store for original designs and easy-to-wear beach clothes and play wear . . . all with elastic waists. But what makes this store extraordinary is the small but ample collection of used and old *huipiles*. We thought we were in *huipil* heaven, but didn't have the bread (beginning at $50 and escalating quickly to near $200) to go for a real piece of art. The store has several chambers and a split personality—if you enter from Avenida Benito Juárez, you must walk forward into the store to get to the *huipiles*. Collectors, this is the find of the century!

MAX, Avenida Benito Juárez 487

DEORELA BAZAR: Pottery, silver, some embroidered dresses, colonial-style furniture, glass (red glass, which isn't found often), and sets of pottery—which do indeed cost over $1,000 for the good stuff.

DEORELA BAZAR, Avenida Benito Juárez 165

▼

CALVIN KLEIN: One of the better shops, with nice casual clothes and jeans for men and women.

CALVIN KLEIN, Hidalgo 224

▼

VILLA MARÍA: A small but choice arts-and-crafts shop, with profits going to charity for local children. One of the finds: an embroidered pillowcase (baby size) that says *"Buenos Noches Mi Amor."* Picture frames, vases, some furniture and crafts.

VILLA MARÍA, Avenida Benito Juárez 449

▼

IRENE PULOS: A local designer who makes resort clothes with a touch of the native and a strong personal influence. Some appliqué work; some dresses with ribbons. Unusual and well-made. Also rather expensive. Interesting belts.

IRENE PULOS, Avenida Benito Juárez 479

▼

CYAN: New versions of colonial furniture—and they ship!

CYAN, Avenida Benito Juárez 533

▼

GALERÍA ARTE HUICHOL: This shop only sells this one art form, from the Huichol tribe, which includes intricately beaded embroidery work. Will knock your socks off!

GALERÍA ARTE HUICHOL, Ramón Corona 164

▼

ST. VALENTIN: One of our favorite stores in town, even though it's narrow and hard to move around in. We can take the claustrophobia because we are jammed in with the most wonderful tiles, and pots, and dolls, and artworks—and can barely move, or breathe, or possibly buy it all, even though we want to. In the back, they even sell the kitchen sink. Well, they sell sinks, anyway. Also handpainted tile signs that say *"Mi Casa es Su Casa."* You'll go nuts here.

ST. VALENTIN, Avenida Benito Juárez 510

▼

POLO/RALPH LAUREN: One of the nicest-ever branches of the Lauren chain in Mexico. Two levels of store with top-quality merchandise for men, women, and children.

POLO/RALPH LAUREN, Ignacio Aldama 109

▼

RUBEN TORRES: One of the better Torres shops. Torres reminds us of Benetton back in the days when a Benetton shop was still rare enough to be special. The clothes are obviously designer-created, because they have that certain snap, crackle, and pop that ordinary clothes don't have. Brightly colored beach clothes, sweats, and good running shorts. This spare, gray store has high-tech features and loud music. A top Mexican designer; a top place to buy.

RUBEN TORRES, Paseo Diaz Ordaz 592

▼

ACA JOE: Between Aca Joe and Ruben Torres you can be dressed for the weekend for the rest of your life.

ACA JOE, Paseo Diaz Ordaz 588

Welcome to Ixtapa

After Fonatur created Cancún and saw what a wonderful job they had done (with their little computer), they created Ixtapa, another artificial community. This one is on the Riviera.

Ixtapa is absolutely perfect. In fact, it is Beverly Hills perfect. While it does have a lot of big, modern, gorgeous hotels, for some reason the area is not as crass as Cancún. It's a jewel . . . like Beverly Hills.

One of the reasons we like it here so much is that you really get everything that Mexico has to offer in one fell swoop. With Zihuatanejo (say Zee-wah-tah-nay-ho), a mere four kilometers away, you add an authentic Mexican fishing village for shopping, bargaining, and funky fun, and then you can sail through the lush hills back to your plush resort in Ixtapa for more of the charmed life. The charmed life includes one giant shopping center complex that has a branch of every store you'd ever want to visit, and resorts such as the Camino Real that come complete with their own shopping arcades. Thus Iggy-Ziggy, as some people call it, has it all. And we want it all.

The Lay of the Land

Ixtapa, since it is an artificial city, is actually made up of a hotel zone along the Palamar Bay. All of the big hotels have beachfront properties and lovely views of the bay. There really isn't much of a downtown.

You can taxi from the pier to Ixtapa (about $4), you can get out at the shopping center

(Los Patios), or you can ask for a tour of the hotel zone and then get out at the shopping center. If you're going to Ixtapa to shop, there is no reason to go any farther.

The siesta is solidly observed here (2 to 4 P.M.), so you can shop the center, have lunch there—or at one of the Ixtapa resorts—and then spend the afternoon in Zihuatanejo—ideally, anyway. Now for the bad news: If you're on a cruise, Princess Lines ships stay in port for only half a day, so you'll have a lot of running around to do. But you do have time to see it all (and shop it all)—so don't panic. But plan ahead and know what you want to do.

Shopping Ixtapa

The joy of Ixtapa is its resort attitude. The shopping centers are as gorgeous as the resorts. There are about five of them, with different names, but they are all on the same plot of real estate, so you don't even need to know the names. As more shopping centers come to town, they locate in this same portion of land, making it easy for the visitor to take a cab to one address (Los Patios) and then wander contentedly . . . probably for three days.

Hours in Ixtapa are from 10 A.M. to 2 P.M. and from 4 to 8 P.M. daily. Almost every store in the shopping centers closes for the siesta. So if you want to do this, and your ship docks at 11 A.M. (as the southbound Princess does), hightail it directly to Los Patios when you arrive. There are several places to eat lunch here, which are of course open during the siesta.

You will have little trouble getting a cab from Los Patios back to the pier . . . or anywhere else. But don't get in without first agreeing on the price.

Booking Ixtapa

O f all the Mexican resort cities (we haven't been to Las Hadas yet, so we may change our minds someday)—we are most likely to want to spend a hunk of time in Ixtapa. Should you be doing the same, note that all the major hotel chains have spectacular hotels here. As usual, the Camino Real is the fanciest hotel in town; it has its own shopping arcade (since it is located a bit out of the zone) with a branch of **TANE** and a good crafts shop, **LA ESPERANZA.** The Sheraton is directly across the street and therefore within walking distance of all of the shopping malls, as is La Hacienda del Sol Hotel (which we haven't checked out from the inside). Krystal has a big hotel, Presidente has one of their new, spiffy refurbished hotels here, and there is a Holiday Inn.

Shopping Centers

LOS PATIOS: This is the main shopping center of the group with its modern face to the road. It is directly across from the Sheraton hotel and the Hacienda del Sol hotel. Among the tenants: **ACA JOE, BENETTON, BYE-BYE, POCO-LOCO, POLO/RALPH LAUREN,** and **MARACA**, a name you might recognize from Rio (women's sportswear).

SCRUPLES: This is more like a department store on a strip than a center, and is adjacent (as they all are) to Los Patios. Scruples is a large, freestanding structure, a beige villa with a waterfall over rocks right there in the front yard. The names **BILL BLASS, CHRISTIAN DIOR,**

260 ▼ THE RIVIERA

and **CALVIN KLEIN** are written in the windows. These are licensed goods. The store is closed from 3 to 5 P.M. for the siesta, so the hours are a bit different from everyone else's.

PLAZA BUGAMBILIAS: This shopping center is behind Los Patios and kitty-corner to Scruples; you'll know it by its terra-cotta–painted stucco. There are about six shops here: an antiques shop, two or three arts-and-crafts shops, a jeweler, and a café.

IXPAMAR MALL: Directly behind La Fuente, you'll get to the next group of stores, which are a little bit hidden—you have to know there's yet another mall back here. This one is built around a patio and has several shops such as **CALVIN KLEIN** and **FILA**.

CENTRO COMERCIAL LA PUERTA: This appears to be part of Los Patios, but isn't. Some of the best and most original stores are in this mall, including the artsy-craftsy store **FLORENCE** (see page 261). There's a little mini-market as well as a cute Italian restaurant.

CENTRO COMERCIAL LA FUENTE: This is next door to Los Patios on the opposite side from Scruples, and is a two-story building with a patio and shops on both levels. There is also a tourist office and a long-distance phone office upstairs; it's one of the larger malls.

Finds

LUISA CONTI: Possibly the most incredible find in Ixtapa, mostly because you don't expect something like this here, is the shop owned by designer Luisa Conti, who makes handmade jewelry. Almost every piece is different. Her style is big and bold and dramatic, often incorporating semiprecious stones and in many mediums—brass, copper, wood, etc. Some of the pieces have an ethnic look to them; some would go with a Chanel summer suit. Prices are higher than souvenir prices, but this is important work. Sold wholesale in the United States through Affix Jewels, Inc., in North Miami Beach.

LUISA CONTI, Centro Comercial La Fuente

▼

FLORENCE: A gallery–cum–crafts shop selling fine examples of handicrafts at slightly-higher-than-necessary prices. Many pieces here that you won't see anywhere else.

FLORENCE, Centro Comercial La Puerta

▼

EL TESORO DE MOCTEZUMA: Another gallery–cum–crafts and housewares shop. Diego Rivera posters (gorgeous ones) are sold here, but they cost $20! Since a Frida poster costs $6 at Fonart, we have trouble telling you this is a steal. But you won't have any opportunities to buy a real Diego Rivera. Some pewter here, also some silver and *alpaca,* woven wallets, and some sculpture. Best news: They do not close for the siesta!

EL TESORO DE MOCTEZUMA, Centro Comercial La Puerta

▼

DIANE ANTIQUEDADES: A cute shop with ambience but not a lot of stock, and very high prices. You might get lucky. Worth a look because it's so nice here.

DIANE ANTIQUEDADES, Plaza Bugambilias

▼

POLO/RALPH LAUREN: A two-story modern boutique looking very American and nice and bright. Men's, women's, and children's clothing.

POLO/RALPH LAUREN, Los Patios

▼

AFRICAN: A local version of Banana Republic that isn't Explora (there is an Explora shop down the walkway, at the very end of Centro Comercial La Fuente) and is worth looking at. The painted zebra lamps are cute.

AFRICAN, Los Patios

▼

WANDA AVIERO: A Mexican designer in the Norma Kamali mode at moderate prices.

WANDA AVIERO, Los Patios

▼

LA FUENTE: The kind of sportswear shop we are used to in San Antonio, where everything looks alike, and fits alike, but is well made and has a resort/ethnic air that feels Mexican without looking like you're ready to start work in a floor show. Easy-to-wear, bright cottons with a strong mix of sizes; many clothes appropriate for a woman over forty. High prices, in keeping with the Beverly Hills clientele, but one of the best sources for this kind of thing anywhere.

LA FUENTE, Centro Comercial La Fuente

▼

CHERRY SILVERSMITH: An excellent resource for *alpaca* picture frames.

CHERRY SILVERSMITH, Ixpamar Mall

EL HUIZTECO: A gallery for collectors of masks and native art.

EL HUIZTECO, Ixpamar Mall

▼

ARMANDO'S: A famous Mexican name for original designs in the Mexican mode—but not quite in the native style. Expect appliqués and ribbons. It's kind of San Antonio–ish. More branches in Acapulco, but there's no reason to wait. Some of the designs are big and loud and exactly what you want to wear on holiday or on board the ship; others are perfectly suitable for life in the American Southwest.

ARMANDO'S, Ixpamar Mall

▼

HAPPY HOUR: The Poco-Loco of beer and tequila T-shirts.

HAPPY HOUR, Centro Comercial La Fuente

▼

ESPRIT: You know the stuff, but it's made in Mexico.

ESPRIT, Centro Comercial La Fuente

▼

COCO: One of the best T-shirt shops in all of Mexico, with original silk-screen designs by Julie, Ramon, and Carlos, whoever they are. Wonderful, special graphics! A real winner! This shop is upstairs; don't miss it.

COCO, Centro Comercial La Fuente

▼

WILD WILD WEST: Another upstairs shop you don't want to miss. This one would turn Ralph Lauren green with envy. The interior of the shop is designed like a corral. They sell Western wear and boots, with a small amount of silver jewelry. The women's fashion moccasins are great too. Much fun.

WILD WILD WEST, Centro Comercial La Fuente

▼

LADDI GUICHI: A small shop, mostly for carpets, but with some Oaxacan carvings and folk art.

LADDI GUICHI, Centro Comercial La Fuente

▼

TANGA: Bathing suits and beachwear that are original, cute, and worth considering when you're ready to go local. Could hold its own on the French or Italian Riviera.

TANGA, Centro Comercial La Fuente

Welcome to Zihuatanejo

This is perhaps our favorite port on the cruise. Yes, Puerto Vallarta is perfect, and we love it there. But Zihuatanejo is imperfect—and that makes it better. Despite the hordes of tourists who come through, the fishing village is not totally ruined. (Yet.) It's not a sleepy little town anymore, but it's an adorable little town filled with vendors who are willing to sell you everything you came to Mexico to buy. If you have not bought a thing on the entire cruise, and you don't even care to go into Ixtapa, you can have all the Mexican shopping thrills there are right here in an hour or two. Don't miss a few contemplative moments sitting at the *Zócalo* looking out at the sea.

The Lay of the Land

Zihuatanejo isn't very big, and most tourist shopping is concentrated around the pier, the beachfront *Zócalo,* and the pedestrian streets Calle Pedro Ascención and Calle Cuauhtemoc, which leads from the *Zócalo* right into the heart of the shopping zone.

The central *mercado* is not in this area, and since you are on a tight schedule, you must bear the extra expense of $1 or so for a taxi. This is a small but rather good market; see page 267.

Locals shop on the road leading out of town toward the central roundabout (Calle Morelas), but this is mostly too real for tourists. There are some nice paint stores here; many of them sell excellent vinyl.

Shopping Zihuatanejo

Legend has it that Zihuatanejo was a fishing village. Beats us. We'd swear its sole purpose for being was to sell *tchotchkes* to tourists. Get out your $1 bills; have lots of 5,000-*peso* notes on hand. This could be the start of something big.

One note: Your ship will tender you ashore (at least, ours did), so make sure you can carry everything you buy. You might want to go ashore with an empty tote bag, lest you be forced to buy an unwanted one on shore. Furthermore, should you have to buy a tote bag on shore, the $20 asking price for a straw job is outrageous (pay $10; tell the vendor to take it or leave it) and you can buy a large (very large) plastic *bolsa* (bag) in the *mercado* for about $4.

Strolling the Square

One of the best things about Zihuatanejo is that the *Zócalo* is right on the beach front. Here you have your basic granite bust of Vicente Guerrero and all the little colored rowboats painted with their names (*"La Gloria"*) on them, pulled up on the sand. If you are standing at the *Zócalo* looking at the ocean, the pier is to your right and the town is behind you. You stroll the main street, which borders the *Zócalo,* Paseo del Pescado, then you cut back to the side streets. At the **MUSEO ARQUEOLOGICO "EL PATIO"** they sell Frida posters. **CASA MAMINA** is a shopping center of sorts on the *Zócalo,* as is **EL COLIBRI,** your basic tourist shop, selling everything from dolls to rugs.

The best shopping is from the vendors who are set up on the walkways of the pedestrian streets, one block off the *Zócalo.* These streets form a T pattern, and should be wandered with ready delight.

Bargain fiercely for everything—from silver earrings to sombrero ashtrays to carved bunny rabbits to hammocks for one or two.

Finds

ARTESANÍAS ADRIANAS: This is a tourist shop (with something special for the true collector), selling everything you expect and then some surprising pieces of handcarved folk art and a wide selection of complete pottery sets. We saw a three-foot-tall, handmade, wooden Ferris wheel in the back of the shop (it's probably still there) that cost a little over $100 and was worth many times that. It was just a little big to get home. The Ferris wheel, representing the circular route life happens to take, is a big Day of the Dead item, by the way—often seen with tiny skeletons in each seat.

ARTESANÍAS ADRIANAS, Calle Juan de Alvarez, at corner of Cuauhtemoc

▼

MERCADO CENTRAL: It's off to the right of the *Zócalo* (if your back is to the ocean), and not within range of tourist fire. Go to Avenida Benito Juárez. After all, when it's time to go shopping, it's time for the central *mercado*. There are two covered buildings here, one for foods and one for dry goods. There is the usual system of stalls in a row, with a few stalls to compete with each other, but not a lot. Pottery is at the far end, while baskets are close to the food end. Good selection of vinyl, hair ornaments, cheap jeans, and tote bags. No panniers.

MERCADO CENTRAL, Avenida Benito Juárez

Welcome to Acapulco

Years ago, and we mean years ago, Acapulco was considered the seat of the jet set. Anyone who was anyone had a villa at the Villa Vera. Even when we first went there, in the early 1960s, the shopping wasn't great. But people never came to Acapulco to shop. They came to party.

Acapulco is a dance-all-night, sleep-all-day kind of place. It's far easier to find a frilly strapless pouf than a simple silk dress. What you will also find is a lot of resort chic—people who'll pay $48 for a beaded Las Brisas T-shirt (only sold in the Las Brisas Pink Shop) in order to go into town wearing said shirt so the world can know they are a Las Brisas kind of person.

So it is with the demi–jet set.

We love it in Acapulco, don't get us wrong; but what we love is staying in our pink stucco villa, looking out at the ocean, sitting down at the La Concha Beach Club, and then, at nighttime, taking our *paseo* from Edificio Esteban to Carlos 'N' Charlie's for dinner. With a trip to the *mercado* in the morning. Amen.

The Lay of the Land

Acapulco has a large and beautiful bay with a main drag (the Costera Miguel Alemán) running all the way around it. While there are hotels on both the beach and nonbeach side of the main drag, the real action in Acapulco is up in the hills. Hotels located in the hills (with their private vans into town and to the beach below) are the cat's meow. People in town for more than a day usually rent a Jeep in order to get around, as they are bound to be isolated.

This city is hot—so hot that you can't really consider shopping much during the day. Store hours are 9 A.M. to 1 P.M. and 5 to 9 P.M. daily. Most tourists shop after 5 P.M.

If you feel compelled to get into a store during the day, Plaza Bahia is an air-conditioned mall and does not close during the siesta.

Getting Around

f you are in town for only a day or two with a cruise, you don't need one of those Jeeps. You can hire any of the taxi drivers who swarm outside the pier office, for a set price that is posted on the board. This includes a flat rate for driving you all over on a per-hour basis.

You can also take the city bus right into the shopping district. Catch the bus right in front of the pier and take it to **PLAZA MARBELLA,** a shopping center in the thick of things at the Diana Circle, or to **PLAZA BAHIA,** more toward the center of town. Simply return to the ship on the bus that runs on the other side of the street. The bus from town to the pier should say *"Hornos"* on it.

From the pier you can walk to Sanborns, to the old downtown, the *Zócalo,* and even the Ralph Lauren factory outlet (see page 275). If you faint in heat, think twice about walking anywhere. It's a $2 taxi ride to the flea market, **VIEJO MERCADO DE ARTESANÍAS,** from the pier; pay in American dollars. (See page 272.)

About addresses: While there are some, most addresses and directions in town are given in terms of hotels. "It's near the Hyatt" or "Across from the Golf Club," etc., is the usual address given to a shop or such.

Shopping Neighborhoods

The Pier Terminal

The pier is small, but it has a duty-free (**RAY'S**) as well as a **POLO/RALPH LAUREN** shop, and a few other shops. The pier itself is not in any particular neighborhood, so to get anywhere, you must walk or taxi.

Downtown

This means El Centro to the locals, and is their part of town. It's not very far from the pier (you can walk), and is not very charming. There is an old *Zócalo*. There are branches of some of the bigger names here, but they are big names to locals, not to tourists. (Except for Sanborns.) There is no reason a tourist would come downtown if in an American frame of mind. (We don't mind it at all, but it's not for most.)

Diana Circle

The midpoint of the Costera Miguel Alemán is the Diana Circle. This is a *glorieta* (roundabout) with a statue of the goddess Diana in it. There are stores, malls, and hotels right here.

Golf Club

The section of Costera Miguel Alemán near the Golf Club is considered the hot new retailing location, and is still being built up. It is farther away from town and closer to the swanky hillside resorts (Las Brisas, Princess, Sheraton), while still being down in the flats. In the evening, on your *paseo,* you can walk from here all the way to the Diana Circle; but not during the heat of the day.

La Vista

Calling this a shopping center is being generous, but it is a neighborhood—a small group of fancy stores and a restaurant on a hillside down the street from Las Brisas but up above the bay. As the name suggests, there's a great view.

Tianguis

MERCADO CENTRAL: The central market is a rather rambling sort of a thing with many, many huts and shacks and places of business— few of which have seen a gringo before. Tell your taxi to take you for *canastas,* which means baskets, so that he drops you at the right part of the market. Needless to say, this is not the part of town you want to be wandering aimlessly about. Signs are, of course, in Spanish, and label the various parts of the market: *Nave de Ropa* (clothes), *Nave de Comida* (food), *Nave de Zapatos* (shoes), etc. To get to the *Nave de Canastas,* your driver will have to turn right on Avenida Constituyentes. You'll know the market by the ceramic pots outdoors.

Indoors you'll find straw, pottery, flowers, *piñatas,* horse and donkey fittings (bridles, saddles, no panniers), and those dry goods that real people need. Bargain fiercely. We've been here several times and just adore it. This is the most authentic shopping experience you can have in Acapulco.

MERCADO CENTRAL, Avenida Constituyentes

▼

NOA NOA: This is a flea market touted down at the pier, and we have disdain for it because it is set up specifically for tourists. And it isn't even very good. Our advice: Noa Noa.

NOA NOA, Costera Miguel Alemán

▼

VIEJO MERCADO DE ARTESANÍAS: The old city market used to be here, but now the government has moved the artisans in—in one of the biggest tourist rip-offs we've ever seen. This place is outrageously expensive! Just because of its downtown location, you'll think this is the real thing. We suggest otherwise. You are being taken. Know prices before you pounce.

VIEJO MERCADO DE ARTESANÍAS, Centro

▼

AFA: AFA (Artesanías Finas Acapulco) is a government-agency crafts shop (the warehouse kind) that is off the beaten track and bills itself as a *tianguis* and bargain basement. We call it K mart without Martha Stewart. Right behind the famous disco, Baby O's.

AFA, Avenida Horacio Nelson

▼

TIANGUIS PAPAGAYO (LADA): This is another giant warehouse (two warehouses connected with a cashier), where at least you can get a free Coca-Cola while you browse. This one is not as offensive as AFA, but it's not great, either. Both shops have incredible selection, true, but it's *junque*. Papagayo does have a lot of onyx dining-room tables, but we can't figure out how to pack these. Most tourists don't even know this shop, deep in the heart of a lovely park, even exists. But then, the owners don't know how to spell papagallo, so it's even. Any taxi driver who brings you here will get a percentage of what you buy.

TIANGUIS PAPAGAYO (LADA), Parque Papagayo

▼

JOYERÍA MERCADO: This is a *mercado* like we are Mexicans. It's another giant warehouse tourist trap with tons and tons upon tons of silver jewelry, and then the rest of the tourist souvenirs upstairs. It's not as bad as some of the others, but the prices are a bit steep.

JOYERÍA MERCADO, Costera Miguel Alemán

▼

TIANGUIS PRINCESS: Should you be stuck in the outer reaches of town, at either the Princess or the Pierre Marquez, don't worry; on the strip of land between the two hotels there is a regular *tianguis* where locals will be happy to sell you the usual junk. We would much rather shop here than in many of the so-called *tianguis* that are out to get you. Why not be gotten outdoors and under thatched huts? Divine fun of the Princess sort.

TIANGUIS PRINCESS, Princess Hotel

Shopping Centers

PLAZA BAHIA: The best and the brightest of the local malls, with fancy architecture, fancy stores, and fancy clients. Don't let that scare you away. This is the most American (and upscale) place in town; it's fully air-conditioned, and the stores don't close for the siesta! You can eat in the full food court or in the American-style café. If you insist on shopping in Acapulco, this could be your first and last stop, and you could leave mightily impressed. **ESPRIT, BALLY, LASERRE, FIORUCCI, OSHKOSH, BENETTON, BYE-BYE,** etc.

PLAZA BAHIA, Costera Miguel Alemán

▼

EL PATIO: A very, very nice mall built in the hacienda style with a patio (how did you guess?) and many lovely shops, including **GUCCI** and **CALVIN KLEIN.**

EL PATIO, Costera Miguel Alemán

▼

GALERÍA ACAPULCO PLAZA: A big, glitzy mall that doesn't have a lot of soul to it, but does include branches of **FILA, EXPRESS, VIVA MÉXICO, GUESS,** and **ELLESSE.**

GALERÍA ACAPULCO PLAZA, Costera Miguel Alemán

▼

CENTRO MARBELLA: Sort of a villa strip in the California style with hacienda-type architecture and a series of shops, mostly jewelry shops but also a **MARTI** for sporting goods. There's **CARTIER** as well as **SUZET'S BAZAAR** (upstairs) for crafts, **NIKE,** and **WANDA AVIERO.**

CENTRO MARBELLA, Diana Circle

▼

PLAZA ICACOS: Right where you start to go up the hill to Las Brisas, on Icacos Beach, this small strip mall is upscale and tony, with **LA CASITA** and **LOREA.** Very nice.

PLAZA ICACOS, Costera Miguel Alemán

▼

POLACA MALL: It's a word made from joining "Polo" (as in Ralph Lauren) and "Aca" (as in Aca Joe). A small, jazzy strip mall next to Centro Marbella with an Espirit shop as well.

POLACA MALL, Diana Circle

Finds

POLO/RALPH LAUREN: A brand-new shop fit to beat the band. There is a factory outlet downtown that we don't think is worth venturing to, but you can see if you're in the mood. We saw $50 sweatshirts at the outlet for $23, but they were very damaged. That's not our idea of fun.

POLO/RALPH LAUREN, Polaca Mall at Diana Circle
EL SEGUNDO (Ralph Lauren Seconds), Hidalgo 20–2

▼

ESTEBAN: Locals and jet-setters know this is the place for couture. Set at the edge of the main drag, in the Golf Club neighborhood, Esteban is an American who grew up in Mexico and now dresses royalty and movie stars. The shop is small and not outrageously fancy, but the clothes range from better-than-average to sensational. Although he will happily custom-order, Esteban makes a high-quality ready-to-wear garment that cannot be matched this side of Martha on Park Avenue in New York. Look at his 1960s-style dresses that are ever-so-Holly-Golightly, and his dress-up frills and poufs. There is a sale room upstairs; an art gallery is next door.

ESTEBAN, Costera Miguel Alemán (at El Cano Hotel)

▼

ACA JOE: The original Acapulco Joe himself. You know what to expect by now. Popular resort clothes all around town.

ACA JOE, Costera Miguel Alemán (at El Presidente Hotel)

▼

RUBEN TORRES: Nice bright sportswear for men and women.

RUBEN TORRES, Costera Miguel Alemán (at El Presidente Hotel)

▼

MAD MAX: A great store for kids; we can't wait for them to open up in the United States!

MAD MAX, Costera Miguel Alemán (at El Presidente Hotel)

▼

SANBORNS: The one downtown is service-able, but this one is delightful. A typical Sanborns department store selling everything from postcards to maps, souvenirs, clothes, and health and beauty aids. Also a coffee shop.

SANBORNS, Costera Miguel Alemán (at Es-trella del Mar)

▼

VILLADRIANA: Upstairs at Plaza Bahia, a home-furnishings shop that sells pewter frames (a tad expensive) and fabulous drop-dead, painted, colonial-style furniture. They will ship. And they don't close for the siesta. In our opinion this is the best store in town.

VILLADRIANA, Plaza Bahia

▼

ANTIQUA: A Moorish-style exterior with gift shops including **SUZETT'S BAZAAR** for handicrafts.

ANTIQUA, Costera Miguel Alemán

▼

MOY: Oy, oy, oy, will Moy make you smile. This is a cowboy shop with Western-style clothes, leather goods, and boots, and it is fun to visit. It also is famous for its quality and moderate prices. Make sure that any exotic leather you pick out (and they have some doozies) is legal to bring into the United States. (Remember turtle-hide and ostrich-hide are not allowed into the U.S.)

MOY, Costera Miguel Alemán (at Centro Com-ercial Kennedy)

▼

NICCOLINO'S: Another place for boots and wild leather goods, including chicken-skin boots. (Could we make this up?) Lots of fun even if you're just browsing.

NICCOLINO'S, El Patio

▼

GIGANTE: This is the local grocery store but it sell everything, á la K mart, and is within walking distance from the cruise pier.

GIGANTE, Costea Miguel Alemán

▼

AIRPORT MALL: This two-level mall is right in the airport terminal and features booths selling everything from souveniers to necessities. Prices are higher than in town but it's last-chance shopping. After you've paid your exit tax check out the duty-free shop.

AIRPORT MALL, Acapulco Airport

Size Conversion Chart

WOMEN'S DRESSES, COATS, AND SKIRTS

American	3	5	7	9	11	12	13	14	15	16	18
Continental	36	38	38	40	40	42	42	44	44	46	48
British	8	10	11	12	13	14	15	16	17	18	20

WOMEN'S BLOUSES AND SWEATERS

American	10	12	14	16	18	20
Continental	38	40	42	44	46	48
British	32	34	36	38	40	42

WOMEN'S SHOES

American	5	6	7	8	9	10
Continental	36	37	38	39	40	41
British	3½	4½	5½	6½	7½	8½

CHILDREN'S CLOTHING

American	3	4	5	6	6X
Continental	98	104	110	116	122
British	18	20	22	24	26

CHILDREN'S SHOES

American	8	9	10	11	12	13	1	2	3
Continental	24	25	27	28	29	30	32	33	34
British	7	8	9	10	11	12	13	1	2

MEN'S SUITS

American	34	36	38	40	42	44	46	48
Continental	44	46	48	50	52	54	56	58
British	34	36	38	40	42	44	46	48

MEN'S SHIRTS

American	14½	15	15½	16	16½	17	17½	18
Continental	37	38	39	41	42	43	44	45
British	14½	15	15½	16	16½	17	17½	18

MEN'S SHOES

American	7	8	9	10	11	12	13
Continental	39½	41	42	43	44½	46	47
British	6	7	8	9	10	11	12

Pesos-to-Dollars Conversion Table

First determine the daily exchange rate of the peso. Choose the closest rate on the horizontal scale above the chart below. Go down this column until you reach the peso amount you wish to convert, as seen in the vertical column on the left. The answer is the approximate dollar value of this amount.

PESOS	2000	2100	2200	2300	2350	2400	2450	2500	2550	2600	2650	2700	2750	2800	2950	3000	3050
50	0.03	0.02	0.02	0.02	0.02	0.02	0.02	0.02	0.02	0.02	0.02	0.02	0.02	0.02	0.02	0.02	0.02
500	0.25	0.24	0.23	0.22	0.21	0.21	0.20	0.20	0.20	0.19	0.19	0.19	0.18	0.18	0.17	0.17	0.16
1,000	0.50	0.48	0.45	0.43	0.43	0.42	0.41	0.40	0.39	0.38	0.38	0.37	0.36	0.36	0.34	0.33	0.33
5,000	2.50	2.38	2.27	2.17	2.13	2.08	2.04	2.00	1.96	1.92	1.89	1.85	1.82	1.79	1.69	1.67	1.64
10,000	5.00	4.76	4.55	4.35	4.26	4.17	4.08	4.00	3.92	3.85	3.77	3.70	3.64	3.57	3.39	3.33	3.28
20,000	10	10	9	9	9	8	8	8	8	8	8	7	7	7	7	7	7
50,000	25	24	23	22	21	21	20	20	20	19	19	19	18	18	17	17	16
80,000	40	38	36	35	34	33	33	32	31	31	30	30	29	29	27	27	26
100,000	50	48	45	43	43	42	41	40	39	38	38	37	36	36	34	33	33
200,000	100	95	91	87	85	83	82	80	78	77	75	74	73	71	68	67	66
300,000	150	143	136	130	128	125	122	120	118	115	113	111	109	107	102	100	98
400,000	200	190	182	174	170	167	163	160	157	154	151	148	145	143	136	133	131
500,000	250	238	227	217	213	208	204	200	196	192	189	185	182	179	169	167	164
1,000,000	500	476	455	435	426	417	408	400	392	385	377	370	364	357	339	333	328
5,000,000	2,500	2,381	2,273	2,174	2,128	2,083	2,041	2,000	1,961	1,923	1,887	1,852	1,818	1,786	1,695	1,667	1,639
10,000,000	5,000	4,762	4,545	4,348	4,255	4,167	4,082	4,000	3,922	3,846	3,774	3,704	3,636	3,571	3,390	3,333	3,279

INDEX

About the Authors

SUZY GERSHMAN is an author and journalist also known by her maiden name, Suzy Kalter. She has worked in the fiber and fashion industry since 1969 in both New York and Los Angeles and has held editorial positions at *California Apparel News, Mademoiselle, Gentleman's Quarterly,* and *People* magazine, where she was West Coast Style editor. She writes regularly for *Travel and Leisure;* her essays on retailing are text at the Harvard Business School. Mrs. Gershman lives in Connecticut with her husband, author Michael Gershman, and their son. Michael Gershman also contributes to the *Born to Shop* pages.

JUDITH THOMAS was an actress in television commercials as well as on and off Broadway. She left the theater in 1970 to work at Estée Lauder and then Helena Rubinstein. In 1973 she moved to Los Angeles, where she studied for her ASID at UCLA and formed Panache and Associates Inc., a commercial design firm. She now lives in Pennsylvania with her husband and two children.